DOROTHY FULDHEIM

The <u>FIRST</u>
First Lady of Television News

Patricia M. Mote

Quixote Publications
Berea, Ohio

Quixote Publications
209 Best Street
Berea, Ohio 44017-2639

10 9 8 7 6 5 4 3 2 1

Library of Congress Cataloging-in-Publication Data

Mote, Patricia M., 1930-
    Dorothy Fuldheim : first First Lady of television news / Patricia
M. Mote.
        p.   cm.
    Includes bibliographical references and index.
    ISBN 0-9633083-5-1 (alk. paper)
        1. Fuldheim, Dorothy   2. Television journalists--United States-
-Biography,   I. Title.
PN4874.F77M68   1997
070'.92--dc21   97-11135
[B]   CIP

*For Mother and Dad, who taught me
that faith and hard work often can make the impossible happen*

Excerpt from "Dorothy" by Bill Gordon reprinted with permission
from *Cleveland Magazine;* February 1990 issue.

Excerpts from "Dorothy Fuldheim and Mother News" by Terence Sheridan
reprinted with permission from *Cleveland Magazine;* April 1973 issue.

Excerpts from *A Thousand Friends* by Dorothy Fuldheim reprinted with permission of Doubleday, a division of Bantam Doubleday Dell Publishing Group, Inc.

Excerpts from *This is Milwaukee* by Robert W. Wells reprinted with permission of Larry Sternig/Jack Byrne Agency.

Acknowledgments

To Tamara Sanderell for her sensitivity and perception in editing and her meticulous attention to details of production;

To Ken McCarthy for his creativity and cooperative spirit in designing the cover and to Susan Peck for her artistic depiction of Dorothy Fuldheim as a child;

To the *Thanks Be to Grandmother Winifred Foundation* for believing in a proposal for a biography of Dorothy Fuldheim and generously granting funds for my research; To those who graciously contributed countless memories and details, and even, in some cases, took photographs from their walls and loaned them: Chris Bade, Jean Bellamy, Stephen Bellamy, James and Yvonne Breslin, Mary Cayet, Rabbi Armond Cohen, Randy and Shirley Culver, Judith Diehl, Taffy Epstein, Eleanor Fanslau, Joseph Gibbons, Bill Gordon, Richard Gildenmeister, Fred Griffith, June Kosich, Bill Kozel, Sam Miller, Ted Ocepek, Greg Olsen, Donald Perris, Bishop Anthony M. Pilla, Tony Poderis, Joel Rose, Ann Sidoti, Wilma Smith, Congressman Louis Stokes, and Sister Bernadette Vetter;

To others who assisted in locating and accessing resources: Annajean Slater, The Book Cellar; Brian Tomek, Star Bank; Dr. Alan Stephenson and Jim Sislo, Media Archives, John Carroll University; Nancy Birk, Jeanne Somers, and Eric Linderman, Special Collections and Archives, Kent State University; Cleveland Press Archives, Cleveland State University; Jean Collins, Photo Collections, Cleveland Public Library; Donna McCarthy, Gorman's Photo and Art; Helen Rathbun, Baldwin-Wallace College; the staffs of Berea and Fairview Park branches, Cuyahoga County Library; Gary Robinson and Terry Moir Cheplowitz, WEWS NewsChannel 5; Carol Starre-Kimiciek, Women in History; Judith Simonsen, Milwaukee County Historical Society; Thomas Steman, Milwaukee Urban Archives, and Sylvia Turner, Undercover Books;

To my friends and colleagues of the Northern Ohio Publishers Association for their encouragement and willingness to share their expertise;

To my husband, Newton—challenger and valued critic—for his genuine interest, pride, and day-by-day involvement in this undertaking, and to our adult children, our grandchildren, and other family members and friends who have contributed ideas and enthusiasm—I am deeply grateful.

P. M. M.

Contents

Preface

Dorothy Fuldheim was not my aunt. In fact, I never knew her. But when I moved to the Cleveland area in 1975 and her television presence came into my life, I felt as if she should be my relative. She and my favorite aunt, Alice Nelson, were cut from the same bolt of cloth. Both were born in 1893. Both were super-achievers in fields of work not yet open to women of their generation. Each remained with a single employer for several decades. Like Dorothy Fuldheim, Aunt Alice had a bold, forthright manner, coupled with a generous and compassionate spirit.

Thus, as a newcomer in the city, I felt drawn to the vivacious red-haired woman on my television screen. Not only did she dazzle me with her wardrobe and her jewelry, but also, and more importantly, she impressed me with the amazing reservoir of information she kept at her fluttering fingertips. Her fierce intensity challenged me to think and to investigate matters I would probably have let slide by. I began having some of her commentaries taped for students in my high school government classes to view.

Eagerly, I read her books, although I had to search used bookstores to find them all. When I tried to learn more about this world-renowned news analyst who had served her city and her country with such distinction, I was frustrated that little was available. Because she had opted to remain in Cleveland and did not become a network personality, Dorothy Fuldheim's name does not appear in many directories and books written about television news reporters and analysts. Yet, her reputation was legendary among world leaders. She was known as a bold, critical thinker who set high standards for the television industry.

"Somebody should write a book about that lady," I kept hearing in bookstores and libraries.

With the encouragement and unwavering faith and support of my family and friends, I took up the challenge. A grant from a national foundation gave impetus to my research as well as heightened my own confidence in the project. Wherever I went, I met people who were enthusiastic and helpful, agreeing that a biography of this remarkable individual was overdue.

This book offers a tapestry of Dorothy Fuldheim's life, woven from strands of her own books, her commentaries and interviews, conversations with her cooperative friends and colleagues, and of material from both print and film archives. The result is, I hope, a vivid and engaging account, illuminating as faithfully as possible many facets of the remarkable persona of Dorothy Fuldheim.

Berea, Ohio   Patricia M. Mote
April, 1997

1

"Everyone Ought to Have Been Born Poor"

Milwaukee 1903

Anyone watching the stocky girl with flaming red hair who darted in and out of 6th Street storefront doorways in a Milwaukee slum might have thought she was a runaway. One minute she'd stop at a drug store, as if the grimy window's papier-mâché fisherman advertising cod-liver oil enthralled her. Next she'd zigzag along the teeming, littered street, dodging fruit vendors with sagging shoulders and rowdy afternoon newsboys, all the while stealing backward glances as if fearing attack dogs in pursuit.

Her jaw was clenched and her blue eyes steely with resolve. Not more than ten, she wore a faded, school-rumpled cotton dress, barely covering her knees, black stockings and scuffed, high-topped shoes.

Clutching her school satchel to her chest, she walked faster now, as if her goal was in sight. With a bird-like glance in either direction, she bolted into a narrow alley where a few drab clapboard houses huddled together like beggars in the shadows of dingy stone tenements. A stifling stench rose from piles of garbage that offered themselves to hordes of green flies, while a mangy, one-eared dog slobbered over a splintered bone.

The girl sidestepped a pile of horse droppings and lifted a rusted latch. A creaking gate swung open in a sagging fence that boasted startling mounds of blue morning glories, now closing their daily show.

One more time, she thought, *I've done it. I got home from school without anyone seeing this awful, ugly street where I live.*

Inside the gate Dorothy Violet Schnell arrived in her own secluded world: a minuscule plot of stubby grass, a rope swing tied to a struggling weeping willow, a bench made of a discarded shutter and a few bricks. Here she entered her private retreat, her sanctuary from the filth and din of the streets around her.

Off came the hightopped shoes and darned cotton stockings. Next, Dorothy pulled from her satchel the book she had borrowed yesterday from the next-door neighbor, Mrs. Dehni. She often ran errands for Mrs. Dehni and her many lady friends who came and went over there. In return, she was allowed to borrow books from the shelves at the top of the back stairs. Propping herself against the bench, she wriggled her bare toes in the grass and fondled the book before opening the cover of *Lady Randolph's Lover.*

Wafting over from next door, the sumptuous fragrance of Mrs. Dehni's solitary lilac bush wrapped Dorothy in a dream world. Nothing smelled as heavenly as lilacs, Dorothy thought. She often told her mother she would like to sleep on a bed of lilacs and have them strewn on her path wherever she'd go. Her mother, who believed her children were exceptional, always told her she could do anything she wished. So what was so impossible about sleeping in lilacs, already?

Soon Dorothy was reveling in her book, totally shutting out the thumps and whacks coming from the open cellar door of the Schnells' meager house. If she heard them at all. These were everyday sounds. Her brother David, four years younger and already home from school, was probably perched on an apple box, swatting away rats while their mother did the family's laundry.

With a little luck Dorothy could read a chapter or two before her mother would emerge from the cave-like cellar. Squinting in the afternoon sunshine, she'd call Dorothy to help hang out the Schnell family's tired-looking, tattered laundry. The warm May breeze would dry it before supper time.

Dorothy turned the pages eagerly. Even a borrowed dime novel was a luxury. In the Schnell household there was scarcely money enough for rent, food, and scant clothing. Dorothy dreaded the trips she'd make to the butcher when he'd say, "Tell your mother I have to have something on the bill." Many times there was no meat in their house for days. Apples and potatoes were cheap, and Bertha Schnell made vast quantities of soup from each to help keep her family warm and their stomachs full.

Still, Dorothy's own life was not nourishment enough. She turned to books to feed the hungering of a young soul, yearning for romance and beauty, a respite from the poverty in which she lived.

Herman Schnell, Dorothy's father, was a good man, but making a living for his family wasn't his long suit. He tried to sell insurance; he tried to sell clothes. He wasn't very good at either, but he had a great reverence for learning and for the beauty of language. One thing he and Bertha agreed upon was the importance of their children's education. Both parents had left their native lands while still in their teens, arrived penniless in America, and mastered a new language to enable them to survive in their new surroundings. Herman had come from Germany, Bertha Wishner from Russia. They had met and married near the east coast of their new country, but after the births of their two daughters, Dorothy and Janette, they had moved to Milwaukee. David was born soon after their arrival. Milwaukee had a large German immigrant population and the Schnells had relatives there. Herman and Bertha had hopes for a brighter future in Milwaukee, but life had remained harsh for them.

With flimsy coats and holes in their mittens and their shoes, Dorothy, Janette, and their brother David trudged the two miles to school and back through torrential rains and blinding snowstorms. They never had three cents for a bowl of soup at school but ate an apple and stale gingerbread for lunch instead.

"A great wall separated the children who had three cents for soup and a nickel for ice cream and those who had no money for such luxuries," Dorothy was to write decades later. "No one who has not known poverty, lived in it, with it, and been ground down by it, can understand its terrifying effect." She never forgot the humiliation of poverty. In her mid-eighties she told *Cleveland Plain Dealer's* Mary Strassmeyer, "Everyone ought to have been born poor. You have more respect for people when you become successful."

Twice a week, in spite of searing summer heat or the most bone-chilling winter day, Bertha Schnell allowed Dorothy to walk twelve blocks to the Milwaukee Public Library and twelve blocks back. Her only caution to her book-starved older daughter was that she wear a bonnet to protect her face and neck from the summer sun or mittens, ragged though they might be, to prevent frostbitten fingers in winter.

She needn't have warned Dorothy about this, for the girl was already careful about her fair skin. Secretly, she longed for a graceful white neck and fluttering hands like her Aunt Molly's. Dorothy adored her Aunt Molly, her mother's younger sister, who modeled dresses at a department store. Remarkably, by age twenty-five, Molly Davidson had buried three husbands and adopted their collective group of nine sons. When she came to visit Dorothy's mother, the Schnells' shabby house exhaled an aura of luxury for days afterward. Aunt Molly's perfume wafted through the boxlike rooms, punctuated by the lingering sound of her staccato-laden syllables. She enunciated her own unique brand of wisdom: "The morning sun is best for sleep. That's when your strength and health are fortified." She also said, "Tea is good for only one thing: to be a conveyor of jam. And it has to be peach jam. It kisses your cheeks and makes them glow."

Aunt Molly must surely have been the most beautiful woman in Milwaukee. She had an hourglass figure, and she moved sinuously, using her God-given grace to her best advantage. Few males did not fall victim to her coquetry and beauty. But she was not destined to be a married woman for much of her life. Her first two husbands fell to their deaths at their work, and the third died after a brief illness. Fortunately, there had been a total inheritance of $16,500 and a large house from Husband Number Two. The indefatigable Molly insisted she would keep all nine of her stepsons with her—to the consternation of her practical-minded sister Bertha. She warned Molly that boys would be hard to raise and that she was letting herself in for a fate worse than a job.

Molly would toss her pretty head and sniff into her scented, lace-trimmed handkerchief. "So, what am I to do? Throw these boys out into the street? Of course, they will stay with me . . . they are mine, and God wants me to keep them." Dorothy would watch her aunt's luminous blue-violet eyes brim with tears as she gathered the boys, aged three to the thirteen-year-old twins, around her. Bertha Schnell would shake her head and pour her sister another cup of tea. There was never any use arguing with Molly when she related her conversations with God.

After Aunt Molly's visits Dorothy would peer at her own prepubescent image in the cracked mirror in the kitchen when no one else in the family was looking. Were her eyes as wide-set as Aunt Molly's? True, Dorothy had the thick auburn hair, but when she was allowed to wear it up, would hers look as gloriously elegant?

Tying a tattered bedsheet around her waist, she would practice swishing when she walked, as Aunt Molly did. "Don't walk straight, swish a little," Aunt Molly had told her. "This makes a man feel you are not a waitress or a grocery store clerk but you are a woman whose business is to be a woman."

Dorothy longed for some perfume, for her aunt had told her that she put a different perfume on each of her petticoats, just as the Medici women did in the time of Leonardo da Vinci. But perfume was as out of reach for Dorothy as the diamond rings her aunt wore—one from each of her husbands. Once Dorothy's brother David came in and found her arrayed in her sheet and swishing across the rough, bare floors of their home. He ran back outside to get their sister Janette, and the two of them poked fun at Dorothy until she flung the sheet off and ran outside to the solace of her willow tree and her books.

If it was her day to go to the library, she could escape her brother and sister for hours. On a stifling summer day, Dorothy would hurry to catch up with Jack, who delivered ice to everyone in the neighborhood for their iceboxes. She'd politely beg slivers from his wagon. After carefully wiping the sawdust from the jagged pieces he'd hand her, Dorothy would savor their soothing coolness on her parched lips and picture herself sipping tall, frosty drinks on the deck of a luxurious ocean liner, her deck chair surrounded by a cluster of admiring swains.

Near the reeking Milwaukee River, Dorothy would pass one of the city's largest breweries. The air around there hung in dense, malt-laden sheets, prickling Dorothy's nostrils with unpleasantness. Workers huddled in groups over their dinner pails, and a lethargic game of horseshoes was in progress on a dusty strip of grass. A few workers waved, for Dorothy, with her armload of books, was a familiar passerby. "There goes little Miss Library Lady," one grimy worker called out in a friendly tone.

These twice-weekly trips to the library were Dorothy's keys to locked doors of enchantment and wonder. By the time she was ten or eleven, she had unconsciously realized the mental limitations of Mrs. D's library of dime novels and yearned for more challenging reading. She discovered Shakespeare at an early age and read and re-read Dickens' works, easily putting herself into their settings of London's slums. The novels of Thackeray, Jane Austen, and Charlotte Brontë utterly consumed her romantic young soul.

Once she had selected her quota of books to borrow and had checked them out with the waspish librarian who cluck-clucked her approval or occasionally frowned an objection over her choices, Dorothy was ready for her special treat. No trip to the library was complete without "The Stairs." She stole out of the main reading room and waited, cat-like, until there were no people near the twin marble staircases on either side of the lobby.

Creeping to the top of one of the stairways, her books cradled in one arm, Dorothy lifted the train of an imaginary green taffeta gown and began her promenade down to the street level. The train rustled luxuriously as she glided down, smiling and nodding graciously to the awed stares of friends and would-be suitors she pictured watching her. Reaching the bottom, she turned, a portrait of elegance and grace, dropped her train, and blew kisses to the crowd.

Whether she was an actress, a duchess, or an operatic soprano never cluttered Dorothy's mind. But always the dress was green taffeta with a train that rustled, always she reveled in the adoring attention of her admirers.

Someday, she'd vow, *I'll have all the taffeta dresses I want, and people will clap and cheer for me.* So enfolded was Dorothy in her make-believe world, she never noticed the knot of library clerks bunched at the top of the stairs, watching her descend. Dorothy, with her stocky figure and her flowing red hair, had become an accustomed sight, but none of them would disturb her flight of fancy. Had she known they were watching, she would probably have waved and flung them kisses.

Cleveland 1973

A strident see-sawing of strings, brook-like ripples of flutes and clarinets, and the oboe's authoritative note drifted up toward the frescoed ceiling. Members of the Cleveland Orchestra shifted in their chairs and arranged their music, readying themselves for the Thursday evening all-Strauss concert.

A mushy, early-April snowfall, not unusual for Cleveland, had slowed concertgoers' arrival, but Severance Hall was filling steadily now. Outer garments exhaled the pungent aroma of wet wool, a contrast to the baskets of fragrant flowers on the stage apron. The only sounds from the audience were discreet coughs and the rustle of programs as seasoned music lovers poured over their program notes.

18

When the clock's hands crept past eight, a barely perceptible stir rippled through the hall. Coughs were more frequent. Heads began turning. A low hum of voices rose as patrons reminded one another that the Cleveland Orchestra's Thursday night concerts dependably began on the hour. Ushers positioned themselves sedately along the aisles, their faces locked passively, as if their presence evidenced a normal state of affairs.

At 8:23 a whispered swell swept forward from the rear of the hall. Two ushers were escorting a bustling, diminutive, red-haired woman, followed by a younger female companion wearing oversized glasses and a halo of white-blond curls, to the only two still-vacant orchestra seats. The redhead—gracious, chatting—smiled up at one usher, then at the other. Patrons seated near the aisle caught a drift of French perfume, a flash of a heavy jeweled bracelet, and shoes dyed to match the rustling, green taffeta dress. They also heard words of sincere regret for her late arrival, caused by a traffic tie-up.

With brief greetings to those seated nearby, the two women scarcely settled into their seats when the house lights dimmed. Maestro Lorin Maazel entered to sedate applause and took up his baton. The Cleveland Orchestra's evening with Strauss could now begin.

In the next to the last row, two out-of-town businessmen, who were passing the evening hours by taking in a weeknight concert, exchanged puzzled looks. One remarked to the other that he didn't realize Cleveland boasted royalty.

This story circulated with alacrity in Cleveland in the mid-1970's. Truth or legend, it symbolizes the homage and respect the city paid Dorothy Fuldheim, pioneer television commentator and analyst. She was an anchorwoman before the term was coined, and her then quarter-century string of years in the television industry surpassed legends like Edward R. Murrow and Ed Sullivan.

Far more than achieving vapid celebrity status, Dorothy Fuldheim attached herself to every Cleveland family. Though her fans might not always agree with her, they felt free to tell her so. ("Hey, Red, you were all wet last night," a truck driver once called out as he passed her at a downtown corner.) But a window washer delighted in telling her that his wife thought she should run for President. A friend to drivers of cabs as well as members of Congress, Dorothy Fuldheim daily affirmed the worth of every individual she met. "She was a queen, but she didn't act like one," one close associate is fond of saying. Shouts and greetings followed her wherever she went, and people frequently sidled up to her in crowds and asked if they could touch her. At an opening day for the Cleveland Indians, she attracted more attention than the city's civic leaders or the president of the American League.

By 1973 Dorothy Fuldheim, at age eighty, was the longest running personality on television. She came to Cleveland's flagship Scripps Howard station, WEWS-TV, in 1947 when she was fifty-four. Not just a news reader—a talking head—she was a news analyst and a commentator in the true sense of the word. With no model to follow, she had fashioned her television news broadcasts in a format which pleased her—and evidently pleased her superiors, her sponsors, and her viewers. She would continue to hold forth for more than another decade. In 1984 she conducted her last interview, by satellite with then-President Ronald Reagan, only hours before she suffered the first of several strokes that would leave her helpless for the remaining five years of her life.

Despite her powerful intellect and awe-inspiring storehouse of knowledge, her lightning-quick mind and years of globe-circling to interview the affluent, the powerful, and the infamous, Dorothy Fuldheim grappled throughout her life with fears borne of a childhood of grinding poverty. She endured devastating tragedies in her adult life, particularly the death of her beloved daughter, Dorothy Louise. In her commentaries emerged traces of a wistful searching for a truth and serenity not found in erudition and science. In some of her interviews, especially in the 1980s, a yearning surfaced for a dimension of happiness she saw in others' lives but never experienced in her own.

Only those closest to Dorothy Fuldheim sensed this longing for something more in life. It was a carefully concealed facet of her nature. Generally, she lived and moved and worked in the aura of confidence and ebullience she had created for herself.

Yet, Sam Miller, the cherished friend who became her guardian in the final years of her life, had these words from Ecclesiastes inscribed on her tombstone in Cleveland's Park Synagogue Cemetery: *With much wisdom, there is much sorrow.* "She was the unhappiest woman I ever knew, a tragic figure," Miller says. But through the decades, to her friends and colleagues and to the world at large, the phenomenal, durable redhead was Ultimate Authority–Mother Confessor–Best Friend–A Window on the World.

2
Growing Up in Milwaukee

Although Herman Schnell was not much of a provider for his family according to his daughter, he had several interests. One was a lodge which he attended faithfully as did many immigrant men. Lodges provided the comforting embrace of the European village amidst the coldness and commotion of an alien city. Another special interest was his three children upon whom he doted.

At one time he undertook to blend these two interests by organizing an entertainment for the lodge members: the featured performers would be none other than his children. By this time, David had revealed himself to be gifted at the piano. In fact, he was what was then called a child wonder. At age three, when he sat down at a neighbor's piano, his chubby hands played any piece he had ever heard that anyone would request.

Fortune smiled when, in a moment of beneficence, an uncle blessed the Schnells with a battered upright piano. Even though David's tunes bounced off the family's "music room" with its bare floors and only one pair of lace curtains divided between two windows, David had his piano and eventually there was, somehow, money for lessons. His sisters took orders for Larkins' household products to buy new lace curtains to cover both windows. Dorothy remembered decades later that nothing she ever bought gave her the same satisfaction as those lace curtains did.

Graceful Janette, with her raven hair and violet eyes, yearned to become a ballerina and worked in a grocery to make money for dancing lessons. Thus, Mr. Schnell had a son who could dazzle people with his piano playing and a beautiful daughter who could dance on her toes. But what could Dorothy do? Her father at last decided she could make a speech for the lodge entertainment. There is no record of what Dorothy's spoke about. In truth, she remembered feeling that the lodge members were really bored with her but tolerated her speech in order to enjoy the greater talents of David and Janette.

The children were a great hit and continued to perform at a number of lodge meetings. Amateurish though they were, those speeches sowed the seeds of a speaking career that would span eight decades. "I learned from this early experience," Dorothy wrote in 1966 in *I Laughed, I Cried, I Loved* "that words must be used as an artist utilizes his colors and brushes—with care and subt[i]lty." Later in her memoirs she enlarges upon the comparison of a successful lecturer's accomplishment to that of an artist:

> To fill an hour with words, and when you have finished, to leave with an audience a picture, an idea, or a conviction is an achievement. It is very much like an artist, applying paint to empty canvas; as the colors and form emerge[,] the image in the artist's mind is reproduced. A fine speaker does the same with words: there are words that burn with fire, there are words that are noble, there are words that are exalted. These are the colors a trained speaker uses— elegance and brilliance and wit and passion.

Herman Schnell's third consuming interest was listening to lawyers argue cases at the Milwaukee County Court House. This pastime satisfied a longing for the education he never had. "For my father, good language, rolling sentences and eloquent phrases were like music." Thrilled when he would beckon to her to come along, Dorothy hopped and skipped alongside her father's long strides as they made their way through the people-packed, littered streets. She didn't mind going even on the hottest summer days. In winter her parents would allow her to miss school on the occasion of an appearance by an outstanding legal personage. Always, when the judge appeared and the proceedings began, she would immerse herself in the logic and heated polemics of the lawyers. Tugging at their rumpled suits and mopping perspiring faces, these men knew how to choose words powerfully in ways that might or might not make a difference in the fate of the person accused of wrongdoing. At jury trials Dorothy always watched the faces of the jurors to see if they revealed whether or not they were swayed by the particular attorney's defense or prosecution.

Although most of the cases she heard argued in the Milwaukee County Court House did not involve brilliant legal minds, some must have been eloquent and impressed her cognizance with the power and mechanics of legal argument. She made mental lists of new words she heard the lawyers and the judge use so she could look them up in her dictionary when she got home. When her brother and sister called her "Dictionary-swallower," she remained unruffled. Dorothy's mind was filled with an insatiable desire to know—and to know—and to know. "I learned the power of words at the courts, but I didn't know what I was learning at the time."

"The power of words," my father told me, "is greater than guns or cannon. Learn to use them. See what Lincoln did with a few words, and consider the Bible," he told me. "The words in the Bible have influenced mankind more than any armies or generals."

Perhaps Herman Schnell could not pay the butcher regularly, but with his love of eloquent language, respect for skillful rhetoric, and his yearning to become an impresario, he surely helped her to expand her mind and propelled her toward the career that was to be known as the "Fuldheim Phenomenon"—America's longest running television personality.

At age twelve Dorothy took a job at The Boston Store as a cash girl. This was only on Saturdays—from 9 A.M. to 9 P.M.—during the school year, for the Schnells would not allow working to interfere with their children's education. Dorothy received $1.75 each week for her task of carrying purchased items to the bundler who would wrap them for the customer. The job was poorly named, since the girls did not carry the cash at all; a wire basket on a cable would speed it to an unseen presence where deft fingers and a mind reliable with figures would swiftly return the proper change.

Every Saturday night when Dorothy would proudly hand over her pay to her mother, Bertha Schnell would always say, "Someday you will have as much money as you want; you wait and see." Dorothy later wryly declared that her mother was usually right in her predictions but not in this particular one.

At work Dorothy made friends with a girl named Seraphim Dobinsky who lived nearby. *How wonderful it would be*, romantic

Dorothy thought, *to have such a magical-sounding name.* The two girls walked home together on Saturday nights, past the breweries and the brothels. Caught up in gossip and exchanging confidences, they were oblivious to the sordid neighborhood. Dorothy later wrote that neither she nor her parents knew what went on inside those dingy houses. Though her parents were naive about some American ways, one would hardly believe they were unaware of the nearby activities of members of "the world's oldest profession." More likely, they chose to ignore the existence of these brothels, thereby keeping their children's innocence intact.

By the time Dorothy was fifteen, her department store career had expanded to selling dresses. She learned how to estimate the dress size of every woman she saw for the rest of her life. And, more significantly, she acquired a passion for beautiful clothing that would also stay with her forever.

When Dorothy stepped into The Boston Store from the teeming street, she felt as if she were entering into a world of grandeur and grace. Even the store's name called up an image of a seacoast city with a dignified heritage, not a raw-boned, Midwestern sprawl like Milwaukee. She always tried to arrive a few minutes early to linger on the first floor near the perfume counters. If no clerks were yet in sight, she would spray a tantalizing whiff of a fragrance on her wrists from one of the test atomizers set out for would-be customers. The sumptuous fragrance clung to her presence all day like a softly spoken promise. *Someday, someday . . .*

As Dorothy went about her job, arranging dresses on hangers, her stubby fingers lingered on the gowns of whispering silk and satin. Holding up a flounced petticoat, she curtsied to her squat, pale image in the mirror of an empty cubicle-like dressing room. Plumed hats made to frame flirty faces, shoes with shiny buckles, glittering brooches and oversized rings—even of the department store variety—all sent Dorothy's imagination soaring wildly into a drama of elegance and refinement in which she was the central player.

Dorothy and other girls at the store surely would have poured over newspaper accounts that described in detail the wedding gown and trousseau of President Theodore Roosevelt's daughter Alice. The press coverage of the event made the public feel as if they were honored guests at Alice's marriage to Nicholas Longworth in 1905. Her flamboyance and outspoken ways attracted worldwide attention. Alice Roosevelt was determined she would have her wedding her way, although she said, "Father always wanted to be the bride at every wedding and the corpse at every funeral."

The year before when Alice had accompanied her father to Japan to help stave off a war between the Japanese and the Russians, she was received like a princess. Roosevelt would receive the Nobel Peace Prize for his efforts, but his daughter was heralded as the nearest thing to royalty Americans had ever known, and romantic young girls like Dorothy followed her every move. The newspapers recounted her activities, her clothing, her suitors in minute detail.

At the department store Dorothy was entering new worlds every day. She learned the facts of life from a stunning, unreserved co-worker, who had just come back from her honeymoon. Completely guileless, Dorothy sat with her blue eyes transfixed in disbelief through those detailed, minute-by-minute disclosures of shared marital bliss. Then she stared down at an ink stain on the floor, not wanting to look at the other giggling, whispering girls. She could feel her cheeks flaming, as if she had been caught looking through a keyhole.

A far different type of person in an unlikely job, Martha, a buyer in underwear, opened Dorothy's mind and heart to the soaring majesty of poetry. The early years of the twentieth century marked a period of intense popularity of the *Rubáiyát* of eleventh century philosopher, mathematician, astronomer, and poet Omar Khayyám whose four-lined verses explored the most profound and intense aspects of human experience. Dorothy described her introduction to these verses as "exciting wonder and awe." The poems were so popular that Dorothy was able to buy a flimsy paper booklet of them for only five cents. How she longed to be invited to a meeting of one of the Omar Khayyám clubs she had read about. Her philosophy in years hence would reflect the influence of these verses. She would, indeed, live life to its fullest; yet she never could totally embrace a *carpe diem* attitude. She would become too sensitive to the imperfections of this world and too speculative about the world that might exist beyond.

But such verses as these must have etched vivid impressions on an impressionable young girl:

> XXXIV Then to this earthen Bowl did I adjourn
> My Lip the secret Well of Life to learn.
> And Lip to Lip it murmur'd—
> "While you live
> Drink!—for once dead you never shall return."

LX   And strange to tell, among the Earthen Lot
Some could articulate, while others not;
    And suddenly one more impatient cried—
"Who is the Potter, pray, and who the Pot?"

LII   And that inverted Bowl we call The Sky,
Whereunder crawling coop't we live and die,
    Lift not thy hands to It for help—for It
Rolls impotently on as Thou or I.

Dorothy wrote that she later moved beyond the obvious beauty of Fitzgerald's poetry (the nineteenth-century English translator of the *Rubáiyát*) but that throughout her life she preferred poetry that was "straightforward, not the verseless, incomprehensible kind . . . unless I understand what the poet is saying, he is not communicating with me."

Although we do not know if Dorothy read much poetry in later years, she surely would have identified with these lines from Emily Dickinson. They seem to describe her so perfectly that in her mind she would have recast them thus, using the feminine gender:

She ate and drank the precious words,
Her spirit grew robust;
She knew no more that she was poor,
Nor that her frame was dust.
She danced along the dingy days,
And this bequest of wings
Was but a book. What liberty
A loosened spirit brings!

Throughout her youth Dorothy undoubtedly continued her passion for books although friends and a part-time job took up some of her time. Another continued influence was her Aunt Molly, who had always been Dorothy's favorite relative. As Dorothy grew older, she still tried to imitate Aunt Molly's charming manner and wished fervently to grow up to look like her. Her Aunt Molly, Dorothy believed, was ". . . the epitome of femaleness in all its dimensions: sex lure, tenderness, willfulness, courage, and originality. Her eyes were made to flutter with a come-on look; her hands white and soft, to be held; her throat, to be kissed; and her lips to promise sweetness." Of course, Dorothy hoped to have better luck with husbands than Aunt Molly did. Hers always seemed to die.

If Dorothy had attended Milwaukee's Fourth Street School, a forbidding fortress-like structure near the Schlitz Brewery, or if she had ever worshiped in a synagogue, she might have crossed paths with a wide-eyed Russian immigrant girl, five years younger than herself, whose name was Goldie. Ironically, the two were not destined to meet until more than a half-century later when Dorothy (Schnell) Fuldheim would interview Goldie, by then Golda Meir, prime minister of Israel.

Although the population of Milwaukee had reached nearly 360,000 by 1910, most of the immigrant families lived in the same general areas. Frequent moves were commonplace within the area as the immigrants sought to improve their surroundings in their scramble to attain the American Dream. Dorothy's family and Goldie's family followed such a pattern, reducing the likelihood of these two girls ever meeting. Records show that in 1916 the Schnell family lived on 6th street, and Goldie Mabovitch's family lived on 10th Street in Milwaukee. In 1913 the Schnells lived at 623 10th, while the Mabovitches had previously lived on 6th Street.

Goldie and her family were devout Jews who emigrated from Russia in 1906, but there is no record to indicate that the Schnell family identified with the Jewish community of Milwaukee. In fact, Dorothy's close friend Sam Miller, who did not meet Dorothy until the 1960's, says that she was never in a synagogue until he took her. Apparently, in their efforts to become "Americanized," the Schnells abandoned all ties to the Jewish faith.

Dorothy and Goldie both worked as junior cash girls at different Milwaukee department stores, but their age difference probably precluded their getting acquainted. The Mabovitches were a few notches better off financially than the Schnell family. With the help of her daughters, Goldie's mother operated a grocery in one room of their house, and Goldie's father was a union carpenter. Although Milwaukee was the scene of labor strikes and violence during the closing decades of the nineteenth century, by 1910 the unions had dug in their heels, and the city emerged as a center of growth and productivity.

Had they been closer in age, Dorothy might have even benefited from the American Young Sisters Society that Goldie organized to raise money to provide schoolbooks for less fortunate children. Both Goldie and Dorothy would leave Milwaukee soon after they married— Dorothy would go to Cleveland, Goldie to a *kibbutz* in Israel.

Of great influence upon Dorothy was Roseka, daughter of an affluent Milwaukee family, who radiated an aura of romance and opulence that her name suggested. At Roseka's home, Dorothy first tasted wine, used a fingerbowl (by imitating Roseka), and viewed an oil painting. Roseka was the darling of her five brothers, each of whom was being prepared for a different profession. Surely, Dorothy must have basked in the attentions the dashing brothers bestowed upon her, as Roseka's friend.

Dorothy and Roseka, whose last name never appears in Dorothy's writings, remained friends and traveling companions throughout the 1930s and 1940s. In the same way that Roseka's twenty-cent-a-week childhood allowance had treated Dorothy to chocolate ice cream sundaes, her ample means underwrote some of Dorothy's news-gathering trips abroad when she was making her mark as a lecturer.

3

From the Schoolroom to the Stage

Beneath Dorothy Schnell's somber, pensive photo in the 1912 *Echo,* the Milwaukee Normal School's yearbook, is the statement, "I have never found the limit to my capacity." Whether Dorothy herself chose this attribution or whether a perceptive yearbook editor penned it is not known, but no soothsayer with a crystal ball could have foretold this young graduate's destiny more accurately.

A resident of Wisconsin or of another state who declared his or her intention to teach in Wisconsin's public schools paid no tuition to attend Milwaukee Normal, (now the University of Wisconsin-Milwaukee). All others paid twenty dollars tuition per semester. Book rental was five dollars a semester. Dorothy Schnell may not have aspired to be a teacher, but for her any other formal education was unattainable. In fact, few other avenues to higher education were open to women of even average means.

The Schnell family's living standard had still not risen much above the poverty level by the time Dorothy graduated from high school. Although the Normal School did admit students who were sixteen and had completed two years of high school, Dorothy completed high school in 1910 and graduated from the Normal School in 1912, a few weeks before her nineteenth birthday.

Her classes at Milwaukee Normal must have opened vast new vistas for Dorothy's eager mind. The school's objectives state:

> ... preparation for teaching implies more than courses in
> educational psychology and methods of teaching; it implies
> scholarship as well. In the very nature of the case the high
> schools cannot give the breadth of scholarship demanded
> of teachers in progressive communities. The Milwaukee
> Normal School extends the academic work of the high school
> by offering advanced courses in the various branches of the
> curricula of the elementary and high school. These advanced
> courses correspond, and are intended to be equivalent to,
> similar courses in the University. Sound scholarship and
> breadth of view are as much the aim of the Normal School
> as is pedagogy. Without the former the latter is useless.

These two qualities—sound scholarship and breadth of view—
instilled in her by her parents and further refined in her two-year
college experience, characterized Dorothy Fuldheim's entire professional career.

If Milwaukee Normal School lived up to its catalog's promises,
Dorothy's preparation for teaching was perhaps far more adequate
than that of many classroom teachers in America today. Countless
institutions for teacher training have lost sight of those goals—sound
scholarship and breadth of view—and allow their curricula to become mired down in masses of gobbledygook that pass as educational
methodology. Thus, graduates who cannot spell, calculate, read criti-
cally, or write with coherence clutch their teaching certificates and
march into classrooms to instruct children and young adults.

Because of the large immigrant population, children in Milwaukee schools were required to study German, according to Dorothy's
remarks about her career in a televised interview observing her thirti-
eth year in television.

In 1910 three-fourths of Milwaukee's residents either were immigrants or had at least one foreign-born parent. In one ten-block area,
the census takers found forty different nationalities, but 53.5 percent
of Milwaukeeans were described as having a "Teutonic background,"
which included Swiss, Austrians and some others besides Germans.
More than 20 percent of the city residents spoke mostly German while
numerous others were at least as much at home in that language as in
English.

Both Herman and Bertha Schnell spoke Yiddish, according to census reports. Herman very likely spoke German as well. Both learned
English readily, however, and there is no record of any other lan-

guage being spoken in the home. Dorothy surely learned to speak some German from her father as well as what she acquired in school. But she could not have dreamed that twenty years later she would be speaking German with the man who nearly destroyed the world— Adolf Hitler.

When Dorothy faced her charges that fall at a country school a mile from the end of the streetcar line, her salary was fifty dollars a month. Her account of how she spent her first pay shows her hunger for beauty and extravagance. "The first money I earned I spent on perfume and a hat with blue cornflowers. Then I felt I was irresistible. I would have gone hungry rather than give up the perfume."

Frequently arriving at school windblown and disheveled from her mile-long walk, Dorothy would struggle to put up her luxurious red hair and assume a dignified decorum. When the only other teacher on the staff, a male, complained to the school board that Miss Schnell's hair distracted the older students, Dorothy emerged the champion of a battle of principle. The school board, headed "by a man with twinkling eyes," ruled that a woman's hair was her crowning glory, and Miss Schnell could wear hers up or down as she chose.

Academicians in the United States in the early decades of the twentieth century boasted that America's schools were built on the "factory model" so productive in the industrialization of the country. With millions of immigrants swelling the population, schools faced a Herculean task in enculturating as well as educating the newcomers and their offspring. Schools, therefore, laid down a no-nonsense brand of curriculum, strongly laced with the Puritan work ethic. Although drawing and crafts appeared in American schools by 1907, most art education focused on integrating art in the curriculum systematically and incidentally. This meant students might look at pictures of the Pyramids while learning the geography of Egypt or draw pictures of mountain ranges when studying Switzerland. Some art classes took a vocational approach, emphasizing the contribution of design in vehicles, homes, and commercial buildings.

In industrialized Milwaukee, in particular, early strides were made toward establishing a vocational curriculum. The state legislature passed a law that permitted communities to establish continuation schools for children who had dropped out of grade school to go to work, a common practice, especially among immigrant families.

By the end of 1912, Robert E. Cooley, a teacher from Fredonia, Wisconsin, had a school of more than two thousand such pupils working toward a high school diploma. His goal was to make Wisconsin the first state to provide part-time schools for working children. Cooley's experiment led to the creation of the Milwaukee Vocational School, which erected its own six-story building by 1923. Now called the Milwaukee Area Technical College, it is located in the heart of the city and said to be one of the largest and best-equipped schools of its kind in the world.

In such an educational environment, time was not likely allotted for the arts in any of the public schools. But Dorothy Schnell would let the arts filter into her classroom by injecting bits of poetry or quotations from Shakespeare. One can imagine her standing at her blackboard and writing in her sloping Palmer method for her students to copy their graceful, looping l's—

> I wandered lonely as a cloud
> That floats on high o'er vales and hills,
> When all at once I saw a crowd,
> A host of golden daffodils,

If a cynic in the corner questioned her as to how a cloud knew it was lonely, Miss Schnell would have seized the opportunity to discuss the differences between cumulus and cirrus and nimbus and stratus clouds. She would have been instructing in an interdisciplinary fashion, even though pedagogy had not yet coined the term.

Near the end of each day, Dorothy probably saved a few precious minutes to share with her students from an ongoing work of fiction— Dickens, perhaps. The characters that were the companions of her grim childhood now took life in her classroom. She would vary her voice and expression to portray Bill Sykes or Tiny Tim, strut like the Artful Dodger or shudder in terror like Ebenezer Scrooge at the sight of Marley's ghost. Who knows how many impressionable yet reluctant young minds were indelibly affected by those afternoon readings.

Still living at home, Dorothy continued to contribute much of her earnings to the household. This pattern was established early. Dorothy, Janette, and David had all worked in after-school hours and contributed to the family's welfare, and several changes of address indicate that perhaps the family's fortunes had improved somewhat. Still, luxuries were still few and hard to come by. In later years, when she wore designer dresses and furs, she remarked wistfully that girls should have pretty dresses when they are young, when they can most appreciate them.

Facing a classroom, being well dressed, and assuming a position of authority—even among young scholars—gave Dorothy self-confidence. Climbing a few rungs higher on the economic scale added to her poise. The Schnells now had "not only two curtains at every window, a front entrance, a garden, and a telephone that rang constantly." Dorothy had so many swains that her father, always the romantic, took to making a list of them.

Having many friends was something new and different for the redhaired girl who had spent much of her childhood in a make-believe world of books. "I never had a date in high school," she told *Cleveland Press* TV-Radio Editor Bill Barrett in 1980. "Not one, not until I graduated—I was just sixteen and wondered why all the other girls had dates and I never did. . . . I always felt the boy would be doing me a favor if he went out with me. That all changed when I began feeling that the BOY should feel proud and lucky to be with ME. That was a bewilderingly wonderful feeling. And it still functions."

On the occasion of her ninetieth birthday, Dorothy would still remember her first date with someone in an automobile. "His name was Herbert, and he took me out in his carriage. He was an awful bore, but I was in an automobile. I can remember the gas, the flame, coming out the back."

With the years of hardship and grueling poverty dimming in her memory, Dorothy wrote of this period, "Life was magnificent. I could hardly wait for the morning to come—the days were so wonderful."

The family began breaking apart about the time World War I ended. Dorothy wrote in later years that David was fifteen years of age when he left home to pursue a musical career. Milwaukee census records, however, show him living with the family through 1918. He was listed as having no occupation in 1917 and as a musician in 1918. Based upon his age given in the 1910 census, David would have been twenty-one years of age that year. According to Dorothy's writings, David did gain a reputation as a composer and eventually became conductor of MGM's studio orchestra in Hollywood.

Less is known about Janette, (spelled Jeanette in the Milwaukee records). She is listed as a stenographer or secretary in various city directories until 1918. According to Dorothy's reminiscences, Janette continued to study dance and performed professionally with a vaudeville troupe before her marriage. "In her pink ballet costume, she was breathtakingly lovely," Dorothy wrote.

In 1918 Dorothy married Milton H. Fuldheim of Cleveland, which was eventually to become Dorothy's permanent home. There is no record of how they met. They were married in Milwaukee, however, and they lived there at 501 Marshall Street. Janette is listed as living with them for a part of that year. She was still living in Milwaukee in 1958 when her mother's death notice listed her as a surviving daugher, Mrs. [Janet] Meyer. Milton was a graduate of the Cleveland Law School (now Cleveland Marshall School of Law at Cleveland State University). Milton's occupation, however, for 1918 was "adjuster," but in the 1920 directory he was listed as having "no occupation."

As they became adults, all three Schnell children kept in close touch with their mother. She believed in them, inspired them, challenged them. "She was our sanctuary and our haven," Dorothy wrote after Bertha's death. Bertha Schnell seemed to accept as her due the luxuries her successful grown children could bestow upon her in her later years. As Dorothy wrote later, "Wasn't that why one had children? That was a different generation. Parents were not shunted away and treated as a burden. They were taken care of and given outward respect even [in cases] when there was no great affection."

After the children left, Herman and Bertha continued to move frequently; four different addresses are given in the Milwaukee City Directory for them between 1918 and 1923. Actually, the 1923 and 1924 entries are for Mrs. Bertha Schnell only. Herman, whose occupation is listed variously as "salesman," "commercial traveler," and "sales," was listed as "Hyman" Schnell, "agent," (husband of Bertha) in 1922. After 1922 Herman Schnell is listed only once, in the 1927 directory—and at a different address from that of Mrs. Bertha Schnell. In 1929 Mrs. Bertha Schnell is listed as "wid [widow] Herman," living at 429 Martin Drive, Apartment 6.

The few pieces of information Dorothy records about her father show him to be a romantic, somewhat of a ladies' man. At least, she seemed to sense this and offers veiled comments on the subject.

> My father was a man of charm and must have had a good deal of sex appeal, because my mother was always suspicious of him. The baker's wife, a red-cheeked, high-bosomed woman, gazed fondly at him; and even when there was no money, we had no trouble charging the bread and milk at the baker's shop. I recall one time, in spite of the fact we had no money my mother refused to go to the baker shop.

> It must have been a period when the baker's wife was *more*
> than cordial to my father.

As stated, Herman was devoted to his children, however, and perhaps he and Bertha found they had little in common as the children grew older and moved away. This is mere supposition, but the information from the directories indicates he did not live with Bertha during the last few years of his life. Also, he did not die in Milwaukee County, according to a search made of the death records from 1922 through 1929, the year when the city directory first lists Bertha as Herman's widow.

Various newspaper stories describe Dorothy's teaching career as being as brief as one year. She was still listed as a teacher in *Wright's Phone Directory* in Milwaukee and the *Milwaukee City Directory*, however, in 1920, eight years after her graduation from Milwaukee Normal.

Although she wore new dresses and perfume while listening to her pupils read from their McGuffeys or watching them practice their Palmer penmanship method, Dorothy's life lacked the mental stimulation she would realize was as indispensable to her as life's own breath. From deep within—nourished by her mother's ironclad confidence in her abilities, by the passionate pleas of attorneys she had listened to with her father, hour after hour, and by the vast sampling of the world's literature she had already digested—a fervent, soul-wrenching need to express herself more completely was crying out. She longed to identify more fully with the human condition. "I felt so confined," she explained in retrospect. "I had all this emotion within me and had to find a release for it."

In a fortuitous choice Dorothy found an outlet for this emotion and passion in a local little theater group called The Wisconsin Players and, without realizing it, took another step on her professional journey. Her first leading role was that of Juliet in *Romeo and Juliet*. Although she wrote later that she felt the best Juliets were older actresses who could understand and evaluate the anguish of young love, her performance under the stars in an outdoor theater was well received and led to other leading roles.

Recalling the redhaired girl who less than a decade before had swept regally down the Milwaukee Library's marble staircase in an imaginary green taffeta dress with a train, her transformation into the winsome Juliet who captivated Romeo's heart at the Capulets' ball is not difficult to imagine. The young girl who grew up listening raptly to defenders of truth and justice could easily give credence to such lines as these:

> 'Tis but thy name that is my enemy.
> Thou art thyself, though not a Montague.
> What's Montague? It is nor hand nor foot,
> Nor arm nor face, nor any other part
> Belonging to a man. O be some other name.
> What's in a name? That which we call a rose
> By any other word would smell as sweet;
> So Romeo would, were he not Romeo called
> Retain that dear perfection which he owes
> Without that title.

Decades later, Dorothy interviewed the inestimable actor Charles Laughton for WEWS-TV few months before his death in 1962. To his delight, his hostess played Juliet to his Romeo in a few scenes. She wrote of the magic he could create—that no singer could move an audience any more than he could with his speaking voice.

Dorothy acknowledged that most female voices by nature are higher than male voices, thus often causing them to be unpleasant to listen to for long periods. She described working with a voice coach who helped her compensate for this quality by rigorous vocal exercises. She could tell the positive effect these exercises had upon her speaking voice, and when she failed to do them she recognized the difference.

The stage offered a natural outlet for the emotion Dorothy had stifled within her that needed release. Acting must have been a pleasurable experience for her and one which, perhaps, she tended to be nostalgic about in her later years. "I'm sure I would have remained an actress if fate hadn't decreed otherwise," she told *Plain Dealer* reporter William Hickey in 1972. Perhaps she even had some regrets, for a few years later she told another reporter that . . ."the stage is where I really belong." She went ahead to state, however, that she is different: she has an erudition not usually associated with actresses.

Since Milwaukee records never list Dorothy Schnell as having any occupation other than that of a teacher, we can assume her stage career never progressed beyond that of a local theater group, perhaps only during her summer vacations from school. The actors did travel to some surrounding cities, including Chicago, which would eventually be of great benefit to Dorothy.

Even before she became an actress, Dorothy's ideas were taking shape by events she observed and experienced in the burgeoning world around her. All around her were changing political and economic situations. Milwaukee was now an industrial city instead of a trading center. The city election of 1910 was the highwater mark of Milwaukee Socialism that had been gaining strength along with trade unionism since the turn of the century. The city would have a Socialist mayor for thirty-eight years. Although not Marxist in philosophy, the Socialist party had inherited the support of "a considerable portion of the labor movement along with a German reform tradition that went all the way back to the Forty-eighters, liberals and intellectuals who fled an unsuccessful revolt.

The Socialist tradition in Milwaukee was at once radical and conservative—the party members wanted to try new things, but only if things they wanted to try proved to be impossible. Under the city's charter, they couldn't do much more than talk about public ownership and at the end of the Milwaukee Socialist era the city did not own any public transport, municipal power plants or much of anything else a capitalist might have wanted.

Dorothy would have followed the national political scene with interest also. At the turn of the twentieth century when Dorothy was seven years old, William McKinley was elected President for a second term. A few months after his inauguration, he was shot by a fanatic and died in September. From the time Dorothy was eight years old until she was sixteen, Theodore Roosevelt occupied the White House. His ebullient nature and fervent oratory kept him in the national spotlight as dramatic speaking tours and newspaper interviews by insightful reporters fueled a meteoric rise in the popularity of a heretofore obscure vice-president. The frequent references by today's politicians to "TR's bully pulpit" attest to his ability to use his office to lead the nation along the path of reform and thereby to aid in nationalizing a progressive movement already strong and popular at local and state

levels. Autocratic and charismatic, TR championed many social re-
forms which now exist in this country. His populist point of view
more than likely appealed to Dorothy and influenced her thinking as
she grew older.

President Theodore Roosevelt made several visits to Milwaukee,
one of which was in 1910 when Dorothy was just starting college.
Although she never refers to being present at one of his speeches, she
surely would have read them. In fact, Herman Schnell, with his passion for rhetoric, very likely read the fiery President's views aloud to
whichever family members would listen.

Two years later, the year she graduated from Milwaukee Normal,
TR was trying for another term as President, running on the Bull
Moose ticket. He again visited Milwaukee, and the dramatic incident
that occurred during his visit to her home city would have no doubt
profoundly affected the young about-to-be teacher.

As he was making his way to Milwaukee Auditorium to speak, the
President was wounded in an attempt on his life by John Schrank,
who was later judged insane. Despite a critical wound, President
Roosevelt insisted upon going on to the hall and delivering his speech.
When the audience failed to take seriously Henry Cochem's bumbling
introduction that attempted to describe the President's condition, TR
ordered him to sit down. Pulling aside his coat and vest and facing
the audience, the wounded President shouted, "I perceive that you
fail to understand that I am the man who has been shot." A hushed
and shocked audience could see the blood drenching through his clothing. Although doctors tried to convince him to go to a hospital, he
talked for eighty minutes. The fifty-page speech that he had carried
inside his coat had slowed the bullet's entry and saved his life.

Other events taking place in the world at the time Dorothy entered adulthood must have aroused in her a myriad of feelings and
emotions. A few weeks before her college graduation, the H.M.S.
Titanic struck an iceberg and sank on her maiden voyage from
Southampton, England to New York, plunging more than 1,500 souls
to their watery graves. Hundreds of those were immigrants, steerage
passengers who were not even permitted on the deck from which the
inadequate number of lifeboats were launched. Ironically, the owners
of the White Star and Cunard Lines reaped two-thirds of their rev-
enue and one-half the profits from these city-sized ocean liners from
the millions of immigrant passengers they carried each year. As a
young woman whose parents had arrived as immigrants little more

than a quarter-century before, Dorothy would surely have identified with those unfortunate victims. She would have poured over the accounts of the investigations into the negligence of the White Star Line and followed the subsequent legal actions on both sides of the Atlantic.

Her romantic instincts would perhaps have quickened when she read of the admission of the nation's two newest states—Arizona and New Mexico. She would long to escape the acrid fumes and malt-heavy air of Milwaukee and to travel beneath cobalt-blue skies and breath the bracing desert air. To read accounts of Roald Amundsen's successful venture to the South Pole must have aroused her sense of adventure and to see a woman—Madame Marie Curie—accept the Nobel Prize for Chemistry and an American statesman—Elihu Root—receive the Nobel Peace Prize must have filled her with pride. Her college class on government perhaps inspired her to read H.G. Wells' *The New Machiavelli*, and while outside of class she would likely have devoured Theodore Dreiser's newest novel, *Jennie Gerhardt*. Possibly, she read newspaper stories written for her own city's papers by young reporters named Carl Sandburg and Edna Ferber.

Dorothy found herself at the center of a kaleidoscope of bold, shifting changes in the world revolving about her. How would she fit the colors and the pieces together to shape her adult life?

4

On the Lecture Circuit

The brush with fate that cut short Dorothy's acting experience and catapulted her to the lecture platform involved none other than Jane Addams, the leading social reformer of the early twentieth century. With her Hull House well established as a refuge and skill-building center for women and children, Addams was crusading for the world peace movement that flourished after World War I. She happened to attend a performance in Chicago where the Wisconsin Players presented Sada Cowan's *The State Forbids*. In this drama Dorothy Schnell Fuldheim portrayed a mother of two sons, one a young man who is being called to war, the other, a young child who was an imbecile from birth.

> [The mother speaks] The State won't let us women help ourselves. We must have children whether we want them or not. And then the state comes and takes them from us. It doesn't ask. It commands. We've got to give them up. [Shrilly.] I've got to give my boy. [Again bitterly.] What are we, we women? Just cattle! Breeding animals . . . without a voice! Dumb—powerless! [An instant's pause, then in intense rebellion.] Oh, the State! The State commands! And the State forbids! Damn the State!
> [In vain, the mother begs the doctor to put the unfortunate child to sleep.] Years ago you wouldn't help me to end the suffering of an innocent soul. You wouldn't even turn your back while a THING went out into the darkness. But now

you've come to take him from me. You'd take the boy I've watched grow big and strong . . . a man . . . and you'd leave THAT. [Points to the child.] . . .You said to put that child out of the way would be murder. The State would call it murder. Well, what's this? Tell me. Isn't this murder? Isn't this life you're taking? [Savagely.] Oh, I hate you. I have hated you for ten long years. But I never knew how much until today.

Moved by Dorothy's stirring performance, Miss Addams visited her backstage and invited the young actress to tea at Hull House the next day. "I was awed. She was a great and noble human being, and the whole world revered her," Dorothy recalled. This experience alone would have been an event to be remembered forever, for Jane Addams would share the Nobel Peace Prize in 1931.

But a discerning Jane Addams had seen in Dorothy's gifted performance more than an actress who could project roles others created. Instead, she wished to tap the young woman's abilities as a stage presence, to enlist Dorothy to her cause as a lecturer for social justice and world peace.

"You have one week to prepare," she told the dumbfounded young actress.

"So I went to Philadelphia," Dorothy recalled, "and I assure you I knew nothing about public speaking. I wasn't sufficiently educated. But apparently I did have some fire because women, my God, started taking off their jewelry and men started writing checks."

In Philadelphia Dorothy shared the platform with the noted Hendrik Willem Van Loon, who, Miss Addams had confided to Dorothy, lacked fire and enthusiasm. Dorothy wrote later that she was too ignorant to understand how momentous the occasion was and how it would influence her whole life.

> I told the audience of an Australian, Thomas Skeyhill, who had been blinded in the war. His poems had been read in the Houses of Parliament and had roused the English to a frenzy.

> England, oh England, thou art calling me.
> Sweet sounds thy voice o'er the soft azure main,
> And all that I have I offer thee,
> Flesh of my bones and the blood of each vein . . .

> I described his stand at Gallipoli, how he had been brought
> to this country, how an American surgeon had restored his
> sight. I lamented about the many who were tapping their
> way through the streets of the cities of the world, blinded in
> the war, doomed to darkness forever and ever. . . . For me,
> Jane Addams' thanks were enough.

In recalling her maiden speech on another occasion, Dorothy seemed more modest. She told William Hickey of *The Cleveland Plain Dealer*, "I don't think I added much fire to the proceedings, but I certainly added to the confusion. I really didn't know what I was doing. I wasn't dumb, but I was ignorant of many things that were taking place in the world at that time. At least I learned that much from the experience."

Hickey, who by this time knew Dorothy Fuldheim as a revered twenty-five-year television news journalist, commented that though Dorothy "may have lacked universal knowledge and oratorical finesse [at that first Philadelphia speech] . . . her arresting and passionate approach was no doubt a natural consequence of possessing a spirited soul and the ability to dramatize its restless searchings."

As a reviewer of books and a freelance lecturer, Dorothy's reputation would reach mythic proportions in the next three decades, but not before she had to make a new start in unfamiliar surroundings. Not long after the Philadelphia speech, she and her husband and baby daughter, also named Dorothy, moved to Cleveland. The young couple was struggling financially. Milton Fuldheim was not well, presumably suffering from a poor heart which plagued him for most of his adult life. The young Fuldheim family rented an apartment on the fourth floor at 12467 Cedar Road at the juncture of Fairmount Boulevard. The building was solid, built of dark red brick with a tiled foyer which to Dorothy probably looked like marble. Even though there were seven other families in the building, this was the nearest thing to elegance she had ever had to call home. Milton took law offices just down the street in the Heights Center Building.

The Fuldheims became permanent members of the Cleveland Heights community, although they moved several times. As finances allowed, they later moved off teeming Cedar Road to what is now known as the Roosevelt Apartments at 2450 Overlook Road where they occupied a ground floor suite. The streets were lined with lordly elms and oaks; young couples strolled in the fragrant evening twilight holding their children's hands. On nearby Euclid Heights Boulevard stood a spacious, gabled cottage with a wide side porch that Dorothy and Milton must have passed many times. Eventually, this became their home, probably the first time in her life Dorothy had lived under a roof that was not shared with other families.

But there were many lean years before Milton and Dorothy were able to purchase the Euclid Heights Boulevard home.

> One day I was walking on the street and a woman stopped me . . . I wish I could remember her name . . . and she said 'Aren't you the woman I heard in Philadelphia?' She said, 'You're the answer to a dream!' or something like that. She said, 'We need a book review at the City Club—the Women's City Club.' I'd never heard of a book review in my life, didn't know what it was, but if it was about books, it was all right with me, and I agreed to do it.

She recalls that first review was of H.G. Wells' *The World of William Clissold*, a story about supermen ruling the world. She gratefully accepted a stipend of ten dollars and stood on tiptoe (literally!) at the threshold of a reputation as a book reviewer par excellence.

Dorothy's unique style of reviewing a book could enthrall an audience. She used no notes. Not satisfied only to relate the story to her audience, she dramatized the characters' roles.

"I had a sense of drama, you know," she said, "even if I didn't have anything to eat. I had the clothes that would do it and the groups that featured me would raise their funds for the year. That's how I started."

Times were still lean, however, in the Fuldheim household. On her way to Cleveland Heights High School, Taffy Epstein (known then as Harriett Gombossy), who years later became a neighbor and close friend of Dorothy's, remembers walking to Cleveland Heights High School and seeing tiny Dorothy Fuldheim waiting for a streetcar to take her "down to [Rabbi] Silver's Temple to do a book review. Her skirt flapped in the cruel, cold wind. She evidently didn't own a winter coat."

Dorothy managed somehow to acquire the clothes she needed for these public appearances. Although she had grown up in a household where her mother made dresses from discarded curtains, even if Dorothy had been skilled with a needle, reading and preparing book reviews and caring for a family filled her time. Perhaps she structured some creative financing or a lending policy with the Higbee Company (department store, now Dillard's) to outfit herself stylishly enough for her early public appearances.

However Dorothy dressed, her book reviews became an institution in Cleveland where she would hold as many as 1,800 persons mesmerized in Higbee's auditorium on Mondays for more than an hour. Dorothy Fuldheim's rising popularity and her gift for self-promotion commanded respect, and before long she could insist that the decorating scheme for the auditorium be color-coordinated to the dress she would wear on a given day. Charitable organizations sponsoring her book reviews could count on raising their funds for the entire year. Her success left the only other book reviewers in the city, both males whose presentations were unremarkable, shaking their heads.

With her voracious appetite for books cultivated from childhood and nourished by the Milwaukee Public Library, Dorothy had unwittingly prepared herself for this next level of her career. She claimed to read as many as twelve books a week during this period when she was reviewing books for a living. Never, she explained, did she read every word. Instead, she read diagonally, omitting the insignificant words. Her stage experience aided her in memorizing and delivering the lengthy dramatic passages that so captivated her audiences. Even those late afternoon sessions of sharing her passion for literature with her students in a musty schoolroom were building blocks in the foundation of the career that was to follow.

Always eager to supplement the family income and to broaden her circle of influence, Dorothy Fuldheim, who was acquiring strong opinions about issues of the day and realizing she could make people listen to her, registered in the late 1920s with a lecture bureau operated by a childhood acquaintance from Milwaukee, Rickley Boasberg. Fate, it seemed, had placed them side by side in Cleveland.

Her relationship with Mrs. Boasberg's agency was to last for more than thirty years and was one of mutual advantage. "It doesn't matter if you don't like her," Boasberg told a *Cleveland Press* reporter in 1959. "Hire her to speak at your organization and she'll raise the money you need. I've had her on every major platform in the Midwest in the last 30 years and I've never heard an adverse opinion of her as a speaker."

Dorothy called the agency "one of the finest and most scrupulous, as well as most conscientious and very successful." She points out that lectures were the means by which people saw celebrities in those days, and as long as you did something that commanded attention, the lecture bureaus would come rushing at you, even if you could not speak well.

In what seems a prehistoric era—before television, before bombastic speakers hurled their rhetoric across family dinner tables—the lecture circuit existed as a significant cultural and educational force in the United States. The "Lyceum" movement, an ambitious educational movement started in the first half of the nineteenth century, aimed for "a universal diffusion of knowledge" and for self-improvement by citizens, even in very small communities. At first, Lyceum series relied mostly upon hometown talent, but citizens eventually clamored for visiting speakers. Assisted by such notables as Ralph Waldo Emerson, James Russell Lowell, Oliver Wendell Holmes, Horace Greeley, and Edward Everett Hale, lecturing attained the status of a profession.

Speech making was not reserved for quadrennial political campaigns. Orations on controversial issues of the day, delivered with fire and conviction, not read in a monotone, were commonplace throughout the nation's history. As the railroad brought people together in groups and speakers could travel greater distances, respect for oratory rose to great heights. Crowds thronged the capitol in Washington in 1850, for example, to listen to "The Triumvirate"—Senators Daniel Webster, John C. Calhoun, and Henry Clay—debate the conditions of what became The Compromise of 1850, which would stave off the Civil War for another decade. Not many years later, the celebrated Lincoln-Douglas debates brought thousands streaming across the Illinois prairies to solidify their views on burning sectional issues and, as a result, raised Lincoln to a nationally known figure.

Following the Civil War, lecturing was given a boost by the Chautauqua, a popular adult education program founded in western New York state in the 1870s. Major thinkers of the day frequently held forth under large tents where spellbound listeners stood for hours, only interrupting their rapt attention to cheer and applaud. By 1910, clones of the Chautauqua movement fanned out across the nation. The Chautauqua circuit brought literary, musical, and arts presentations, often featuring the nation's best thinkers and performers, to cities and even small towns. A typical Chautauqua circuit program was a combination of music and dramatics and lecturing.

The American Chautauqua speaker without parallel was three-time unsuccessful presidential candidate, William Jennings Bryan. He was thought by some, however, to display a lack of dignity by going on the circuit with vaudeville acts when he was Secretary of State. A response he made to this criticism elevated lecturing to the status of a profession; Bryan's unequivocal reply was that "lecturing was a legitimate activity, that President Wilson approved, and that he needed his lecture proceeds to support himself and his family."

Of course, all people who toured the lecture circuit in the early decades of the twentieth century were not even familiar names. Although the nation had healed itself somewhat after its divisive Civil War and had "fought the war to end all wars" in Europe, speakers harangued on issues galore—suffrage for women, prohibition, the peace movement, child labor abuse, unionization of labor. For a lecturer to draw a following, he or she must possess intelligence, compassion, and the ability to assimilate the gist of America's social problems and communicate them to others—preferably with a dramatic flair. Dorothy Fuldheim had a natural talent for professional speech making.

By the late 1920s, as the era of flappers and flivvers drew to a close, Dorothy was being paid what was then a hefty fee for her lectures. She used no notes, believing that they were an obstruction between her and her listeners. She regarded each lecture as a performance and felt her audience deserved her full projection. Vastly more satisfying to her than her former careers, lecturing permitted her to flaunt her own ideas—not those of a textbook writer or a playwright—ideas clothed in words of her own selection.

She had to combat stage fright, confessing in later years that "it would take a full fifteen minutes after I had begun talking to get command of myself and get into the subject with feeling and expression."

To project her views, Dorothy moved from a general statement and supported it with specific examples and illustrations she knew her listeners would identify with. Her technique was much the same as the gospel of a wise sociology professor in a Midwestern women's college who drilled into her students' consciousness a timeless maxim. "Define—and il*lus*trate—when making statements in this classroom," she would thunder from her platform. Fresh-faced young women trembled in their saddle shoes when called upon to speak in Dr. Clara Helen Mueller's classes, but they learned to make forceful, significant arguments. Perhaps young Dorothy Schnell experienced a Dr. Mueller at Milwaukee Normal, or maybe her hours spent with her father, observing lawyers presenting cases, provided her with repeated examples of proceeding from the general to the specific as the most effective way to reach an audience.

The young girl whose siblings had taunted her with the nickname, "Dictionary-swallower" had become a professional who could use language to move, convince, cajole, or stimulate her listeners.

She told a reporter years later: "Many people underrate my erudition because I sound so simple on the air. But simplicity is the result of tremendous erudition and knowledge and my ability to put it in simple words."

Dorothy Fuldheim tried to appeal to the man or woman in the building trades or the corner bar as well as the ones in the board room and the ivory towers of academia. She perceived herself as an intellectual, charismatic bridge between her vast storehouse of knowledge of world affairs and her viewers.

An attribute Dorothy felt every speaker must possess was wit. Not given to attempting a stand-up comic routine, she admired humor such as the subtle variety of Adlai Stevenson, for example. When he was campaigning for president against Dwight Eisenhower in the 1950s, Stevenson looked out over a crowd and began his remarks by telling of a very pregnant woman in the front row at the last rally who carried a placard saying, STEVENSON'S THE MAN. In the still-sexually repressed Fifties, the comment at once put the audience in Stevenson's back pocket.

Dorothy Fuldheim recognized the importance of establishing rapport with her listeners at the outset and claimed she could have them in the palm of her hand within the first few minutes. Uncontrived humor often did the trick. Dorothy was a quick study and made the most of sometimes difficult situations to ingratiate herself with her audience.

Even in her later years, when she had gained renown as a television news analyst yet continued her countless lectures, she knew she could defuse a likely situation that spelled trouble with a bit of humor. "I'm never unaware of my [e]ffect on the audience . . . It is as though I were holding their pulse. I know when to switch from seriousness to humor."

At a high school graduation in Aurora, Ohio, where she was the featured speaker, Dorothy spotted a baby sleeping on a mother's lap in the front row. Throughout the introduction by Principal Roger Sidoti (who happened to be the baby's father, she learned later), Dorothy eyed the sleeping child warily. When she rose to speak, she drew herself up to the podium with the immense dignity and *savoir faire* that she possessed despite her short stature. (Sometimes she stood on a box, hidden beneath the podium, so she could reach the lectern.) Peering down at Mary Sidoti and her child, she prefaced her remarks with, "Madam, you had better keep that child quiet—or I will take her home with me!" The audience erupted with good-natured laughter, and it was all Dorothy's. Little Ann Sidoti slumbered peacefully throughout the address.

Occasionally, though, Dorothy was unable to sidestep a disturbance created by an even smaller creature. At a white-tie dinner in Mansfield, Ohio, she became aware during her address that the man next to her at the speaker's table was striking the train of her dress with his napkin. Finally, she turned and questioned him. "There's a mouse running up your train," he told her calmly. Just as calmly, she asked, "Did you get him?" only to hear him say the creature had left the platform and was now running about the auditorium. Every woman sat with her legs drawn up throughout Dorothy's lecture, and the question period was very brief.

Dorothy Fuldheim measured her effectiveness as a speaker by the cohesiveness of the audience. If they were moved, she looked for signs of tenseness or alacrity. If they were listless or easily distracted, she acknowledged to herself she was not communicating with this audience the way she had planned. Never tied to a prepared text, Dorothy would vary her illustrations to help her listeners relate to her main thesis more readily. From the vast storehouse of her vocabulary, she chose words skillfully to embody her ideas. She prided herself on her command of "noble language," her refusal to talk down to her audience. Dorothy's dramatic pauses and her see-it-my-way gestures added the cultivated touch to the spellbinding quality of her delivery.

5
While Storm Clouds Gathered

Regardless of how skillfully a speaker uses words, regardless of his or her ability to be convincing, a message must contain ideas, and those ideas must be bolstered with facts. By the mid-1920s Rickley Boasberg was booking Dorothy Fuldheim as a lecturer throughout the nation. She still did book reviews in her home city of Cleveland, but her lectures required extensive research and more preparation time. Not content to form her opinions from newspaper editorials or to rehash other people's ideas, Dorothy Fuldheim began to travel in Europe to observe for herself the threatening situation that was festering there. Her insatiable curiosity to experience situations firsthand and to identify with the people whose lives she was describing brought her shoulder to shoulder with the power-hungry political leaders and average citizens—many of whom were unemployed and wondering where their next meal would come from.

On a visit to Germany in 1934 she bought a sandwich for a starving prostitute in Hamburg and learned over the lunch counter of the hope and magnetism that Adolf Hitler's message conveyed to the masses of unemployed. At that time Hitler was rising in popularity as the leader of the burgeoning National Socialist, later Nazi, party. In Dresden a few days later, when Dorothy befriended an unemployed tutor, bought her a meal, and gave her a pair of her own shoes, the grateful woman repaid her American friend by taking her to a rally to hear Hitler speak. Dorothy could not believe the pompous little man was to be taken seriously.

> I could not follow every word but I understood perfectly well when he said that Germany had been defeated by the

Jews, [in World War I] who had betrayed the German people. At that a roar in which my companion joined went up from the crowd. Had I but known it, in that roar could be sensed the overtones of death and the smell of the ovens of Buchenwald and all the other camps. "Follow me!" he thundered, "The glory of Germany will be restored; we shall take our rightful place as the leaders of Europe! Follow me and every man shall have a job! The robbers who have taken our wealth, the Jews, shall be forced to give up the plunder they have taken from us!" On and on it went for three hours. I was exhausted but aware that the man had magnetism and answered something in the hungry souls and bellies of the listeners. But like everyone else, [outside of Germany], I believed that he was saying these things only to stir the crowd and had no intention of ever making his promises a reality.

Nearly every newspaper and magazine profile ever written about Dorothy Fuldheim alludes to her personal interview with Adolf Hitler. Most mention it in passing, often in tandem with Churchill's name, as if to give credence to the statement that she interviewed the world's most powerful people. What few accounts relate, however, is that Dorothy's meeting with Hitler occurred, as she describes it, more "by accident than by plan."

Following the speech in Dresden, she heard that Hitler was leaving for Munich where he would be meeting with members of the Nazi party at the Brown House, the party's headquarters. On an impulse, Dorothy went to Munich to try to get an interview with him.

Call it accident or call it fate, Adolf Hitler walked into the very office where Dorothy was trying to convince a secretary to schedule an interview. In later television interviews she sometimes says she met him outside on the steps. Wherever it was, she had to summon up ironclad nerve and moxie to approach him and, in her faltering German, request a personal meeting.

The resulting twenty minutes that he imperiously granted her very likely magnified Dorothy Fuldheim's voice as one to be listened to about world affairs. To her dauntless question as to how he perceived Germany's historical role, Hitler launched forth the same tirade Dorothy had heard in the Dresden speech, blaming the Jews for Germany's defeat in World War I. When Dorothy pressed him to admit that the

Allies were also responsible, he fastened the blame upon "the Jewish international bankers."

Regrettably, no photographs exist of this impromptu conversation between an audacious, diminutive American newsgatherer with flaming red hair and a power-crazed, would-be warlord who was not much taller than she. She apparently persisted with her questions and refused to be intimidated by his arrogance. In her memoirs she perceptively described him with a graphic metaphor:

> He carried a riding whip and every so often struck it against his boots. He was the circus trainer and the world was to jump through the hoops at his command. Alas, the German people did, and the hoop became a ball of fire, encircling the world.

Recalling the historic meeting in an interview for a 1972 profile, Dorothy told *Plain Dealer* reporter William Hickey, "Luckily, he didn't even know I was Jewish." Hickey went on to state that because Dorothy Fuldheim continued, in the years preceding World War II, to give "many speeches in which she pointed out the dangers of dictatorships and the loss of personal freedoms they caused, she was declared *persona non grata* in Germany and Italy as well."

At home, even among sophisticated audiences that she regarded as the easiest to reach, her pre-war warnings about Hitler fell upon deaf ears and closed minds. A 1937 New York Town Hall address was regarded as "too dramatic." Americans there and elsewhere could not be persuaded that Hitler was serious in his intentions and that his brazen scheme to elevate Germany to a superpower of Europe was within the realm of possibility.

Dorothy writes of making five different trips to Europe in the 1930s, observing and gathering firsthand information about the mounting crisis there. Her well-to-do girlhood friend Roseka was her traveling companion on some of these trips, and in at least one case and very likely more than one, she helped finance them.

Yearning to go to Italy later in 1934 to inspect the changes being brought about by Mussolini, Dorothy found herself with no available funds to travel. At that time she was still a freelance lecturer with no regular sponsorship or backing from any organization. Her household responsibilities had eased somewhat since her mother, Bertha Schnell, widowed since 1929, had moved to Cleveland to make her home with Dorothy, Milton, and now-teenaged daughter Dorothy Louise.

Bertha Schnell assuredly was a positive and stable influence upon the young girl. Just as she had always encouraged her children and bolstered their faith in themselves and their desire to achieve, she undoubtedly took a similar interest in her granddaughter. Now that she had leisure time and lived more comfortably, Bertha accepted as her due the amenities of her daughter's home, quickly acquiring manners and tastes far removed from the slums of Milwaukee. Dorothy remembered that her mother never came downstairs, even in her later years, without being powdered and perfumed. Not only was she beautiful with delicate skin and shrewd, knowing eyes, she was charming.

Dorothy mentions that Bertha sometimes visited David in his fast-paced, west coast surroundings and went to parties with him given by Hollywood celebrities. Her permanent membership in the household must have been an advantage during Dorothy's frequent absences. By this time Dorothy surely employed some domestic help, but the value of her mother's presence and the importance of her influence on Dorothy Junior were immeasurable.

A phone call from Roseka one day came as an answer to Dorothy's fervent wish. She claimed to have two tickets to Italy, offered to her by one of her prosperous brothers. Would Dorothy like to go along? Dorothy was no doubt mentally packing her bags before she hung up the phone.

Dorothy and Roseka were fun-loving, well-dressed American women, bound to attract notice. Their visit to Venice, city of gondolas and balconied hotels, brought them attentions from two Englishmen who befriended Dorothy when she lost her purse. After the Italian police returned the purse (for a small fee), the gentlemen invited the two women to dine with them. Impulsive Dorothy, who had always pictured herself being serenaded on a balcony, while wearing a flowing white gown and holding a single, long-stemmed rose, demanded a serenade as a condition for accepting the invitation.

With typical wry English humor, the gentlemen approached the American ladies' balcony singing, "K-k-katy, K-k-katy, over the cowshed," instead of "I Love You Truly," or some similar heart-tugging lyric. They dined together, nevertheless, and the Englishmen eventually drove the ladies to Florence for the next remarkable episode of their journey.

Although Dorothy and Roseka mingled with prominent people in their travels, Dorothy's memoirs frequently recount her in-depth contacts with nameless, prosaic individuals she met. At an audience with the Pope, she speaks of the Pope's graciousness to visitors and of witnessing him blessing a group of children in a "scene of rare and beautiful solemnity." Then her memoir switches off into a tale of borrowing a lace scarf to cover her head. When she returned the scarf afterwards, "the florid English woman," a retired teacher, offered Dorothy a ride back to Rome in her sports car. The car was small and the owner over two hundred pounds, so Dorothy huddled against the passenger door. But "she was a good sort and regaled me with some boisterous stories," Dorothy recalled. Although the woman is nameless, the rollicking ride was a serendipitous adventure she felt worth recording, almost in the same breath, as it were, with her visit to the Papal Chamber.

Dorothy met Mussolini unofficially, though not a chance meeting as the one with Hitler had been. She and Roseka were invited to a party where more than two hundred guests gathered in his honor. Unobserved, Dorothy was able to watch him for some time.

> His face was stony and his eyes were quiet not like the nervous moving eyes of Hitler. He had a magnetism that results from the exercise of almost limited power; it exudes from dictators and is impressive and awe inspiring. . . . Unlike Hitler, Mussolini had sex appeal, at least one was aware that he was a male.

When he was presented to her, rather than she to him, she rankled a bit at this and later observed that "royalty and dictators reverse social customs as well as political history." She resented his inane question about whether she was enjoying shopping and retorted that she was observing his rule in Italy and how it would affect Europe. Undaunted, she continued by taking him to task about the four hundred and nineteen signs she had counted on the streets reading *Viva il Duce*—long live Mussolini. He retorted by trying to embarrass her. "It shows how many of my people wish me well. Are you going back to America and tell about this also?" Dorothy made no comment but later wrote, "I stood my ground." As she walked away, Il Duce was commenting upon the strangeness of American women.

She knew that she was unpopular in Italy because she had articulated her opinion about Mussolini (even before coming to Italy). Nevertheless, she relentlessly pursued angles for stories to use as illustrations for her lectures. One bit of news she did not know was that Mussolini had banned the sale of the current issue of the American *Fortune* magazine that contained a critical appraisal of him. Although the penalty for possession of the inflammatory magazine was arrest and imprisonment, Dorothy flaunted it at the American embassy.

After finally heeding the warnings of their countrymen at the embassy, Dorothy and Roseka returned to their hotel and proceeded to destroy the magazine, a page at a time. But what would they do with the telltale pieces? They considered burying them in the Catacombs, scattering them around the Coliseum, or even hiring a plane and strewing them as if they were ashes. All were regarded as too risky. The ultimate solution resulted in the flushing of several pounds of *Fortune* into the plumbing of the Flora Hotel, putting it completely out of working order. The two women, pumped up with their daring, departed for an evening of wine, food, and merriment. When they returned, hours later, to their amusement, the plumbing was still not in working order.

In America during these years, the power of the spoken word was asserting itself in a new way. Perhaps one of the most familiar images of the Depression years is the family gathered about that wonder of wonders, the radio. Now serving his second term in the White House, Franklin Roosevelt was using the radio to great effect for his "Fireside Chats." His voice, with its nasal, New York intonation, became as familiar as a favorite uncle's, and his optimism placated the fears and bolstered the sagging spirits of a haggard nation. Whether or not one approved of all of his New Deal policies, FDR's spirit of unbridled confidence and courage was indisputable. Although his upbringing was a privileged one, Americans admired how doggedly he had fought against heavy odds when polio crippled him at age thirty-nine. He never was photographed, however, in a way that would emphasize his handicap. This was not because his condition was a secret; it was a matter of respect. Seasoned White House photographers are said to have bashed cameras belonging to over-eager newcomers who violated this unwritten policy. The nation knew that Roosevelt's great strength came from his keen intelligence and gregarious nature, not from his legs.

Dorothy Fuldheim must have approved the President's elegant, powerful use of language, calculated to inspire his people to believe in themselves and their country. She must have soundly embraced Roosevelt's mantra that he gave the country: "The only thing we have to fear is fear itself."

Although none of Dorothy's memoirs detail an interview with President Roosevelt, she is said to have interviewed him and every succeeding President of the United States until her final interview in 1984 with President Ronald Reagan. Certainly, many of FDR's programs implemented to relieve the agony of the Great Depression must have won her approval. Yet, particularly in his re-election to unprecedented third and fourth terms, she would, in all likelihood, have understood the apprehension of many citizens who saw Roosevelt as a would-be despot.

During World War II Dorothy continued her lectures, and since foreign travel was restricted, she possibly resumed more frequent book reviews to alleviate the grim, depressing aura of wartime.

Dorothy could appear practically at a moment's notice. She could pack in a flash. Her naturally wavy, wash-and-wear hair kept her independent of beauty salons. Minor inconveniences of travel Dorothy took in stride. The tug-down roomettes on trains, the lonely station platforms or stagnant air of airport waiting rooms, hotel rooms with cold water, the consumption of endless cups of coffee that she said would "stretch to the moon"—all of these were but minor discomforts. Only once in all of her years of travel does she record feeling lonely. She was spending a long, solitary holiday in New Delhi, India, while she was covering President Dwight Eisenhower's world tour. Sitting unaccompanied in a dining room, she remembers the present she gave to herself was "knowing I could go home in a few days. It was desolate to spend Christmas alone."

Dorothy never quite conquered her fear of flying, although she hopped on and off planes as easily as if she were alighting from her front porch. As is often the case, her nearest brush with disaster came close to home. A friend who piloted her own plane had offered to fly Dorothy from Lancaster, Pennsylvania, to Akron, Ohio. Her lecture service had booked the two appearances with little time to spare.

When Dorothy stepped off the plane at the Akron-Canton airport, she thought her friend would also leave the plane and let the maintenance workers service it. Her friend, however, began taxiing the plane to the hangar herself. Though Dorothy seldom wore a hat, on this occasion she was wearing a hat with a long quill. When she started walking toward the terminal, the quill caught on the propeller blade. As she described the incident, if the whirling wooden blades had not struck the heavy silver chain she was wearing around her neck, a souvenir from a trip to Italy, she might have been much more severely injured.

Dorothy's first thought was that she'd been shot by someone who didn't like her remarks about her impressions of her recent visit to Germany. A stretcher appeared and she was flown back to Cleveland where, after several days' rest, she met her regular Monday speaking engagement. Dorothy was a mass of bruises from her throat to her waist but proudly claimed to be the only person who walked into an airplane propeller and lived to tell about it.

6
Radio: A Brief Interlude

A cable television network offers a popular nightly program called *Biography*. Affable Jack Perkins and Peter Graves host these hour-long, candid studies of the lives of notable personalities. Many are distinguished in fields such as politics, science, the arts; some are infamous, notorious criminals such as mobster Al Capone and war criminal Heinrich Himmler. Through the adroit use of still photos, film clips, and live commentaries from the persons themselves (if they are still living), as well as those of family members, associates, and biographers, the series effectually preserves intimate portraits of renowned individuals. Producers of the series make a conscious bow to objectivity, yet often introduce little-known details illuminating the subjects' personalities.

Viewers who might never read a full-length biography can gain an awareness of contributions to or influences upon society of persons from history, from the distant as well as the immediate past and present. *Biography* episodes profile such diverse persons as Moses and Marilyn Monroe, Edgar Allan Poe and Paul Newman. The host seats himself on the corner of a comfortably furnished set's antique desk and hooks the viewer by relating a tantalizing event or fact about the evening's subject. Then as the unseen continuity or anchorperson, he moves the life story from one narrator to another. Reappearing after commercial breaks to pick up the narrative, Mr. Perkins or Mr. Graves picks up the narrative and zips it up neatly at the end, bridging the story to the present time.

Now, in contrast to the multimedia *Biography* series, imagine one indivdual *telling* the story of a person's life. You can hear only that one voice, and you can see nothing but the tacky brown and gold threads of the fabric covering your table model radio's speaker. Occasionally, a whoop of static blots out the speaker's voice. Wavering organ music separates the various segments of the life story you're hearing, but no commercials interrupt this hour-long solo drama. You sit, enthralled, as the speaker spans centuries, and through her voice alone you are Marie Antoinette on her tortured way to the guillotine. When the final passion-wrought syllable sounds the anguished young queen's death knell, you stare, frozen like marble, at the blank face of your radio's speaker. For the past hour that speaker has dissolved, in your imagination, into the elegance of eighteenth-century French court scenes against which the tragedy has played. You wait, still captivated, to hear the announcer reveal the name of the subject of next week's biography.

In the 1930s Dorothy Fuldheim's dramatic and articulate talent brought such characters as Marie Antoinette, Cleopatra, Maximilian, Rasputin, Sarah Bernhardt, and George Washington to life on radio. Although historically accurate, the episodes contained little-known, human foibles that presented the historical personages as human beings everyone could relate to. George Washington, for example, refused pay as commander in chief but had a huge expense account. Marie Antoinette's severed head proved that her hair had not turned white from the ordeals she suffered; instead, the dark roots revealed she was without hair dye while in prison. Evidently, Dorothy captivated her listeners. The biography series ran for nearly two years, during which time she characterized the lives of more than one hundred people.

Occasionally, she interspersed political commentary if the subject of her biography was relevant to the present day. When characterizing the Russian communist leader, Nikolai Lenin, in 1946, she declared the Soviet goal of world domination:

> The Soviets . . . will never be satisfied until they demote the free enterprise system into a secondary role imposing communism on the world! They have started and, like some dreadful scourge, have swallowed Estonia, Latvia, Lithuania, East Germany, Poland, Hungary, Czechoslovakia, and wait

like hungry beasts to consume the Arab nations who unwittingly opened their arms to them.

For these views she was branded a communist by listeners whose
comments made the front page of *The Cleveland Plain Dealer.*

In what had become à la Fuldheim in her book reviews, she used
no notes for these broadcasts; they were truly spontaneous, theatrical
monologues. Educators hoped she would put the biographies together
in a book, she said, but she never got around to doing it.

Within a decade Dorothy Fuldheim would emerge as a television
anchorwoman before any such term evolved. The popularity of this
radio series tapped another fathom of her wellspring of talent: her
ability to move an unseen—and unseeing—audience. This undoubtedly delighted her and helped prepare her for her future role.

With her reputation as a lecturer and book reviewer now rock-
solid, Dorothy's entry into the marvelous world of the airwaves was
as if pre-charted. She did not, however, give up her other activities;
she simply added radio broadcasting to her parade of talents. In 1943
she was hired as a regular commentator for WJW radio.

She also did an editorial and news commentary for ABC radio
each Saturday afternoon following the opera. For these brief broadcasts she traveled, usually by overnight sleeping car, to New York, for
there was no feed from Cleveland to the ABC network at that time.
Her fee for the year was $5,000. " . . . they questioned me as though
I were out of my mind. . . . I thought it was too much, but they had
expected me to ask for $25,000. I was so simple then." Her sponsor
was the Brotherhood of Railroad Trainmen; her sleeping car fares
may well have been fringe benefits of the contract.

These Saturday editorials have evidently disappeared into the ether
waves. Regrettably, Dorothy's own reminiscences detail little more
than her concern about whether Milton Cross's final commentary
on the opera would run over into her time (especially if it was a
Wagnerian program) and her people-collecting adventures with her
impulsive, affluent friend Roseka. Living in New York at the time,
Roseka would meet her friend at the ABC studios or come to Grand
Central to see her off. One day Dorothy found Roseka seated on a
pile of assorted bundles and shabby luggage. She was holding an
immigrant woman's hand and proclaiming the glories of life in
America. The woman could understand little, but a crowd had gathered, good-humoredly watching the impromptu scene. Dorothy recalled being embarrassed by the scene, but when the woman's son

appeared, he thanked Roseka for her kindness. The woman herself stood on tiptoe, gave Roseka a kiss, and wished her a "long life and many children."

Perhaps Dorothy, when she saw Roseka's natural ease with someone less fortunate, began following Roseka's example. In her later years, after she became a well-known television personality, Dorothy would grow less concerned about appearances and become more giving of herself to others. Calls from her viewers, for example, frequently came from people in distress—("why won't Blue Cross pay for chemotherapy?") to petty annoyances ("the man next door has an air conditioning unit that disturbs my sleep"). "They call me," Dorothy said, "because after so many years, they look upon me as their friend, and I'm not likely to deny them the right of friendship. They feel better after they've told me their woes."

During World War II Dorothy continued to lecture in her home city and surrounding areas, wherever her agency could find bookings and arrange travel. She mentions a series of lectures she gave during the war to Fanny Farmer candy factory employees throughout the nation. Although she praised the firm for its people-oriented management and the spotless appearance of its stores, giving motivational speeches to candy makers was probably far less appealing to Dorothy Fuldheim than warning a New York Town Hall audience of the dangers of communism.

Her husband Milton, ten years her senior, had set up law practice when they moved to Cleveland. He was an early member of the Cleveland Heights City Club and later became president of the group. He was also one of the city's best bowlers. Dorothy Louise, to be known forever as Junior, graduated from Cleveland Heights High School.

Wartime brought drastic changes to many American families, and at the Fuldheims the changes were tragic in proportion. Dorothy Junior, after studying drama for a while at the Carnegie Institute of Technology and acting in a number of theaters outside Cleveland, had married a high school classmate, Harold N. Urman, six days after the Japanese bombed Pearl Harbor in December 1941. Like thousands of other couples, Dorothy Junior and Hal, as he was known, rushed to the altar before he would be sent overseas. They were married in Cleveland by M.J. Penty, justice of the peace.

Hal was the son of Samuel and Sophie Urman, owners of the Norman Hat Manufacturing Company in Cleveland. Little is known of Junior's and Hal's relationship or even of the length of time they actually lived together with Dorothy, Milton, and Bertha Schnell. Harold's occupation was listed as a clerk in the 1941 *Cleveland City Directory*, but he evidently entered the military service at some time near the beginning of the war. Their daughter, Halla Dorothy, was born on October 2, 1943. By the time she was a year old, doctors determined she was permanently handicapped.

Shortly after Hal returned from military service in 1944, his father, Sam Urman, was awakened by a noise outside his home. He found his son lying unconscious in the family's yard at 1:15 a.m. on July 25. In his pocket was a four-ounce can of calcium cyanide from which about one ounce had been removed. The police were summoned and young Urman was taken to Lakeside Hospital where he died at 2:50 a.m. He was twenty-three years old. Coroner S.R. Gerber ruled "the death in this case was the end result of calcium cyanide poisoning and suicidal in nature." The coroner's report added that "this man had been despondent over domestic difficulties."

Whether Hal was separated from Dorothy Junior and living with his parents at the time is unknown. He had come home from the service without physical injury, apparently, as there were no scars on his body. How much psychological stress he may have suffered is unknown, however. Returning home to find his wife struggling to care for a severely handicapped child he didn't even know may have overwhelmed Hal, and perhaps he was unable to cope with his life as he found it.

The Fuldheims were managing the hardship and expense of Halla's care, although they certainly were not wealthy at this time. They were still living in the Cedar Road apartment on the top floor of a four-story, brownish-red brick building at a busy intersection. A few years later Dorothy joined WEWS-TV for a salary of $125 a week. Milton continued his law practice in the same Cedar Road location.

Seeing her cherished daughter left a widow with a handicapped daughter dealt a heart-shattering blow to Dorothy Fuldheim's optimistic spirit. "She is the shadow over my heart," she would say of Halla in years to come. Dorothy Junior, who had postponed further college for marriage and motherhood, evidently devoted herself totally in those postwar years to the care of her daughter. Later, Dorothy Junior enrolled at Western Reserve University (now Case Western Reserve) and earned a bachelor's degree in 1961, when she was past forty, to be followed with a master's and a doctorate. This was the beginning of a distinguished academic career for Dorothy Junior.

Dorothy Fuldheim (Sr.) at the end of World War II was fifty-two years old, and was probably wondering, "Is this all?" when she viewed her professional life. Her powerful intellect and analytical mind were pressing her to find new audiences with which to share her views. With radio now at the core of the nation's consciousness, Dorothy's experiences on radio had strengthened her professionally and underscored for her the influence of the spoken word when delivered via a mass medium.

She truly stood on a plateau, casting about for a new challenge for her competence—and that something was television. In fact, her radio career lasted only five years. As many who knew Dorothy Fuldheim professionally have agreed, she was, indeed, waiting in the wings at a propitious time—at a time when the fact that she was over fifty years of age and had been a successful lecturer for more than three decades would work to her advantage.

7
Television and Dorothy Debut in Cleveland

The week before Christmas in 1947 Clevelanders paused in their frenzy of last-minute shopping to cluster around store windows and huddle in corner bars, congratulating one another that their city now boasted the only television station between New York and Chicago. With the sign-on of WEWS-TV 5, flagship station of the Scripps Howard Corporation that also owned *The Cleveland Press,* the city welcomed the eleventh television station in the country.

Cleveland had boomed with oil refineries, machinery and railway equipment manufacturing, and steel mills since before the turn of the century. In the 1940 census, just before World War II, the city ranked as the nation's sixth largest with a population of nearly 900,000, and growth soared in the postwar period. New industries were springing up in the city, and payrolls were climbing. Cleveland's potential viewing audience was prospering—agog over and eager to revel in the wonders of television.

Recalling early Cleveland television, Linn Sheldon, whose career on Cleveland television spanned four decades, recalled the most striking thing about the birth of television in Cleveland. In an interview for *The Plain Dealer* during the city's 1996 bicentennial year he spoke of

> . . . the hunger and fascination of the viewers for what we were doing, and we felt the same way. Every day, everything we did had a sense of newness. There was always another 'first.' Both we and the viewers were going through this experience of television in Cleveland together.

Sheldon is best remembered for his role as "Barnaby," a storytelling program for children.

WEWS-TV would not remain the sole television station in Cleveland for long; within two years two other stations were on the scene, destined to become affiliates of NBC and CBS. WEWS eventually joined a third network, ABC, thus giving Cleveland links to three powerful networks by stations that were also recruiting talent and developing creative local programming. Managing WEWS-TV's staff of novices was James Hanrahan, a pragmatic Irishman, a journalist by trade, who understood few of the technicalities of his adopted industry. But Hanrahan was a people person, a follower of hunches, a visionary. All three of these traits led him to recognize the potential in the forthright, articulate redhead who'd been packing Higbee's auditorium to the walls with her book reviews and barnstorming about the country on the creamed chicken-and-peas circuit for years.

Dorothy Fuldheim had actually been hired away from WJW radio to work for newly chartered WEWS-FM radio at about the time the television station was to make its debut. Hanrahan, in his impulsive way, whisked her away to the nebulous land of television, giving her carte blanche to fashion her own news program. The fact that no women in the country were anchoring radio news broadcasts mattered not a whit to him. He knew Fuldheim could draw viewers. But sponsors of the program were not as progressive in their attitude:

In a televised interview, observing forty years of broadcasting, Dorothy gave her own version of how she got into television.

> "God, I was old. Fifty-four . . . but they [the station] needed Cleveland talent to get the license. They could sell me because I was already known, you see . . . I had the first across the board news show between New York and Chicago.
>
> "The sponsor, Duquesne Beer, expected me to use a script. When I told them that wasn't what I did, they said, 'Hell, let her do what she wants. We're not going to keep her anyhow.'"

Dorothy announced to the sponsor that they had never had anyone work without a script because they never had anyone competent.

Duquesne gave in to Hanrahan's insistence that Dorothy would deliver the news, although the sponsors felt that the urbane Miss Fuldheim would last only a few weeks in smoke-and-steel Cleveland. But Dorothy and Duquesne Beer had an eighteen-year relationship. She confessed, however, that her early days of breaching the TV-news sex barrier made her very lonely. She said she always felt like an outsider.

"I owed him [Hanrahan] so much," Dorothy recalled in reflecting on her career. "He was the only man in the country willing to give a woman a chance to anchor a news show." According to Donald Perris, this episode "set the tone that the station would stand by its people, particularly Fuldheim."

Station manager Hanrahan, a wise man who was liberal enough in his views about women in a professional role, realized that Dorothy Fuldheim's role at WEWS-TV would be a stellar one among the station's 170 employees. After all, she had reigned as queen of the lecture circuit for more than twenty years. Thus, he respected her ironclad views about how the news should be reported. When she scoffed at the sponsor's prepared script, her words, "That's not what I do" rang prophetically. *That*, reading from a prepared script, was not what she did—ever—in the forty-seven years of continuous broadcasting that would follow. Eventually, she did use a TelePrompTer, but the words were always those she had written herself, and she often deviated from the written text. "She said what she wanted to say. She didn't care what the TelePrompTer said," says James Breslin, her producer and director for many years.

Once she wrote something she claimed it was in her consciousness. If she saw a way to improve on emphasis or word choice to drive her point home, she would do so. She felt an obligation, also, to give the news a human dimension:

> To be able to humanize the news is the ideal and the newscaster who can do that is bound to be successful, for there are few who respond to abstract postulations and impersonal accounts compared to those who respond to almost everything emotionally. It's ridiculous to hear an anchorman report a killing with exactly the same expression as if he were reporting a recipe to make applesauce. News reported in newspapers must of necessity be impersonal. But a broadcaster is a human being and should cease acting like a feelingless printing press pouring out the news.

65

"Dorothy feels if the news is done well, with warmth and drama," Donald Perris told television reporter Nancy Gallagher in 1959, "everyone, not just the eggheads, will want to understand about the world they live in." Perris came to WEWS-TV as a reporter in 1948. He advanced to general manager and later to president of Scripps Howard Broadcasting. Perris speaks of Dorothy Fuldheim with deep respect and admiration and continued through the years to provide her with the freedom and the support that Hanrahan had established.

The humanistic approach to the news worked for Dorothy Fuldheim, and it endured during five decades—from 1947 until 1984 when she gave her final broadcast. Her news commentaries and interviews were part of the fifteen-minute news program that she anchored for ten years. As news coverage expanded, Dorothy Fuldheim stepped down from the anchor position in 1957. Her contributions were then integrated into three-times-a-day news programming.

The interviewing skills Dorothy had honed while traipsing about Europe were put to good use on television. Any noteworthy person who came to Cleveland in those early days of television hoped to find his or her way to her show, known variously as *Inside Cleveland Today, Views on the News,* and *Highlights of the News.* Sometimes celebrities knew Dorothy Fuldheim only by reputation and that her show would give them good exposure in Cleveland. One was comedian Joe E. Brown. He came in one evening in the early fifties to be interviewed, according to Randy Culver who was then on duty as station announcer. Brown came in through the small newsroom, inquiring, "Where am I supposed to go?"

"Here, go right through here," Culver answered, steering Brown toward the door of Studio C. Brown looked in to find Dorothy Fuldheim seated on the set. In the glare of lights streaming down on her flaming red hair, she took on a spectral appearance.

"What—is that?" Brown's eyes were like pie plates.

"You'll find out. That's where you're going," Culver said.

The interview that followed went well, but Brown was genuinely taken aback by his hostess' wraith-like appearance.

Dorothy fell in love regularly with some of her male guests. One whom she found most urbanely charming was David, Duke of Windsor, the former Edward VIII, King of England. She called him "undoubtedly the most romantic figure of our generation." The Duke had shocked the world when he abdicated England's throne in 1937 to marry the woman he loved, twice-divorced American Wallis Warfield Simpson. In 1951 he wrote a book, *A King's Story*, and was touring American cities with it. Although he had been on television only once before, he granted Dorothy's personal request after twice refusing her producer. The interview, televised according to strict protocol, was not merely a coup for Dorothy; it became something of a royally staged production. The Duke agreed to answer handwritten questions that were submitted by a royal emissary. WEWS-TV employees were required to wear coats and ties to the interview. For years afterwards rumors would surface periodically among the staff that the Duke was Dorothy Fuldheim's lifelong though unrequited love. In 1973 she put these rumors to rest in a *Cleveland Magazine* interview as being "so fantastically erroneous that it is funny."

> "But apparently," she smiled, "I am the type of person around whom myths arise. No, he was not my great love, the man I waited for all my life. Of course, I was a great coquette and I certainly would have waited for him if he had shown any interest. He was a charming man, so diminutive, but with exquisite manners—impeccable! When we concluded the interview—and he had been so nervous!—his feeling for me was the same you have for a dentist who has been drilling and suddenly you find it doesn't hurt.
> "He was so grateful that he said, 'I wouldn't mind doing this often with you.' But there was nothing like that—the silly story of him being my love . . ."

Arguably, perhaps, the 1950s are demeaned as the "Do-Nothing Years," an era of "normalcy" squeezed in between the cataclysm of World War II and the tumultuous Sixties. Several events that captured the nation's attention and stirred its conscience, however, must have prompted strong opinions from Dorothy Fuldheim. Since she is notably silent about some of these in her writings, we can only infer how she reacted.

An emotionally charged issue that jolted the nation in the early 1950s concerned a death knell that was sounded, as it were, to a distinguished military career. The United States was embroiled in the Korean conflict, hailed as a "police action" for deterring the spread of communism throughout the world. U.S. troops were fighting on the side of the South Korean government in a civil strife against communist-controlled North Korea. Strict parameters limiting military intervention in specific areas had been established.

General Douglas A. MacArthur, commander of U.S. forces in Korea, and President Harry Truman clashed over military policy on several occasions. A zealous MacArthur, emboldened by his hero-status as the triumphal leader who had accepted the unconditional surrender of the Japanese only a few years before, urged aggressive action against the North Koreans. MacArthur knew that Communist Chinese troops were massed at the Korean border by the hundreds of thousands, poised to strike against the South Koreans, the U.S. and other United Nations' forces. Yet, he defied his commander in chief on several occasions, instigating military actions he felt would bring the war to a speedy close.

Ultimately, President Truman relieved MacArthur of his command in the spring of 1951 and replaced him with the more moderate General Jonathan Wainwright. By doing this, he preserved the constitutional dictum that the command of the nation's armed forces rests with a civilian, not a military leader.

When MacArthur returned to America, he came back to a tumultuous ticker-tape welcome on Broadway and addressed a joint session of Congress where his heart-rending "Old soldiers never die, they just fade away" speech sparked an outpouring of national sentiment, much of it directed against the President.

President Truman's popularity at that time was low, and in the face-off with MacArthur a large segment of public opinion overlooked that the President had resolved the constitutional question of insubordination and focused upon the fact that he had deposed a national hero of mythic proportions. MacArthur's noble-warrior status and his sense of theatrics contrasted sharply to the bland image the nation had of its President at that time. Upon Roosevelt's sudden death in April 1945, Truman, a little-known vice-president from the Midwest, had assumed the helm of a nation at war. Four months later he made the fateful decision to use the atomic bomb to bring the Japanese nation to its knees. The war ended, but the nation no sooner shifted gears into peacetime than the Korean affair erupted. It would drag on until the signing of a troubled armistice in 1953.

Dorothy appears to have kept silent on this issue of whether or not the President should have relieved MacArthur. Every reference she makes to President Truman, however, depicts him in commendatory terms. She interviewed him first at the White House when he was still Vice-President and was impressed with his straight-from-the-shoulder demeanor. As his responsibilities increased, she asserted that Truman grew greater in stature and that he was ever conscious of the dignity of his position. In 1966 she wrote,

"Never, I believe, has a man who became President of the United States risen to meet the high demands of the office of the presidency as did Harry Truman. . . ." History has confirmed Dorothy's judgment. In recent years Harry Truman has emerged as a far more illustrious leader than most Americans regarded him during his presidency.

Senator Joseph McCarthy, a Republican from Wisconsin, commandeered a national witch hunt that began in 1950 with a speech the blustering senator made in the unlikely setting of Wheeling, West Virginia, McCarthy asserted, almost parenthetically, that the State Department was riddled with communists and communist sympathizers. This triggered his relentless search for domestic communists, largely targeting the Democratic party but also aimed at many well-known figures in the arts and entertainment fields. Riding on the popularity from his war record, which had nicknamed him "Tailgunner Joe," McCarthy had brought with him to the Senate a bundle of insecurities and fears collected from his early life as an Irish kid from the wrong side of the tracks. He appealed to a myriad of class-conscious attitudes and political fears of a nation that had rebounded from war and was now forced into a new era of co-existence with communism. Communist China had signed a thirty-year treaty with the Union of Soviet Socialist Republics, and longtime respected Chiang Kai-Shek was now only the leader of Nationalist China.

McCarthy cloaked his accusations in vague and imprecise language and labeled as treason what was really political naivete. The press ballooned the circus-like atmosphere surrounding what seemed a never-ending stream of accusations from McCarthy, and he was page one news for four years. Tension mounted, fear spread like the plague, and numerous senatorial campaigns of the early fifties became exercises in red-baiting, including those by Richard Nixon, Everett Dirksen, and John Foster Dulles. (He lost an unsuccessful Senate race in New York.)

Finally, wanting to give McCarthy an opportunity to disprove her accusations, Dorothy phoned him to invite him to appear on her show. "He came, and I interviewed him; and though I differed with him in judgment, I found him to be an utterly charming man. If his veracity had equaled his charm, he would have been invincible."

Even persons with whom she disagreed vehemently could kindle Dorothy's respect if they displayed charm and good manners. This is not to say that she would permit a person's demeanor to sway her opinions; she simply had the courtesy to respect others' views, especially if they were framed in intelligence and civility. She could have had the familiar words, usually attributed to Voltaire, posted on the set, above her guest's chair: "I [may] disapprove of what you say, but I will defend to the death your right to say it."

During McCarthy's witch hunts, Dorothy Fuldheim criticized his methods and his merciless grilling of persons at the expense of their privacy and their careers. One who particularly suffered at McCarthy's hands was CBS news correspondent and analyst Edward R. Murrow, noted for his reporting during World War II and his documentaries in the years that followed. In March 1954 he devoted an entire newscast, documented with film clips, to condemning Senator McCarthy's tactics. He attacked the Senator's abuse of his investigative power, saying that he had stepped repeatedly over a fine line between persecuting and investigating. The result was an overwhelming outpouring of gratitude to Murrow from his colleagues in the arts, broadcasting, and entertainment industries. Because one man of such professional stature dared to allow himself to be a catalyst against blatant demagoguery, public feeling at last began to run against Senator McCarthy.

In 1954, during the Eisenhower presidency, McCarthy attempted to prove communist infiltration into the U.S. Army. The result turned up only one dentist with Communist sympathies, and the ultimate outcome was that Senator McCarthy was formally censured and condemned by Senate resolution, forcing his resignation.

Shortly before Edward R. Murrow died, he was Dorothy's guest. "No one wrote with higher principles or reported with greater honesty than Ed Murrow," she said. She told Murrow that often she had thought of him "during the years of the McCarthy witch hunt and of his courage in denouncing him." Murrow replied by telling Dorothy something of the loneliness "that accompanies an individual who remains uncorrupted." Dorothy concluded that "incorruptible" was an appropriate accolade for Murrow.

The same year the McCarthy furor subsided, Cleveland osteopath, Dr. Samuel Sheppard was on trial for bludgeoning his pregnant wife Marilyn to death. The trial focused worldwide attention upon the city. Although investigations yielded only circumstantial evidence, the prosperous young doctor was literally tried by the newspapers, many of which, like *The Cleveland Press*, screamed for his arrest and then demanded the death penalty. Sheppard's arrest did not, in fact, take place until twenty-six days after the murder. During this time *The Press* kept such headlines as these on page one:

> **Somebody Is Getting Away With Murder**
> **Why No Inquest?**
> **Why Don't the Police Quiz No. 1 Suspect?**
> **Quit Stalling and Bring Him In**

Throughout the trial's six-month duration, *The Press* published 399 articles about Dr. Sam, whose name became as synonymous with "alleged wife-killer" as O.J. Simpson's would become in the 1990s. Many of the stories focused on Dr. Sheppard's reported extra-marital activities.

Sheppard appealed his conviction of second-degree murder on the grounds that the press had created "an inhospitable atmosphere for a fair trial." The Supreme Court agreed and in 1966 ordered a new trial at which Sheppard was acquitted, after having spent ten years in prison. The appeal specifically cited prominent journalists who had incited the unfavorable atmosphere, among them noted celebrity correspondent, Walter Winchell.

The terse facts of the outcome of the Sheppard case are the only references to it found in Dorothy Fuldheim's writing. These references exist incidentally in a story she told about her friendship with Ariane Sheppard, Dr. Sam's second wife, a native of Germany. She happened to be a half-sister to the wife of Hitler's minister of propaganda, Joseph Goebbels. Dorothy asked Ariane to confirm the story of the death of Goebbels and his wife and children by suicide. In doing so, Dorothy briefly explained that Ariane married Dr. Sam after he had spent ten years in prison and that she worked tirelessly throughout the appeal for his second trial at which he was acquitted. Although the trials attracted attention in Europe as well as throughout the United States, no comments by Dorothy exist about the circus-like atmosphere created by the press in the original trial.

Dorothy could not help but have been caught up in this case which she said had, "all the elements of a Greek tragedy." Both of Sheppard's parents were dead within a month of his conviction. His mother took her own life, and his father, Dr. Richard A. Sheppard, died of a hemorrhaging gastric ulcer. Dorothy referred to Ariane as her friend and related that "hers [Ariane's] and Dr. Sam's should have been one of the great love stories of the century . . . but ten years in prison must do things to man's nervous system. Perhaps he was no longer disciplined to take on the responsibility of marriage." Sam and Ariane Sheppard divorced not long after his acquittal.

Since the original trial was in 1954, television coverage was limited to newscasts, and its effect was negligible in comparison with today's in-depth trial reporting. But with the headlines of *The Cleveland Press*, a well-established Scripps Howard newspaper, raging night after night, demanding "justice," Dorothy must have felt she was in a paradoxical situation. Her conscience would have cried out that any man should be allowed a fair trial, unhampered by a hostile, revenge-seeking press. Yet, her loyalty to the Scripps Howard organization and her admiration for powerful *Press* editor Louis Seltzer may have tempered her remarks. Starting as a reporter in 1915, Seltzer had been editor of *The Press* since 1925 and editor-in-chief of the Scripps Howard Newspapers of Ohio since 1937. In the Sheppard case, Seltzer maintained he acted in the best interest of the city to focus on a situation he felt was a roadblock against the law. Seltzer said in his 1956 book, *The Years Were Good,*

> I have a simple philosophy, by which my whole newspaper life has been guided—especially as editor of *The Cleveland Press*. It is that whatever is in the ultimate best interest of the community is selfishly in the best interest of *The Press*. It is up to us to help the community grow and prosper, to fight those things which are harmful to it and to fight with equal vigor for those things we believe will make the community a better place in which to live.

He declared furthermore that the paper was independent of any party, group, or special interest and free to make its own choices to fight for or against whatever was felt to be right or wrong. Seltzer's editorials asserted that Dr. Sheppard received protection from the mayor of Bay Village [where he lived] and the staff of the hospital where he was taken after the murder. Dr. Sam Sheppard was hospitalized at the Bay Hospital, which the Sheppards owned and operated, for a neck injury he claimed he received at the hands of an intruder.

Dorothy often said, "If I have to apologize for what I say, I'll say nothing." Perhaps she took a neutral stance in the Sheppard case to avoid the public embarrassment of the fledgling television station, as yet not ten years old, finding fault with its older relative, *The Cleveland Press*. If there were commentaries she made to the contrary, they no longer exist. With her respect for the achievements of scientific discovery, Dorothy would be absorbed in the current DNA findings which seem to point to yet a third trial.

In the early days WEWS-TV did not sign on until late afternoon after the test pattern, a constant geometric reminder of wonders to come, had dazzled viewers for a few hours. A popular man-at-the-bus-station program with Paul Hodges gave Clevelanders a chance to see themselves on the tiny screen, uttering their inane, quavering responses to questions from the light-hearted Hodges. Then the test pattern resumed while the operations crew took a dinner break. Dorothy Fuldheim's news broadcast came on at 7:15 following *Seven Serenade* with vocalist Randy Culver and organist Crandall Hendershott. Douglas Edwards followed with the CBS news. (This preceded WEWS-TV's affiliation with ABC.)

Cameras shifted from set to set within a studio, and cables snaked across the poorly lighted floors. "One evening, as I began to sing my last number," Randy Culver remembers, "I looked out into the studio just in time to see Dorothy Fuldheim coming toward the set. Suddenly, she tripped over a cable and fell to the floor. I was horrified but had to keep on singing. Others who were off camera rushed to her aid. Like the genuine professional that she was, she insisted on going on with her show, but the next day she appeared with a cast on. Her arm was broken."

Many of the renowned persons Dorothy Fuldheim interviewed in these early television years are mentioned briefly in her book, *I*

Laughed, I Cried, I Loved, published in 1966. Sometimes her comments are meaningful and give the reader an insightful glimpse into the guest's personality. At other times, she focuses on trivial characteristics of the individual. Here is a sampling:

She wrote of a memorable visit with Leopold Stokowski, the celebrated conductor: "His individualism is so marked . . . that being with him is almost like meeting someone from another planet." After his concert she entertained the maestro at her home, where she served a full-course catered Hungarian dinner. During the evening he used her telephone to make a lengthy call to his wife, Gloria Vanderbilt, who was in the process of leaving him.

Of Teamsters' Union leader James Hoffa she said, "[he] may be all the awful and horrendous things they say about him . . . I found him a powerful personality who spoke openly and candidly of his humble beginnings."

Margaret Mead, renowned anthropologist, Dorothy found "to have a somewhat brusque, astringent personality." Ms. Mead is one of the few persons about whom Dorothy Fuldheim could find little that was ingratiating. Another recollection described her as "brilliant, but supercilious."

Rachel Carson's *Silent Spring* incited the chemical world's awareness of the folly of tampering with the balance of nature. Dorothy found Miss Carson to be soft-spoken, serious, honest, and forthright in her answers.

Dorothy told of the historic, stirring concert by African-American soprano Marian Anderson at the Lincoln Memorial. She felt Miss Anderson's appearance issued a national rebuke to the Daughters of the American Revolution since that organization had denied her a concert in Constitution Hall because of her race. "What a superb picture for history to enshrine in its textbook!" The audience "was entranced by her great poise and her magnificent voice." Dorothy wrote that Miss Anderson was hesitant to be interviewed. Although Dorothy says she stayed up all night to familiarize herself with Anderson's background, she makes no comment about the interview itself, other than to describe Miss Anderson as a woman of great reserve.

Cleveland-native comedian Bob Hope thrilled Dorothy whenever he appeared on her show. "It makes no difference how much money he has made, how much homage he has received, it can never be enough to compensate him for the delight he has given countless numbers of people."

Sir Edmund Hillary, who scaled Mt. Everest, caused Dorothy to reflect upon "The great inextinguishable spirit of man that must conquer all obstacles! That fearless little equation of matter called man, pitted against the universe and the endlessness of time, setting out to conquer nature and to wrest from her the secrets of creation itself!"

Sir Alexander Fleming, who discovered penicillin, left Dorothy feeling very submissive. "What does one say to a man to whom mankind owes so much? It's a very humble feeling, indeed, to meet and talk with a man of that kind."

She described playwright Tennessee Williams was "the most nervous author I've ever met. He was apprehensive about his play, which was opening that night at the Hanna [theater], and he paced up and down until the curtain went up." In instances such as this, the reader wishes for a more perspicacious comment from Miss Fuldheim offering more insight into the guest's personality.

The unique, adventuresome spirit of WEWS-TV persisted until the mid-1970s, according to Greg Olsen, thirty-year veteran advertising salesman for the station. "There was a unity, a togetherness. We were not drowned by MBA's and attorneys." Today's media, Olsen feels, is as fenced in as if it were in a Mediterranean country.

Former station manager Don Perris cites the station's newspaper heritage as responsible, in part, for its reputation as combining innovation in a new medium with responsible journalism. "You said what you believed. There were ratings, and we were concerned about them, but we still stood by what we believed."

According to former WEWS-TV personality Wilma Smith, Don Perris was the person who was able to help Dorothy to maintain her aura and keep her strong in the marketplace. He could see what value she was to the market. Smith feels other managers with less foresight would not have recognized her continued value. They would have thought having an older woman as a news analyst would be so unusual that it would not work. On the contrary, Smith feels because it was this way was what made it work. "WEWS-TV was unlike other stations that would go as young as they could find—cheaper, prettier—even if the quality of work was less," she says.

DOROTHY FULDHEIM

After the formative years of television and what would, in retrospect, seem the comparative calm of the Fifties, Dorothy Fuldheim and WEWS-TV would face undreamed of challenges in news reporting and analysis in the turbulent Sixties and Seventies. Her interviews with dignitaries and personalities, both fascinating and controversial, continued to be an integral and unique part of news programming at WEWS-TV.

8
The Incomparable *One O'Clock Club*

By 1957 WEWS-TV had moved from East 13th and Euclid, the former Women's City Club building, to roomier headquarters at the present location, 30th and Euclid. More space meant better opportunities to offer innovative programs such as *The One O'Clock Club*.

At one o'clock every weekday a hundred or so persons squeezed around card tables spread with linen cloths and set for a dessert course. What made this scene unusual was that it took place in Studio C at WEWS-TV, where these selected viewers who came downtown by busloads would watch and participate in the live-live production of *The One O'Clock Club*, co-hosted by Dorothy Fuldheim and Bill Gordon. There was always a waiting list to be in the audience.

In the beginning the men wore formal morning suits with swallowtail coats and striped trousers. Dorothy appeared in elaborate gowns. Later on, the men would forego the formal attire, but Dorothy would continue to grace the set with the sophisticated wardrobe to which her viewers had grown accustomed. The format of the show was totally ad-lib, off-the-cuff, accompanied by a live orchestra directed by Joe Howard.

Bill Gordon reveals that *The One O'Clock Club* actually owed its inspiration to the southern end of the state where at WLW-TV in Cincinnati another one-of-a-kind lady named Ruth Lyons hosted her midday *50-50 Club*. Lyons made her mark as a philanthropist by championing deserving causes on her program and emerged as a civic icon in the Cincinnati viewing area where the *50-50 Club* would run for a couple of decades. Dorothy was more of a multidimensional talent than Ruth Lyons but, as Gordon unabashedly states, "She [Dorothy] needed Bill Gordon to make a format like *The One O'Clock Club* go." The show's producer, who hired Gordon for the job and paired the two, was Betty Cope, eventual president and general manager of WVIZ-TV, Cleveland's public television station. Fuldheim and Gordon, an incomparable team, played off each other like a pair of seasoned vaudevillians. After a show that didn't go especially well, Dorothy would turn to her partner as they walked to her office and say, "Wasn't that audience *terrible*?" But if it had been a good day, she'd ask, "Wasn't I wonderful?" With a what-can-I-say shrug to the now-vanished audience, Gordon would pat his partner's shoulder with genuine affection.

Gordon remembers that Dorothy had what you call *presence*. Despite her short stature, she would somehow manage to sweep into the studio and stroll (a combination of a strut and a flaunt) toward the stage to the collective awe of the viewers. In Gordon's view, Dorothy was the "epitome of confidence. Her detractors might have called it *chutzpah*, but whatever you called it, it sure paid off."

What perhaps even Gordon, her co-host, didn't know was that a few moments before Dorothy did her strut-and-flaunt into the studio, she had been back by the projection room saying, "Randy, hold my hand. I'm so nervous." This happened every day, according to Randy Culver, who was a vocalist in those days and later switched to continuity to round out a WEWS-TV career of thirty years. "Once she got on, she was fine," he recalls. Fine, indeed. Whether she was doing book reviews, interviews, or near-slapstick with Gordon, Dorothy Fuldheim delighted thousands of visitors to *The One O'Clock Club* during its seven-year history.

Since Cleveland has long been a home to major league baseball and football teams, sports figures frequently appeared as guests on *The One O'Clock Club*. These were roll-in-the-aisle occasions, since what Dorothy knew about sports would fit into a teacup. Here's an example as recalled by Bill Gordon:

> "So, tell me, Mr. Gr-r-roza, how high do you kick it (the football)?" Gordon . . . interrupting, "No, no Dorothy, you don't ask Lou-the-toe Groza, the Number 2 placekicker and scorer in the National Football League, 'How high you kick it?' You might ask 'How far; how accurately; what was the

toughest kick you ever made? but you don't ask 'how high.'
It's not a question of 'how high.' It's simply a matter of you
not knowing anything about football."

"Well, personally, I find it a bore. I have my gingersnaps
for breakfast and I never go into the kitchen and I don't
know how to cook or clean and I never watch football."
Audience applauds and laughs and thinks it is all a big put-
on. It never was. It was for real . . .

But Dorothy never changed. When interviewing world heavy-
weight champion Rocky Marciano, she inquired, "How many home
runs have you hit?" As far as baseball and football were concerned,
she could never separate home runs from touchdowns; now she
was mixing them up with boxing. Sometimes, though, comments
Randy Culver, you wondered how much was calculated. Remember,
Dorothy was an actress. Yet, the audience anticipated her confusion
whenever a sports figure was introduced—and they loved it. She played
it with all the arrow-straightness of old-time radio's Fibber McGee
opening his closet for a couple of decades. Although listeners knew
the years of accumulated clutter would come crashing down, they
looked forward to Fibber's opening the door and to his milk-toast
remark,"Gosh darn it, Molly, someday I've gotta clean out this closet."
Howls never failed to erupt from the studio audience. Dorothy
Fuldheim on sports was a guaranteed Fibber McGee-like crowd-pleaser.

The One O'Clock Club often featured book reviews. Dorothy persisted in her no-notes approach to book reviewing, dramatizing the
characters' roles and making a book come alive in her viewers' minds.
Often the camera would pan the studio audience and discover them
literally in open-mouthed intent, oblivious to their coffee cups and
dessert dishes. Not only the viewers but also the camera crews, lighting and sound technicians were mesmerized. Sometimes Dorothy arranged herself on the steps leading from the audience to the set, pleated
skirt spread out in a swirl, eyes transfixed somewhere off the set,
while she verbally sculpted the moors of Scotland or the plantations
of Georgia.

In these enchanting moments, Dorothy reverted to her role as an
actress. Studio C could have been a Broadway theater as far as she
was concerned. She gave the part her all. Bill Gordon, who probably
watched every one of these book reviews, sums it up: "Dorothy
Fuldheim was an actress. She would go into her role, but the main

thing is, she wasn't kidding. She meant it. She was convinced she was greater than any movie star, stage actress, news commentator, anchorperson, book reviewer, whatever; she was in [Mohammed] Ali's words, *The Greatest*. And she showed it."

Just as she never knew how many of her students she might have held spellbound by her dramatic readings when she stood in her Milwaukee schoolroom, Dorothy Fuldheim never knew how many lives she touched with the magic of her voice. She breathed life into literature they would perhaps never have known otherwise

One of these lives was that of Mary Cayed, a young bride who moved from Baltimore to Cleveland in the early 1950s. She had met her husband Lou, a Cleveland native, while he was in the service and stationed near Baltimore. The young couple rented the second floor of a home that belonged to a Dr. and Mrs. Kellum. "Mrs. Kellum lived by Dorothy Fuldheim . . . thought she was just the greatest. She'd say, 'Come on down, Mary. Dorothy's on.'" Cayed would join her landlady downstairs in her living room to watch *The One O'Clock Club*. "The book reviews were the best part," she recalls. "She never used a note or read from her book, but she made it so real. You felt you were right there—in the story."

In an existing tape of *The One O'Clock Club*, Dorothy was at ease in a floral wing chair, reviewing a short story by Noel Coward called "Bon Voyage." After a succinct comment about the author, she introduced the characters and placed them in the setting, using her hands convincingly to add dimension to her word pictures of the clothing of the countess or the height of the captain. Interestingly enough, although she wore a bright dress with a jeweled collar, on this day Dorothy's hands were bereft of her signature oversized rings. Perhaps she felt they would detract from the story she was telling. She kept her mind-bending vocabulary scaled down, too. The only four-syllable word she used was "diaphanous." Since this described the countess's negligee, the reviewer must have assumed the meaning was obvious. Actually, Dorothy never related the plot of "Bon Voyage" on this particular broadcast; she only re-created the characters and told that they all came together and interacted at the captain's table.

The brevity of this review may well be an example of how Dorothy Fuldheim's television book reviews had to be shortened, regrettably, to fit the format of *The One O'Clock Club*. Her live book reviews, so popular in Cleveland since the 1920s, had always been at least an hour in length. "Unfortunately, they always seemed to lose something on television," Donald Perris says. The studio audience and the viewers adored them, nevertheless.

At one point Dorothy was inexplicably and abruptly removed as president of *The One O'Clock Club* for nearly a year. Upon her return, President Fuldheim said, "Jim Hanrahan [WEWS general manager] told me I was superb." Viewer reaction must have been fiercely pro-Fuldheim, for Don Perris [then assistant manager] admitted that the station had learned a lesson.

A sort of populist notion evolved among women where Dorothy Fuldheim was concerned, Bill Gordon believes. They delighted in hearing her tell how she couldn't cook, didn't clean house, and so on, because they longed to identify with her lifestyle—to have a job that required mental acumen and commanded the respect of others, especially men. To be appreciated for their intellect and ability and to express themselves more fully was appealing to more and more women as the June Cleaver-Father Knows Best era drew to a close.

Dorothy's interviews with persons of renown often took place on *The One o'Clock Club.* Tapes of early interviews show a not-so-composed Dorothy Fuldheim as in later years. She seemed somewhat ill at ease interviewing in the format. One such occurrence was with Dr. Tom Dooley, the brilliant young doctor who at the time of his visit had set up nine hospitals for cancer patients in Africa. This man, whom Dorothy hailed as the American Dr. Schweitzer, would himself die of the disease only a few years later at age thirty-four. Throughout their conversation, Dorothy sat slumped in an oversized chair, both hands jammed into the pockets of a tailored shirtwaist dress—a somewhat defiant and unfeminine posture for her. Perhaps the subject of death and disease was abhorrent to her; she never went to funerals or visited people who were in the hospital. Or she may have been rebelling against a director who'd told her she talked too much with her hands during the interviews. But the expressive hands were là Fuldheim, and, whatever the cause, the hands-in-the-pockets pose was a detraction. Such mannerisms were uncommon, for Dorothy Fuldheim riveted her full attention on her guests. "She had the ability to make you feel you are the most interesting of all people," says Donald Perris.

Timing handed the cast of *The One O'Clock Club* the arduous task on November 22, 1963 of helping its viewers to struggle through the initial shock of news that broke the heart of America. Shortly after the opening theme, during Bill Gordon's live commercial for

Mrs. Weiss's noodles, a news bulletin interrupted him with the chilling news that President Kennedy had been shot in Dallas. Visibly horror-stricken, Dorothy and her colleagues reached out to one another for support and managed to carry on, moving like puppets, through the hour-and-a-half program.

Dorothy probably recalled a story she told many times about British actress Beatrice Lillie, "who was Lady Peel," she'd always add. "When she was about to go on stage to entertain troops during the Second World War, Miss Lillie was told her only son had been on a ship bombed and sunk by the Germans. Her words, in true show-biz tradition, were, "No, I'll go on; I'll cry tomorrow.""

Dorothy's grief was genuine. She admired the young president and particularly the aura of elegance and culture that he and the First Lady had created about the White House. Later Dorothy wrote of that fateful November day, "No one knew then of the strange doom encircling the Kennedy family nor that from that day forth there would be anguish, disorder, and distrust for our nation."

In 1964 *The One O'Clock Club* succumbed to the demon competition, cast in the form of a WERE-TV look-alike—but with big-name talent and paid guests. Mike Douglas, whom no one had heard of at the time, became Bill Gordon's counterpart at WERE, accompanied by a different talent each week to fill Dorothy Fuldheim's co-host role. The WERE-TV show opened with Carmel Quinn, an Irish singing sensation, direct from *The Arthur Godfrey Show*. The following week Zsa Zsa Gabor was sitting in the co-host's chair next to Douglas. Before long WERE-TV was peddling tapes of its show to five other cities, and the New York market began putting together a similar offering. It featured a young man named Merv Griffin as host. "And the rest is history," says Bill Gordon. The Scripps Howard owners of WEWS, however, refused to be drawn into a spending war with their competitors. According to Gordon, a media veteran who still does a weekly talk radio show in Cleveland, the station management became "antsy" as the market fell away and, eventually, handed down the decision that the only practical solution was to cancel *The One O'Clock Club*.

Not many legends are created in seven short years, but *The One O'Clock Club* endeared itself to the hearts and memories of thousands of WEWS-TV viewers.

Susan Peck
Dorothy as a young child. Artist's rendering adapted from a photo that appeared in a 1958 issue of **The Cleveland Press.**

WALKER, MARY.
"Sweet Lavender."
South Milwaukee.

SOLWAY, FLORENCE.
"How goodness brightens beauty."
Menominee, Mich.

KURZ, CHARLOTTE.
"Responsive to her duty."
Milwaukee.

KASTEN, GERTRUDE.
"Bright as the sun her eyes the gazers
strike,
And, like the sun, they shine on all
alike."
Milwaukee.

NIEDERMAN, HARRIET.
"Sprightly and gay."
Milwaukee.

DAVIS, RACHEL.
"Her ways are ways of pleasantness,
All her paths are peace."
Berlin.

SCHNELL, DOROTHY.
"I have never found the limit to my
capacity."
Milwaukee.

PETERMAN, JULIA.
"Her wildest ways are beautiful,—
Her freest thoughts are pure."
Milwaukee.

FARLEY, MARGARET.
"Simple, modest, and true."
Racine.

BEERS, STANLEY.
"Life's a serious proposition."
Girls too."
Sun Prairie.

HEMENWAY, HOMER.
"O, he sits high in all the people's
hearts."
Carter.

VEEDER, MIRIAM.
"True blue."
Mauston.

Both the photo and the caption in her college yearbook hint at young Dorothy Schnell's serious nature.

*This 1934 photo promoted Dorothy Fuldheim
as a lecturer.*

Dorothy gave up smoking in her middle years. She thought it was "a messy habit."

When she entered television in 1947, Dorothy quickly learned to access information from the wire service.

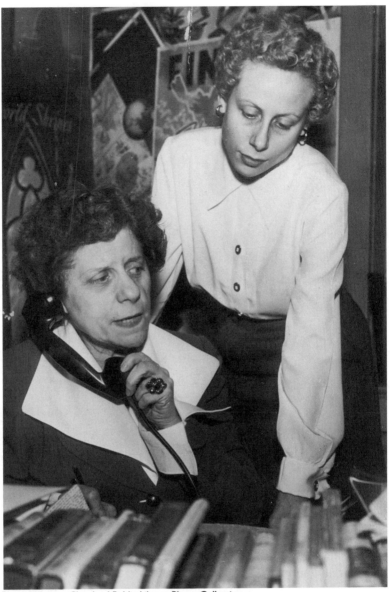

Much of Dorothy Fuldheim's happiness depended upon her daughter, Dorothy, Junior. This photo was taken in 1951.

Dorothy never got over her dislike of flying, but it did not prevent her from traveling throughout the world to pursue interesting people and stories.

Photo courtesy John Carroll University Media Archives/
WEWS NewsChannel 5

*Dorothy's book reviews delighted **The One O'Clock Club** audiences.*

Photo courtesy John Carroll University
MediaArchives/WEWS NewsChannel 5

*The famous "Day-glo" hair could also
be wash and wear if time was short.*

The Duke of Windsor ranked high on Dorothy's list of guests. She called him the most urbane and charming of men.

Photo courtesy John Carroll University Media Archives/
WEWS NewsChannel 5

*Senator Joseph McCarthy's good manners did not convince his hostess to agree
with him in his investigations of Americans who were suspected of being communists in the 1950s.*

Her interview with Helen Keller thrilled Dorothy beyond all others.

Dorothy congratulates Dr. Martin Luther King when he received the Nobel Peace Prize in 1964.

Esteemed movie producer Cecil B. DeMille and Dorothy enjoy a spirited conversation.

Photo courtesy Cleveland Press Archives/
Cleveland State University Instructional Media Services

The Women's City Club, The Higbee Company, and WEWS-TV introduced two of Dorothy Fuldheim's books.

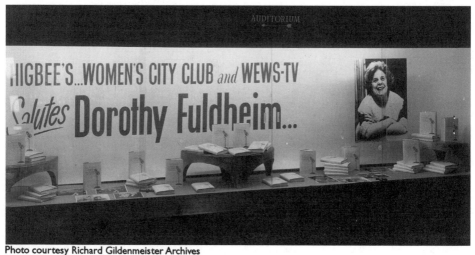

Photo courtesy Richard Gildenmeister Archives

I Laughed, I Cried, I Loved *appeared in 1966. The event was televised live from the Higbee Company's auditorium.*

Dorothy Fuldheim kept her viewers aware and informed about local issues as well as world affairs.

This painting by Sandor Vago pleased Dorothy so much that she used it on the back cover of her first book.

William Ulmer, Dorothy's second husband, earned a reputation as an avid horticulturist.

9
All in a Day's Work

Any reporter who wrote a profile piece about Dorothy Fuldheim felt compelled to reveal her penchant for eating gingersnaps for breakfast. "She liked to *doonk* them, as she'd say, into her French coffee," said Randy Culver, longtime WEWS-TV staff member. Evidently, she started on gingersnaps at breakfast and went on *doonking* them throughout the day. Her palate sensed a character in them, somewhere between an apricot and a sunflower seed. Taste was what counted. The fact that gingersnaps have only thirty-five calories and two grams of fat each didn't make a whit of difference to her. Was that character-laden ginger taste a carryover from her poverty-riddled childhood, when a school lunch consisted of an apple and a piece of stale gingerbread bought for a penny?

A healthful diet was obviously not the secret to Dorothy's longevity, although she once told Larry King she stayed healthy because she liked chocolate. Liked it? She had a passion for it. Her fans sent her boxes and boxes of it. Surprisingly, her taste in chocolate didn't run to the Godiva or even the Whitman's variety. Instead, her desk had separate compartments for stashes of Hershey's Kisses, KitKat bars, and chocolate-covered raisins. Each Christmas the Hershey Company showered her with Kisses, milk chocolate morsels wrapped in red and green foil. Another of her lesser-known cravings, according to her close friend and Shaker Towers neighbor, Taffy Epstein, was hot pumpernickel bread from Davis' Bakery. " I'd pick it up there when it was still warm. We'd slab sweet butter on it, then sour cream. Her daughter thought we were out of our minds."

Actually, Dorothy was hypoglycemic and certainly intelligent enough to know how to eat properly. But, as she said, she was stubborn. She loathed eggs and the hens that produced them. She did recognize she required a lot of protein and, thus, tried to consume a lot of cheese and milk. But food was not important to her. Satisfying her palate—except with chocolate—was inconsequential. She craved mental stimulation. She relished romance and adventure.

Along with the gingersnaps, Dorothy did eat some breakfast, usually prepared by her daughter, Dorothy Junior. Cooking was not among the elder Fuldheim's talents. "We keep Mother out of the kitchen," Junior remarked in an interview televised in the Fuldheim home in 1979. "It's a disaster." Dorothy was quite content to have her breakfast served to her after her daily physical therapy session for relief of her arthritic joints. She nibbled at her food, but she focused attentively upon several of the newspapers she read each day in order to prepare her commentaries. At one time these were reported to be the two Cleveland dailies—*The Press* and *The Plain Dealer* as well as *The New York Times* and *The Herald Tribune*, *The Wall Street Journal*, *The London Times* and *The Daily Herald*.

A career wife since day one of her marriage to Milton Fuldheim in 1918, Dorothy was at least cognizant of the needs of her household. "I run my house, you understand. I entertain," Dorothy Sr. would say with an elegant lilt. "Mildred (Forbes) comes in every day, but I get fussy if the drapes need changing. I lay out the linen . . . But I CAN'T cook. I'm so inept that I can't even do an egg and have it come out right."

The television news queen didn't drive either, once her income had climbed high enough to allow a driver. (Dorothy showed some pique that the station didn't provide a car and driver for her.) After she moved to her Shaker Towers apartment in the 1970's, the building's driver, Toyce Anderson, drove her in her own Lincoln Continental to and from the studio. If she had a midday speaking engagement, she'd take a taxi. Dorothy had high regard for taxis—and taxi drivers. Frequently, she'd pass on to her evening viewers some morsel of philosophy acquired from the driver who'd whisked her off to a luncheon speaking engagement earlier that day. Once, on the way to the Cleveland City Club, a driver looked in his rear-view mirror and informed Madame Fuldheim that her hair was a mess—then let her borrow his comb, after he wiped it on his sleeve.

The discreet hum of that Lincoln Continental's motor alerted ad salesman Greg Olsen every morning. He'd already been at his desk at WEWS-TV for more than an hour, but about 9:30 he'd begin listening for Dorothy's arrival. Greeting her always helped him adjust his mindset before hitting the streets to call on his accounts. A few minutes spent with Dorothy was like a shot of adrenaline.

At first glance, the driver would appear to be alone when he wheeled the Lincoln up to the back door of the studio. Only a few puffs of tangerine-colored hair were visible above the dash on the passenger's side. Dorothy always rode in front with her driver; she'd probably have ridden in the front seat of taxis, too, had she been allowed.

"Good morning, lady," Olsen would say, opening the door and taking Dorothy's tote bag. Every day she'd bring the newspapers she'd already read at home, plus a couple of recent books. She read four or five books a week, sometimes as many as twelve. Using her diagonal mode of reading, her prehensile mind, as she called it, could absorb the relevant facts. She insisted she did not have a photographic mind.

Olsen would sometimes say "Good morning, Red." It depended on her mood. If her spirits really seemed buoyant, he'd even give her a mock serenade as he ushered her into the studio: "Good morning, lady. I'm not a knight in shining armor, but I love you."

To which would come a volley-like reply: "You should have seen me when I was your age, young man. I was quite something."

Once in her office, which was across from his, Olsen would help her with her coat. If it was a fur, she'd delight in saying, "Just throw it there on the couch."

Perhaps she was remembering when she didn't even own a winter coat. The redhead who once yearned for a green taffeta dress now bought more than fifty dresses a year, many with Dior or Chanel labels. Some she purchased locally; others she ordered from New York, a dozen or more at a time. Clothes were not an obsession with her—not quite—but her colorful and eye-popping wardrobe, often complemented by showy pieces of jewelry and dyed-to-match shoes, identified her as surely as her elegant and proper speech.

Cleveland television personality Wilma Smith has a wardrobe that attracts viewers' admiration, but Smith leans toward understated, classic designs. When she was a co-worker of Dorothy's at WEWS-TV, Smith hit upon a theory about the Fuldheim wardrobe: "Flashy dressing was a part of her identity, her persona. Dressing down was not a part of her. She liked frills, bows, bright colors, silks, jewelry. Others could not do this without detracting from their job."

"I may be interesting looking," Dorothy told Diana Tittle in a 1982 interview for *Northern Ohio Live,* "but I'm not a beautiful woman. I had to create the aura of beauty which I think I did." Stephen Bellamy, who knew Dorothy from the time he was a young boy, agrees that this was so. "Something happened when she came into a room," he says. "She was a very sexual woman."

Dorothy detested slacks, although she did admit to owning a few pantsuits. She was partial to dresses of soft, clinging fabrics, especially with wide lace collars and cuffs. Her favorite colors were white and blue. She admitted she didn't keep her dresses long but passed them on to agencies like the Salvation Army. Photos of Dorothy in her travels—climbing on and off planes or walking along cobblestone or dusty streets in Italy or Israel—show her preference for feminine-looking footwear also, whether slingbacks or open toes, whatever was in fashion at the time. She is seldom pictured wearing a hat, even in times when women habitually wore hats and gloves nearly everywhere but their back yard. "I like only large, romantic hats," she once said. Since wide-brimmed, or picture hats as they were called, were neither practical for travel nor especially flattering to a person of her short stature, Dorothy scoffed at convention and traveled the world hatless. Perfume was her passion, and she was never without her signature fragrance, tuberose.

In her office a heady aroma of ever-present bouquets of fresh flowers always mingled with her perfume. Just as Dorothy flaunted showy rings, bracelets, and necklaces, she adored *masses* of flowers. Once, during her brief acting career, she asked the noted Broadway producer, Horace Liveright, only partly in jest, to "strew her path with lilacs" if she came to New York to discuss a role he had offered her. When she stepped off the train at Grand Central, she was ecstatic to find mounds of dewy lilacs delivered to her on the platform, lilacs filling her taxi, lilacs even heaped upon the bed in her hotel room. "What a flair he had! What a debonair personality and what a bold adventurer," she said of Liveright. "I often wondered why I didn't fall for him." She never said if she accepted the role he offered her.

From her early days at WEWS-TV, when she was quite in awe of Dorothy Fuldheim, Wilma Smith tells a favorite "Dorothy story" about flowers. "I was paged to come to the front desk," Smith says, "where I was handed a single rose with a note from the man I had been dating. As I went down the hall to my office to put it in a vase, I met Dorothy. To young, dewy-eyed me, this one, perfect rose was very special, so I showed it to her. With a sniff of disdain and a withering glance, she remarked, 'My dear, you will learn that unless a man sends you three dozen roses, don't bother with him.'"

During the morning hours in her flower-filled office Dorothy researched and wrote her commentaries and readied herself for whatever guest she might be interviewing that day. She would have her assistant hold her phone calls, for she worked in a very tight time frame so that her commentaries would be current. "My chief trouble is finding subjects for them," she once told *The Plain Dealer's* Mary Strassmeyer. "I do 10 a week and each one is different. I might repeat one or another six times in a year. That isn't much repetition."

"How do I do it? It's simple," she said once in an interview. " I do four good ones and six lousy ones." She appeared on the newscasts three times daily for most of her television career—an interview at noon, commentaries at six o'clock and eleven o'clock. The late broadcast was taped earlier before she left the studio for the day, which was usually around six-thirty.

Though concise—only one-and-a-half to three minutes at most— these verbal editorials constantly challenged viewers to consider timely topics, whether of personal, local, national, or global interest. Dorothy wrote them on yellow lined paper, in red ink, then handed them to her assistant, Mendes Napoli, who would decipher them and type them for the TelePrompTer. In later years Tommie Malone took over this job.

Donald Perris, the station's highly regarded manager who took the helm when James Hanrahan retired, always held that "before anything of quality could happen on the television, someone had to sit down at the typewriter and actually think and write." He admonished his reporters to read a daily newspaper and to read books frequently from cover to cover. Dorothy's voracious reading habits, according to him, made her the newsperson she was. "She always knew more, the extra things, that were not in the headlines. She read the *New York Times* when most people in this area did not."

In a complimentary note to then-news executive Fred Griffith, Perris singled out a piece Griffith had done as "Further evidence that it all begins in the typewriter." With a Perris-like touch, two typewriter keys, an F and a G, probably from a vintage Remington, accompanied the note. Although Dorothy did not compose at the typewriter, she definitely fit into Perris' definition of a person who could think and write quality material. This respect for the written word seemed to have pervaded WEWS-TV from the early days. James Hanrahan had been a journalist also, and his bold leadership laid the foundation for the cohesive entity WEWS-TV would become.

Describing Dorothy Fuldheim as the "glue person who held us all together," Perris tells of her intolerance " ... if she thought something was not first class. She hated anything mediocre." Thus, she embraced and helped enforce the high standards put in place first by Hanrahan, then Perris. As her tenure at the station lengthened, her influence as a power figure heightened rather than waned.

"I always thought the best of Dorothy Fuldheim came from the tip of her pen," says former WEWS-TV cameraman Ted Ocepek, who is an aspiring writer himself. Often he'd ask her to critique one of his short pieces before he submitted it to a magazine. He prizes one particular comment from her: "It's too long for *Reader's Digest*," she wrote on his manuscript, "but I wish I'd written that piece myself."

All writers delight in the exhilaration of feeling "the flow," when ideas and words come tumbling out so right and so fast that even the speediest computer can hardly capture them. These are gemlike moments for writers. They atone for the too-frequent, anguished times of searching for that punchy verb or apt metaphor to transmit a particular emotion or idea onto paper.

"When I put something down on paper, it has to flow if it's any good," Dorothy told a *Cleveland Press* reporter in 1980. "On my birthday a year ago, I wrote that piece about 'my house'—my physical self, my body.

"I wrote it in just 45 minutes and never changed a word or a line. I knew it was good because it flowed." Fifteen thousand viewers called the station requesting copies for that essay for which she received a Cleveland Press Club award.

Admitting some of her commentaries are more lucid than others, she told Bill Barrett of *The Cleveland Press*, "There are days when I think, 'God, what a lousy job I did today! Why do they pay me?' And I suffer all that night until the next day when I do a GOOD job—and then I wonder why they don't pay me more."

"It's quite a trick to be able to appeal to Harvard graduates and to a guy who owns a little store and never went beyond the first year of high school. It's a technique which you develop, really, by trial and error," she told a *Beacon Magazine* reporter in 1975. She was then eighty-two years old and had appeared every weekday on WEWS-TV for twenty-eight consecutive years. Her style was her own—unique, and by her own admission, charismatic. "Some people have it and some haven't. But obviously, you couldn't occupy the kind of position I do without some background or knowledge."

Some found her long on style, short on substance. A former WEWS-TV staff member, Joel Rose, who worked closely with Dorothy Fuldheim for many years, does not think she was a particularly a good journalist, per se. "Dorothy knew how to get the drama, the emotional quality out of a story," Rose said.

Others called her silly, outdated, without original insight, according to a 1975 account in *Beacon Magazine*. Some resented her indignation, her opinions, or her irreverence.

Some criticized her style, saying that her commentaries consisted of reiterating a complicated or confused situation, and then topping that off with, 'Now isn't that amazing!'

But, *Beacon Magazine* concluded,

> Dorothy Fuldheim with no plans to retire, is a tradition who has endured for so long that she has transcended the novelty, controversy and the cosmetics of 1970s television newscasting to ease into the category of institution. She commands a huge following, which therefore gives her influence, and at an age by which most people are dead, she continues to work nine hours a day to fulfill what she sees as her duty.

In many interviews she gave to reporters, Dorothy herself focuses attention more on her style, her drama, and her personality than upon her lofty intelligence and keen insight. Perhaps this was but one of the tactics she adopted to maintain her appeal for a multi-layered spectrum of viewers in a heavily industrial city.

Guest interviews most often occurred as part of the noon newscast. Dorothy's habit was to meet her guest briefly and informally in her office to establish rapport and the parameters of the interview before the live telecast. In the areas of politics and world affairs, Dorothy was well versed, asked insightful questions, and gave her guest ample time to respond. She thoroughly enjoyed comedians, causing native Clevelander Bob Hope to remark once, "I'm supposed to be the comedian here." In sports, however, Dorothy frequently let her guest take the lead. She might begin by asking a seemingly innocuous question such as "What do you do?"

Both Randy Culver and director James Breslin tell the Joe Namath story in which that question backfired and the New York Jets' quarterback found himself propelled out of Dorothy Fuldheim's office. After an intense Monday night football game against the Cleveland Browns, Namath showed up at the WEWS-TV studio, flanked by an appropriate entourage, for an early morning taping session with the Queen of Cleveland Television—or so he'd been told.

Settling herself in her highbacked leather chair and surveying Mr. Namath with an agate-like gaze, she inquired, "By the way, what do you do?"

Namath stiffened, eagle-eyed his hostess, and hurled back, "Lady, if you don't know—what am I doing here?"

Without a moment's pause, Dorothy was on her feet, waving them all toward the door. "I don't know," she declared. "Get out of here."

Culver says Namath went down the hallway, muttering, "That's a crazy lady in there." Apparently, Namath did not make an issue of the incident with the management of the television station. Since it did not happen on the air and only a few people were witnesses, Mr. Namath's brief skirmish with Dorothy Fuldheim was not trumpeted about the city.

Most pre-broadcast sessions were pleasant times, and often Dorothy and her guest would visit for a while after the interview concluded. The Honorable Louis Stokes, Ohio's U.S. Congressman since 1968, recalls:

> I always enjoyed watching how relaxed she was both before and during any interview. She never required notes and conducted her interviews from her enormous intellect. Dorothy Fuldheim was a very proud and powerful woman, but she was also a very warm and genuine personality.

The Fuldheim papers, housed in the Special Collections at Kent State University, contain countless notes of appreciation from persons whom she interviewed. Many mention the extra time she spent, talking with them, putting them at ease.

The interview with you was great fun. You asked excellent questions, and you were generous enough to give me time to develop and explain my answers.

John H. Chafee
Secretary of the Navy

Handwritten note at bottom: You are terrific, no wonder you have such a following in the entire Cleveland area.

I enjoyed the interview, but I particularly appreciated your candid observations beforehand over coffee. You know I value your opinions highly.

Senator Hubert H. Humphrey

Rarely have I been interviewed by anybody who presented the challenge you offered last Wednesday. I think your viewers are indeed fortunate. You should be on national television so that the entire nation could benefit from your insight and wisdom.

Nelson A. Rockefeller
Governor of New York

Bishop Anthony M. Pilla of the Catholic Diocese of Cleveland appeared with Dorothy many times and considered her one of the best interviewers. He says,

I really admired her for her skill. Normally, when you get interviewed in the media, there are a certain number of questions the interviewer is going to ask you, no matter what you say. They don't always seem to listen to what you say; they just keep repeating the questions they want answered. But Dorothy Fuldheim never did that. She would let you speak, and she would pick up on what you said and carry it on, so you could deal with things in a substantive manner, in some depth. She didn't let it go because she had five other questions she wanted to ask you, but she would stay with something if she thought it was worthwhile. This was true even in brief interviews. She allowed what she heard to influence the interview, which I always appreciated.

Dorothy assesses her own interviewing skills by concluding that she is sincere, she is interested, she is completely into the subject. "And this," she told a reporter in 1975, "is why I'm effective. I'm genuine. I'm no phoney, you know." She explained her practiced interview technique:

> First of all, I charm them, put them at their ease. And then I find out what they want to say while making an effort not to hurt their feelings. I have been hurt, and I don't want to do that to someone else. Life can be brutal enough. Privately, I may think they're jackasses. But I don't want to be supercilious.

James Breslin sums up Dorothy's success as an interviewer:

> She treated everyone the same, whether he was the paper boy or the President of the United States. She asked them anything. She wanted to get the facts. All I had to do as a director was get her guest up on the stage. She did the rest. A real pro. When she finished with an interview, she knew the true nature of a person.

Interviews often extended off-camera into the lunch hour. Several staff members at WEWS-TV claim to have tried to interest Dorothy in eating lunch. Sometimes her assistant would bring her some soup from a vending machine in the building. Sometimes she'd call Greg Olsen and say, "I feel like a corned beef and Swiss today," and he'd bring her one—along with a cold pop, (of the Duquesne variety), from the Diplomat Lounge next door. Most often, lunch was a sandwich, split with Breslin, from the little lunchroom between her office and his.

One day Dorothy was on the way to her office after concluding her noon interview. She'd usually stop in Breslin's office to pick up her half of a sandwich. Hearing voices in the hallway, Breslin realized she was bringing her guest for the day back to her office. This happened occasionally.

"All at once," Breslin recalls, "the redhead appeared in my doorway. 'Jim—' she stopped short, turning to speak in a syrupy tone to her guest in the hallway. 'Excuse me just a moment, Mr. President.' Back to me, curtly, 'Where in the world is my sandwich?' With that, she sailed on past my door, escorting a somewhat amused President Jimmy Carter, followed by two Secret Service men."

In the afternoon hours Dorothy would continue researching and writing commentaries for another day or update her files for lectures, mostly on world affairs or economics, that she continued to give to all sorts of audiences—civic clubs, high school and college graduations, or presiding at testimonial dinners and fundraisers. She would try answering her own phone again, dealing with questions such as one from Linda of Solon, protesting the discontinuing of the Erie-Lackawanna commuter train or Bruce, a Cleveland steelworker, asking for an explanation as to why foreign steel was purchased for the construction of the [Cuyahoga County] Justice Center.

The documents housed in the archives at Kent State University reveal that Dorothy Fuldheim devised an efficient, yet personalized, method of dealing with her constant flood of correspondence. Unfortunately, copies of her replies are not included with the letters on file, but most letters she received bear a number, which appears to be in Dorothy's handwriting. One would assume she had devised stock replies to letters, and the numbers indicated which of these her secretary would use in replying. When she signed the letter, Dorothy could add a handwritten post script if she wished. Some letters, of course, merited a totally personal response, such as letters from her editor at Doubleday, Diane Cleaver, urging her to do another book or from Cuyahoga County commissioner Seth Taft, asking her to do a commentary supporting a constitutional amendment to permit farm lands to be valued for farm purposes, thereby keeping more land in farming. One wonders what sort of reply she wrote to several letters on file from Rex Humbard, dubious television evangelist at Akron's Cathedral of Tomorrow, seeking to be her guest.

Dorothy's late afternoon talkfests with Don Perris and Greg Olsen supplied her some relaxation before her appearance on the evening news. If she had no evening speaking engagement, she might join friends at a dinner party or attend a play or a concert by the Cleveland Orchestra. She frequently dined at the Severance Supper Club, according to a letter from Tony Poderis, then director of development for the Cleveland Orchestra. He wrote, thanking her for her patronage and a favorable commentary she had done on "the Maazel Elektra concert." He mentioned that he enjoyed seeing her often at the Supper Club.

At another time Poderis invited Dorothy to a pre-concert dinner he was hosting at the Supper Club. He recalls passing her table and hearing her remark to her dining companions, "Now why in the hell did he invite an old lady like me to this?"

After an evening out, when she would return to her Shaker Towers condominium where she lived after 1971, Dorothy would read until around 1:00 a.m. As any avid reader knows, ending the day without some time spent with a book is like eating Thanksgiving dinner without finishing it off with pumpkin pie. Presumably, this was the time when she read for pleasure. Accounts of space exploration fascinated her by appealing to her storehouse of knowledge of astronomy. Biographies, well-written ones, consumed her interest, meshing with her job as an interviewer who sought out unique and fascinating facts about people's lives. "If she were here today, she would be reading Katharine Graham's *Personal History*," says Richard Gildenmeister. His Shaker Square Bookshop supplied Dorothy with her reading material, "bags and bags of books," he says, for many years. "She liked good fiction, too," Gildenmeister says, "such as Rosamunde Pilcher's *The Shell Seekers.*

Public appearances consumed much of her weekend time, especially speeches she continued to give that were not part of her job at WEWS-TV. "She would go anywhere, ran all around, making speeches, even in her later years. She was terrified of leaving her granddaughter destitute," says Sam Miller.

Chris Bade, who graduated in 1984 from Baldwin-Wallace College in Berea, a Cleveland suburb, remembers that Dorothy Fuldheim was the speaker at his June graduation ceremony. As the graduates lined the sidewalk near the college athletic field, Bade recalls seeing tiny Dorothy Fuldheim arrive in a white stretch limousine. In spite of an unseasonable eighty-degree day, she clambered to the platform with less assistance than one would expect for a woman who was then only days away from age ninety-one.

After she had finished her address, she graciously accepted an honorary degree labeled Doctor of Humane Letters. Then she exited the rostrum just as ably as she had arrived and headed toward her waiting air-conditioned limo. Bade admits that with the heat and the excitement of the moment, he remembers her dramatic arrival and departure more clearly than whatever sage advice she imparted.

Saturdays included fitting sessions with a dressmaker since all of her clothes required alterations. She wore a size 14 or 16 in later years, which trailed the floor like a child's dress-ups when she put them on her five-feet, two-inch frame. Earlier accounts describe her as one inch taller. This is understandable since arthritis often causes persons to hunch a bit as they age. She complained vigorously about stylish clothes being made only for women with sylph-like figures and "longed for a divine figure so that when I would move, I'd be like a swaying tree."

She commented that it takes a lot of courage to wear, at age eighty-nine, some of her clothes. But she said she didn't want to dress conservatively. She felt many women her age dressed as if their lives were over. "Now I don't have the kind of figure I did when I was thirty, forty, fifty, even seventy, so I dress in the best fashion that I can, and I get some attention," she said.

A standing appointment with her hairdresser completed her Saturday morning schedule. She admitted to touching up her naturally wavy, trademark red hair—her "Dayglo hair" as viewers and co-workers alike sometimes referred to it, but with respect. The red hair was as much Dorothy as her beaded and feathered dresses, her portrait lace collars, her rainbow-hued shoes, her flamboyant jewelry. Put them all together, they spelled Dorothy—the image she designed and the one her viewers had come to admire and expect.

A Saturday lunch date with her daughter gave the two professional women a chance to catch up on what went on in each other's week. Dorothy, the news analyst, was mother to Dorothy, the professor. Dorothy Junior, who completed a doctorate in Slavic and eastern European languages in 1978, now taught at her alma mater, Case Western Reserve University. Her classes in Russian literature were said to be among the most popular on the campus.

Once when she was asked by an interviewer what it was like to be the daughter of a celebrated television personality of such duration, Dorothy the professor, replied, "It's satisfactory. If I had to choose a mother again, I'd choose her." When she would occasionally sit in for her mother with a commentary when Dorothy was traveling, staff members at WEWS-TV enjoyed Dorothy Junior's hearty sense of humor and unruffled attitude. "Sometimes," Jim Breslin remembers, "her mother would be uptight about something, some breach of etiquette, for instance. Junior would laugh and say, "'Oh, ma, forget about it.'"

In what would be one of their last joint efforts, Dorothy Sr. and Dorothy Jr. co-authored a weekly column called *Fuldheim* in the Sunday edition of the *Lorain Journal* in 1979-80. The subjects focused heavily on world affairs and economics and no doubt contained many of the same views Dorothy Sr. expressed in her speaking engagements. At times, the two Fuldheims addressed more personal problems of their readers—marriage, education, manners, moral leadership. Since the city of Lorain is in the WEWS-TV viewing audience, the columns obviously did not recycle Dorothy Sr.'s television commentaries. Oddly, the columns were written in first person, and the reader is never certain which Dorothy is speaking; surely two such educated and opinionated women, more than a quarter century apart in age, could not have had identical views. Dorothy Junior admitted to a reporter, however, that she and her mother alternated writing the columns, although both bylines were always given—Dorothy Fuldheim, Sr. and Jr.

To announce the column's debut, the *Journal* displayed a full page photo of mother and daughter, captioned **The Thinking Man's Redhead Is Coming to the Journal.** The announcement heralded Sr. as "an award-winning journalist, author, and world traveler who is teaming up with her daughter, a doctor of philosophy and professor at Case Western Reserve University." Surprisingly, Dorothy, the mother and the news analyst, did not renege on the contract when she saw that caption. "If there is one thing that really irks me, it is to be told, 'you think like a man.' I doubt if one's brain were removed from the body whether it could be identified as male or female. My emotions are female, not my brain."

In Dorothy's personal papers is a letter from George Steinbrenner III. He pays her what he must have thought was a glowing compliment on the occasion of her eightieth birthday in 1973. Steinbrenner, who was chairman and CEO of Cleveland's American Shipbuilding Company and currently owns the New York Yankees, wrote: "To be entertaining as well as articulate and logical is not an easy task—and in this era of 'women's lib,' you are a classic example of a splendid female mind." How Dorothy must have bristled at those last three words.

Dorothy also scheduled time in her Saturdays for a practice session at the piano. She said that she played, "but not well enough to make a living at it." Remembering the battered upright in her childhood home and her brother David's musical prowess at an early age, Dorothy surely found satisfaction in disciplining her mind and her hands to acquire a skill at a different sort of activity from her profession. She was wise enough, also, to know that her super-active brain cried out for an occasional respite from constant stimulation of ideas, the interminable hammering of words. She often mentions her Saturday afternoon times at the piano. In her busy week, this was undoubtedly a soothing and pleasant interlude, one she fiercely guarded.

10

The Fuldheim Phenomenon

When Dorothy joined WEWS-TV in 1947, at age fifty-four, she stood in the doorway of an uncharted and innovative industry. She held a passport guaranteeing her arrival at success. First, she claimed twenty-seven years—what today would be nearly the length of an entire career—as an esteemed and sought-after lecturer. Moreover, she possessed a finely tuned, retentive mind coupled with an insatiable appetite for reading. Her rock-solid reputation as a lecturer and as a book reviewer had already won her a following with thousands who were now able to tune in to the new television station. To glean material for her lectures, Dorothy had traveled throughout the world and interviewed the notable and the notorious, as well as men and women whose paths crossed hers in everyday life: a mayoral candidate, a cab driver, a union steward, an elderly woman she met at a street corner who told Dorothy about her two friends, God and her television. For such a diminutive person, Dorothy was in good health and had remarkable physical stamina. As for the demands of her home life, she always had to reconcile the needs of her family with her career; this was a given. She claimed that she didn't work because of a passion to work but to support herself and her family.

Little is known of Dorothy's granddaughter Halla's childhood. As Dorothy Junior worked to earn her advanced degrees and then to become a professor at Case Western Reserve University, a caregiver was always in the home for Halla, who was confined to a wheelchair. A physical therapist came to the home regularly and neighbors grew accustomed to the touching sight of Halla, her legs in braces and aided by the therapist, struggling to walk along the shady sidewalks. For a number of years she attended the Sunbeam School, a Cleveland public school for students with disabilities. As the girl grew older, she became enthused about classical music and delighted in the music and the story line of many operas and symphonies as well. Through her television she experienced as much of her mother and grandmother's world as she could, but she had only limited contact with other people. In her later years, when Dorothy entertained at her condominium, friends agree that Halla was "kept hidden." Her disability did not allow her to mingle with guests, although by the time Dorothy moved to Shaker Towers, Halla was approaching thirty years of age. Some newspaper accounts state that she had cerebral palsy, but her disability usually was referred to, correctly or not, as resulting from polio.

At the time of Halla's birth in 1943, the specter of polio commonly threatened children and young adults; in fact, the disease had struck Franklin Roosevelt, yet he became president. To have a child crippled by polio would seem more respectable, in those days, than to admit to having produced a child who was congenitally disabled. Before the Enlightened Sixties, persons who were disabled were often shunned or avoided.

Emerging from this shadow of grief enveloping her household in the mid-1940s, Dorothy took up the challenge of a new career with determination and drive. Her granddaughter's condition required additional medical expense and household help, and she and Milton had moved their family to a spacious, many-windowed bungalow-style home at 2652 Euclid Heights Boulevard. They still continued to live near the Heights Center Building in Cleveland Heights where Milton maintained his law practice. As her local celebrity status heightened, Dorothy Fuldheim determined to keep her private life separate from her platform and television image. On Mother's Day 1958, for example, she refused a suggestion from reporters to pose with her family for a Mother's Day photograph of four generations—her mother Bertha, herself, Dorothy Junior, and Halla. She may well have regretted she did not have the photograph made, for it was the last Mother's Day she would have her mother with her. Bertha Schnell died the following September, the autumn of her ninetieth year.

"Dorothy Fuldheim was the first woman to be taken seriously doing the news," ABC's Barbara Walters told the Associated Press at the time of Dorothy's death in 1989. Nevertheless, some writers, in documenting the careers of television journalists, have overlooked

Dorothy Fuldheim since she never moved to a major network. She refused to consider leaving Cleveland and WEWS-TV. David Hosley and Gayle Yamada, in their well-researched *Hard News: Women in Broadcast Journalism*, recognize Dorothy Fuldheim's position and sum up her towering success as owing to her unique style as well as her vitality, her professionalism, and personal warmth.

While Dorothy was familiarizing herself with working with lights, cameras, and a floor crew, a few other women around the country were testing the waves in the infant television news industry. One was Pauline Frederick, who signed on at ABC in 1948, then moved to NBC in 1953. Fifteen years younger than Dorothy Fuldheim, Frederick broke into television, as Dorothy did, by way of radio. Having studied political science at George Washington University in Washington, D.C., Frederick had earned a master's degree in international law and was well prepared to shift into a career in political reporting. Nevertheless, she had to inch her way into political reporting since this field was not then open to women. In those early years she devoted her perceptive writing and reporting skills to the minutiae of social and charitable activities of wives of diplomats and political figures. Battling years of gender discrimination, Frederick often heard that "a woman's voice doesn't carry authority." No wonder she remarked in 1981, looking back on her career, "When a man speaks on television, people listen. But when a woman speaks, people look, and if they like her looks, then they listen." Frederick, who possessed a rich, well-modulated voice, developed a tone that was authoritative without being strident. Television columnist and former movie actress Faye Emerson wrote in the *New York World-Telegram and Sun*, "Pauline has been doing a crack job on NBC radio and has just won a highly coveted award, so why not her own TV show? . . . . There is room for a few ladies on television to talk about something besides cooking and fashion. Women have minds, too." Miss Frederick was attractive in addition to her other qualities. *The New York Times* described her in 1948 as a "tall, lissome brunette of mellifluous voice and photogenic figure."

Eventually, Pauline Frederick found her niche and viewers across America inevitably associated her with the United Nations' activities throughout the 1960s and until her [then] compulsory retirement at age sixty-five in 1974. By then she had acquired twenty-three honorary doctorate degrees—in humanities, law, and journalism—and countless awards for her television reporting and interpretation. For the next five years, after retiring from NBC, she commented on international affairs for National Public Radio. As a footnote, Frederick had remained single until age sixty-one when she married Charles Robbins, a former managing editor of *The Wall Street Journal.*

Hosley and Yamada suggest that if Pauline Frederick was the dean of national newswomen at that time, then Dorothy Fuldheim was her counterpart at the local level.

When one looks at the broadcasting career of Dorothy Fuldheim, seeing her in a niche is difficult, even one as prestigious as covering the United Nations or possibly the White House, as Rita Braver currently does for CBS. Dorothy's interests were far too expansive—her genuine compassion for the foibles and frailties of humankind too encompassing, her celebration of its accomplishments too ebullient— to be wedged into a confined, one-topic corner. She was a generalist in all respects. Any subject or event she deemed worthy of notice or concern, she would bring to the attention of her city. Eventually, the station's viewing area would encompass a seventeen-county area. Although her viewing audience was in northern Ohio, her prestige, attracted the world's great, the near-great, and would-be-great to the WEWS-TV news set. Emotionally as well as financially, Dorothy needed to work, to interact with all sorts of people, to explicate her views, to probe and relate to the minds of others, and to interact with them. With this marvelous new medium, she could bring her audiences face to face with people whose lives she considered worthy of examining.

An interview with Danny Thomas in 1978 exemplified her skills. Her technique was to focus totally upon her guest. As she and Thomas discussed success, Thomas referred openly to the poverty of his youth. He said he could see no justification for being poor but spoke of how his poverty in early life had made him appreciative of success and especially thankful for his good health. "For this I have dedicated my life to my Creator," he said, "and I thank him for every healthy breath."

Although Dorothy never made a secret of her humble beginnings, she did not focus upon or inject herself into Thomas' commentary on this topic. He remarked that he attributed his success to hard work and did not regard it as a blessing. "God is not blessing you when you succeed," he said, adding, "My kids say I'm nuts." To which Dorothy replied quickly, "Dear God, give us more 'nuts.' Then she skillfully segued to another topic, asking "Is there a wall of separation between generations?" (Thomas did not think so, even at a time of the ubiquitous buzzword "Generation Gap.")

Unknowingly, Dorothy served as a mentor for the WEWS-TV personality who would succeed her as interviewer par excellence. When Fred Griffith came to Cleveland in 1959, he hosted *Project 1260* at radio WDOK in Cleveland. He joined WEWS-TV in 1966. One day he was asked to sit in as host for a morning program and in doing so found his real strength emerged as an interviewer rather than as news director. *The Morning Exchange,* which the amiable and articulate Griffith co-hosts at WEWS-TV, celebrated its twenty-fifth anniversary in 1997. Griffith says,

> When junketing authors and celebrities came to town, they would 'do Dorothy.' I'd get them at midday, and she'd get them later. I'd tape her interviews and then go home and watch Dorothy. I'd find myself saying, 'Oh, I wish I'd have thought of that,' or 'Maybe I should have put the question this way,' I learned from what she did, interviewing the same subject, probably without even realizing it. It got to be a part of my day to make sure I watched what she did. I think that a lot of the things I do on television come off more as a conversation than an 'I'm interviewing you type of thing' and are a result of skills I learned from Dorothy. She made a big mark on the way I function.
>
> Even before I met Dorothy Fuldheim, I learned from her, and it didn't take long after I came here [WEWS-TV] for me to get to know her. She sort of accepted me as somebody that Don Perris was high on. He liked me because, as Dorothy had done, I had read a lot and could use the language a bit."

Just as Dorothy credits the first WEWS-TV manager, James Hanrahan, for giving her a chance in television, Griffith acknowledges that Hanrahan's successor, Don Perris, saw potential in him to do the interview-type show when consultants and critics felt he had no potential for air time. Perris' assessment proved correct, and Griffith says he has done more than 2,200 interviews. He continues to do five two-hour shows each week with current co-host, Connie Dieken. Many of the shows feature cooking, since Griffith and his wife Linda are gourmet cooks and have co-authored several popular cookbooks in recent years.

Over his desk, the former Dorothy Fuldheim desk, hangs a print by Claude Monet. The French Impressionist painter continued working in his later years, even when his vision was failing. Like Monet and Dorothy Fuldheim, his mentor, Fred Griffith believes in never letting the creativity die.

Fortunately, Dorothy Fuldheim found time to publish a few slim volumes, sharing with the world some of the milestones and crises of her exceptional career in television. *I Laughed, I Cried, I Loved* appeared in 1966 and *A Thousand Friends* in 1974. Both books offer frank and entertaining glimpses of hundreds of fascinating personalities who found their way to *The One O'Clock Club* or to the noon news show at WEWS-TV, or whom Dorothy Fuldheim wangled to her microphone in some corner of the world—Germany, England, Israel, France, the Philippines. In some cases she creates detailed portraits of extraordinary people, whether famous or unknown.

An account of one such visit took place in 1970 in a walled garden in the storybook city of Heidelberg, renowned as the setting for the operetta, *The Student Prince*. The German government had invited Dorothy to visit, and the consulate offered to arrange any interview she wished. She chose Albert Speer, who had been Hitler's architect, then munitions czar for Nazi Germany. Speer, who confessed his guilt at the Nuremberg trials, was convicted and had served twenty years in prison. While in prison, he wrote *Inside the Third Reich*, detailing the bizarre machinations of Hitler's regime. The book had just been published.

Dorothy re-created the tranquillity of the setting—roses blooming, birds singing, a luncheon table elegantly set with fine linen and china, and Herr Speer's impeccable demeanor. How could this cultivated, courteous man have been a part of "the unbelievable design that had drenched the world with blood?" She recorded a conversation she professed as one of her most memorable interviews:

> "Tell me," I asked him, "why did you plead guilty?"
>
> "Because I was guilty," he answered. "I closed my eyes to what was happening because my ambition was so great. Hitler gave me the fulfillment of an architect's dream, carte blanche to rebuild Berlin as I desired. Who would not have paid almost any price for such an opportunity? Then the war came and my dream for a new Berlin was shoved aside and Hitler appointed me czar of all German industries to produce armaments. By then I was too involved to withdraw."

"But, Herr Speer," I asked, "couldn't you smell the dead flesh in the gas chamber, couldn't you hear the cry of little children, didn't you know that behind the trim landscaped concentration camps children were being held naked in their mothers' arms, their clothes neatly piled in great stacks, and shoved into gas chambers? Didn't you realize that you were using slave labor in your factories pouring out instruments of destruction?"

"No," he said. "I closed my eyes to all of what was happening because it was too late. I had no choice or I would have also been a victim, too, for Hitler was irrational."

Appearing on *Donahue* in 1984 Dorothy recalled this interview with Albert Speer. "I asked Herr Speer how he could possibly have been a party to what Hitler was doing. Why didn't he withdraw?

And the handsome German replied, 'Hitler would have hung me like a carcass on the wall.' And I told him, 'It would have been a worthy and a noble death.'"

The former Nazi official recounted the deaths of Hitler and his mistress, Eva Braun, whom he married the day before their suicides, as well as the deaths of Herr Joseph Goebbels, Hitler's minister of propaganda, his wife and six children—all of whom died from injections of poison. In the interview he recounted events of his own twenty years in prison as atonement for his role in the war crimes.

Dorothy concludes the chapter in *A Thousand Friends* by speaking of the eternal struggle for supremacy between evil and good in the human condition. Her words bring to mind the graphic metaphor spoken by Shakespeare's Friar Laurence in *Romeo and Juliet*. As he considers the powers of herbs and plants from which he will ultimately concoct a sleeping potion for Juliet, the Friar likens the healing and destructive powers of plants to the struggle between good and evil in human beings.

> Within the infant rind of this weak flower
> Poison hath residence, and medicine power;
> For this being smelt with that part cheers each part:
> Being tasted, slays all senses with the heart.
> Two such opposed kings encamp them still
> In man as well as herbs—grace and rude will;
> And where the worser is predominant,
> Full soon the canker death eats up that plant.

Dorothy's *Where Were the Arabs?* stands as what is probably her finest piece of writing. In this slim book, only slightly over one hundred pages, she logged her passion-packed, firsthand observations after the Six-Day War that erupted in the Middle East in May 1967 and exploded into an all-out war during the first days of June. She had covered the Palestinian war in 1948 and had been in Egypt and Israel in 1956, and she recognized that the Arabs' encirclement of Israel almost surely meant war. When fighting began, Dorothy was determined she would go to Israel again in 1967.

Her manager, Donald Perris, had other ideas for his stellar news analyst, who was then approaching her seventy-fourth birthday. When he shook his head, saying, "Absolutely not," she followed him down a hallway, saying, "Look, if you had been manager of a station when Octavian was attacking Cleopatra's fleet with his Roman galleys at Actium, would you have refused to allow your chief news analyst to cover the event? Well, this is exactly what is going to happen in Israel! It is too important to miss." She was racing now, trying to keep up with Perris' long strides. *"I am going to cover this war."*

"You certainly are not," he snapped. "I am not going to have it on my conscience if anything happens to you. You are neither cautious, prudent, nor a mere twenty years old!"

Even against such a profound argument, Dorothy refused to let her boss stonewall her. When she did not badger him in person, she left notes on his desk saying, *I am going to Israel.* Finally, he consented, provided she could find a bodyguard. She agreed, provided the bodyguard was "strong, good-looking, bright, and has a good name." Someone volunteered the name of former Cleveland Indian third baseman Al Rosen, who not only proved himself a delightful and resourceful traveling companion but also insisted that armed guards travel with them throughout the trip.

Where Were the Arabs? is a collection of seventeen finely crafted vignettes, each one characterizing the nature and the spirit of the Israelis who saved their tiny nation from annihilation. Dorothy Fuldheim and Al Rosen traveled dusty, rutted roads to visit with the wounded and the dying, with officers and political leaders, with women and children who were left behind. The two Americans' tears of joy mingled with those of the Israelis as the victorious Tenth Battalion surged back into the streets of Tel Aviv aboard battered, captured tanks and trucks.

. . . . I was torn with sobs as I watched the Tenth Battalion come riding back in the captured tanks and trucks. Why? Why were tears running down the cheeks of Al Rosen? We wept because it was not just the Tenth Battalion of the Israeli Army that was returning; marching with them were the dead, the million, million dead. I wept for the anguish of those millions; I sobbed for the million children who were placed into gas chambers. I wept for those burned in the ovens at Auschwitz. I wept for the dwellers and the tortured in the Polish ghettos. I wept for the branded arms of eight million Jews. I wept for their anguish and for their broken pride and their sullied womanhood. I wept for mankind's infinite capacity for wickedness, and I wept with passion at the sight of these bronzed men burnt by the desert sun, these men dusty with the sands of the desert, these men holding guns in their hands.

These men are a new breed of Jews, who have stood up to fate and announced, "We gave the world thinkers, scientists, creators, musicians, but the world's answer was death, death to the Jews. We turned our swords into ploughshares, but the world was not content. Now we, the new Jews, forged out of adversity—for only the ingenious and the resourceful survived the bitter persecutions—have set aside our ploughshares. We have taken the avenging sword in our hands. Life shall not be denied us until the last of us have fallen. We shall not die ignominiously again. No more gas chambers, for if we die we take our enemies with us through the door of death." This is the new Jew. This is the conquering Jew, the victor.

And so I wept for those whose ghosts and whose memory marched with the Tenth Battalion on that boulevard in Tel Aviv on that June day.

The book is definitely pro-Israel, but not necessarily because Dorothy was Jewish. She did not adhere to or practice any religious faith. As was her habit, she championed the cause of the downtrodden, the persecuted. Here was a small nation of only two-and-a-half million people rising up to defeat the combined forces of the Arab world. Dorothy saw the Israeli army as being akin to America's patriots at the time of the Revolutionary War; they were passionate civilians who had left their businesses and their families to defend their homeland.

Because the book opens such a brief window of history, Dorothy's accounts in *Where Were the Arabs?* are tightly focused and intense. She wrote simply but with clearly defined and burning passion. Her design was not to entertain or impress but to inform and arouse empathy and elicit pride among her readers for the Israeli cause. She captures the pulsing milieu of the tiny country and the strong-hearted will of its people. In addition she offers honest and finely chiseled cameo portraits of the war's principal leaders—then General Moshe Dayan, King Hussein of Jordan, Abdul Nasser, the Egyptian dictator, and Mayor Teddy Kolleck of Jerusalem.

As is often the case, those who give of themselves to others are often blessed in ways they least expect. Through her unwavering support of the Israeli nation, Dorothy Fuldheim gained a priceless gift of personal friendship. One evening in the early 1960s, after she had finished the six o'clock broadcast, Dorothy fluffed up her trademark red hair and freshened her lipstick and perfume. Picking up her fur wrap, she peered at the hemline of her peacock-blue sequin-studded dress as she passed a full-length mirror. Then she left the studio and stepped into her waiting car at 30th and Euclid. After threading the car through the now-emptying downtown streets, the driver deposited Dorothy at a hotel where she was to speak at a State of Israel bond rally. Rabbi Rudolph Rosenthal was in charge. Sharing the podium with Dorothy would be Sam Miller, a Clevelander whom she had never met but knew by reputation as an astute businessman and a generous and tireless benefactor of deserving causes.

On that night Dorothy would gain a friend who would walk beside her through the rest of her days. She and Miller discovered a kinship, a common bond, forged by their intense fervor to use their abilities to help make the world a better place, to aid those less fortunate, and to relieve the oppressed. Miller, whose parents had fled Russia and Poland for a new life in Cleveland, had merged his own construction business with the Ratner family's Forest City home building and supplies enterprises at about the same time Dorothy and WEWS-TV began beaming the news to Cleveland.

A five-year veteran of the Seabees, Miller had taken advantage of the education offered to veterans and graduated with honors in business administration from Western Reserve University and earned a master's from Harvard. Eventually, he became chief operating officer and co-chairman of the board at Forest City Enterprises, which had become a far-reaching corporate structure. Since 1960 Forest City has concentrated on the development and operation of shopping malls, including Cleveland's premier Tower City, a tasteful restoration of the railroad terminal into an upscale shopping and entertainment area.

Miller has been twice decorated by Israeli premier Yitzhak Rabin for his persistent and generous efforts for Israel. His office at Forest City houses a treasury of living history. It overflows with awards and citations for his tireless and distinguished efforts on others' behalf. These awards lining his desk, walls, and shelves embrace a wide spectrum of political and religious affiliations. For example, although he is a supporter of Israel, Miller's generosity has extended to Arab refugee organizations as well. One of his favorite sayings, "Suffering has no political boundaries," frames his philosophy.

At the close of their remarks at the bond rally that night in the 1960s, Miller could sense that his co-presenter on the platform, the feisty redhead from TV-5, shared with him what he calls "the same fire in the belly." He suggested that if she felt so passionately about Israel, perhaps she'd like to go with him, along with then-Congressman Charlie Vanik, to visit Israel and observe conditions there first-hand. "We're leaving tomorrow morning," he told her. "If you want to go, be at Hopkins Airport at nine o'clock sharp." Dorothy eyed Sam Miller warily. "I don't know much about you . . . "

At 8:52 the following morning, just as Miller and Vanik were about to board their plane, a car rolled out on the tarmac and a bustling figure with a flurry of red hair emerged. As Don Perris had often observed, Dorothy could be ready to go anywhere with practically no notice at all. She must have rushed home from the banquet and packed her bags.

"Dorothy and I became fast friends," Miller says. "She 'adopted' my wife, Maria."

Not only did Sam Miller and Dorothy share the same humanitarian views, but also they shared the same birth date, though more than a quarter-century separated them in age. The two admired each other for their keen intellect and their common devotion to the causes of the less fortunate.

A few years before her stroke, Dorothy composed a tribute to her friend Sam Miller and gave it, in a sealed envelope, to his wife, Maria. Dorothy asked her to give it to Sam at some special occasion in the future. On June 26, 1996, Sam's and Dorothy's mutual birthday,

Maria Miller permitted *The Cleveland Plain Dealer* to publish that tribute. Among a myriad of sterling qualities, Dorothy described in particular her friend's boundless capacity for compassion and his seemingly limitless generosity.

> . . . He [Miller] has that incomparable gift, the gift of experiencing another man's grief or distress or triumph. He is crucified a thousand times as he listens and understands and feels the anguish of others.
>
> His reaction is instantaneous, and his capacity for giving and understanding what causes another man's agony means that he suffers over and over.
>
> The hundreds, the countless times he has been blessed by those whose tears were dried and who could smile again because of his kindnesses are innumerable. In the highest sense, he has an educated heart.

Although Dorothy was never a practicing Jew, Donald Perris saw her Jewishness as a large part of the way she presented herself, the way she thought and related to others. "She was much more sensitive to poverty and to suffering. This was a big part of what came out [in her commentaries]. But she did not wear it like a badge."

Dorothy's concern for others seemed to encompass the whole of the human condition. For instance, one night she might speak at a glittering banquet to raise pledges for bonds for Israel; the next day she would stoop down to embrace the March of Dimes poster child who was appearing on the noonday news. While Dorothy would be taking phone calls from viewers seeking her advice, a friend who taught in a nearby parochial school might breeze into her office. When the friend left, she would be pocketing a check from Dorothy for coats or shoes, or whatever her students were in need of on that particular day. That night, after her news broadcast, Dorothy might head out to speak in a rural high school gymnasium, urging Farm Bureau members to lobby for alternative fuels, a subject she felt passionately about.

Donald Perris looks back at where Dorothy came from and points out that "she grew up in the eras of Jacob Riis, of Lincoln Steffens. (Both were social reformers of the first half of the twentieth century.) Then came the labor unions, then the civil rights movement. In her thinking she combined all of these threads into America and what she believed it was meant to be."

Judith Reisman, a rhetorician who analyzed a number of Dorothy Fuldheim's commentaries in 1979, agrees that "the premises from which [Ms.] Fuldheim's lines of argument flow are based upon her belief in the great American Dream. She believes that the historical merging of vast natural resources with the genetic pool of diverse cultures created this unique and powerful country, as well as its successful form of democracy." Resiman points out that her commentaries asserted that basic virtues that directed and protected this nation and its emerging people—such as courage, responsibility, diligence, and active, watchful citizenship—are losing their impact upon society. "Thus, she is concerned for the nation's future and carries out her belief by being an activist and speaking what she believes is the truth," Reisman concluded.

In the past ten years increasing attention has focused upon the decline of these same values. Educators deplore their neglect and hasten to develop values-based curriculum materials tested in willing school districts. Politicians harangue about a return to basic values, but do little to head the nation in that direction. Instead, they grapple with an ethical standard that bends and vacillates with the winds of election years. Dorothy Fuldheim's activist news analyses, her adamant position on certain issues, her high standards for her own image—all of these caused her to be a dominant force in molding public opinion in her corner of the nation. Activist she was, indeed, yet she could not be classed as a "bleeding-heart liberal." She supported the position of management in the case of a strike of auto workers, but the next month she cried out in rage against a governor who would send the National Guard to quell a student uprising. She would throw a vulgar Jerry Rubin off her show, but could judge stripper Gypsy Rose Lee as a woman who was fascinating because of her intelligence.

Dorothy's viewers knew she was unpredictable, and they loved her for it. Hers was no Teflon-clad image, propped in front of a microphone by station public relations handlers. Dorothy Fuldheim operated with the same freedom throughout her career that she had enjoyed in television's infancy. Once she took a stance, though, her viewers knew she would hold fast to it.

11
Another Side of Dorothy

Like "Richard Cory," the creation of poet Edwin Arlington Robinson, Dorothy Fuldheim "glittered when she walked" and was "admirably schooled in every grace." To her viewers and co-workers, even to her closest associates, she appeared to reach a pinnacle of accomplishment. Her position earned her the envy of any man and especially of women who had not yet even seen the glass ceiling. Not only did she attain success, but also she maintained her position decade after decade. Beginning her television career at age fifty-four, she would broadcast continually, three times daily, for the same television station, WEWS-TV Cleveland, until she had passed her ninety-first birthday.

Despite the dare-to-wear gowns and ornate jewelry, the chauffeur-driven Continentals, the parade of honors and awards, the attention and adulation of most people, most of the time—Dorothy Fuldheim did not have it all, so to speak. "She had no period of prolonged happiness or joy in her life," asserts her friend, Sam Miller. Although her professional disappointments were few, a series of personal tragedies, like a chain of unanswered prayers, scarred Dorothy Fuldheim's life.

In the home where Dorothy grew up, the Schnells appeared a close-knit and structured family, struggling together to reach out for pieces of the American Dream. Herman and Bertha stressed education and thrift, laced with a yearning for elegance and refinement. The children helped financially at home by holding part-time jobs while they attended school. Through the Schnells' trail of moves from one cold-water flat to another, they remained close, although apparently not buttressed by a stalwart source of strength such as a synagogue or church or even an extended family. There were no grandparents; Herman and Bertha, while still in their teens, had both left their parents in Europe. Dorothy mentions only an uncle, the donor of David's piano, and Aunt Molly, Bertha's sister, thrice-widowed and mother of nine adopted boys.

Bertha came to Cleveland to live with Dorothy and Milton and Dorothy Louise about 1930, as early as can be determined. Dorothy spoke of Bertha with admiration and devotion and several times mentioned that "my mother lived with me until she died." She was an invalid for at least the last two years of her life, according to Jean Bellamy. "I recall seeing her only once, after we became neighbors in 1956. She was carried downstairs for a party," Bellamy says.

Other than once writing of her mother's visiting David in California and going to a "party at the Goldwyns," Dorothy relates nothing about visits with her sister or brother. Had Dorothy herself visited David in his glittering Hollywood surroundings, before his death in 1967, she would surely have recorded her impressions. She does speak of the three of them—David, Janette, and herself—always keeping in touch regularly with their mother. Bertha was their inspiration, their bulwark of belief in themselves.

Dorothy admits to having "a couple of violent, passionate loves" in her life, yet little in her writing or her papers suggests that either husband was necessarily one of the great loves of her life. She was married twice, to Milton in 1918, and following his death from heart trouble in 1952, to William L. Ulmer the following year. Ulmer and Dorothy purchased a squarish, three-story English Tudor residence at 2840 Kenilworth in the same area of Cleveland Heights where Dorothy had always lived. Although the grounds were not spacious, Ulmer's avid interest in horticulture kept lush rhododendrons and azaleas thriving on their property. Associated with a family business, the Ulmer Mortgage Company, William Ulmer also owned a metals business. Shortly after their marriage, Dorothy confided to a friend that her new husband had "lost all his money." Whether this was an exaggeration is not known, but neither of Dorothy's husbands appeared to achieve a great amount of financial success.

Compared with the adventurous and romantic types whose notice Dorothy and Roseka attracted on their European jaunts, both

Mr. Fuldheim and Mr. Ulmer appear to pale into the shadows. One romantically extravagant gesture Dorothy describes, however, was Ulmer's three thousand dollar purchase of a portrait of herself as a wedding gift. Done in oil by Sandor Vago, a Cleveland artist quite popular at the time, the portrait depicts, in Toulouse-Lautrec-like style, the cosmopolitan young Dorothy of the 1940s. Dorothy treasured the painting and had it reproduced on the dust jacket of her first book, *I Laughed, I Cried, I Loved*. At her death, the painting was left to her friends, Sam and Maria Miller.

Both Mr. Fuldheim and Mr. Ulmer were nearly ten years older than Dorothy. Both appear modest in their accomplishments, somewhat limited in interests—at least by comparison with Dorothy's ever-broadening horizon of concerns. At one time, Milton Fuldheim was the president of the Cleveland Heights City Club and one of the city's champion bowlers. He also loved baseball. "My father was a baseball addict," his daughter Dorothy once recalled to a reporter. "I grew up going with him to old League Park and the Stadium." William Ulmer collected art and was enthusiastic about flowers, two interests which Dorothy at least could appreciate. But because of Dorothy's aversion to "anything that crawled," flowers from Ulmer's gardens never graced the inside of their home; Dorothy preferred flowers that came from a florist. By the time she married Ulmer, Dorothy was anchoring three daily news broadcasts and hostessing *The One O'Clock Club*. Dorothy Fuldheim, (the name she continued to use) was becoming an attention-getting, daily visitor to every Cleveland household. Any man, save perhaps the mayor of the city or President Eisenhower would have appeared somewhat overshadowed. William Ulmer accompanied his wife on at least one and probably more European trips. He was an agreeable man whom people remember as having a good sense of humor. Ulmer was eighty-six when he died in 1971.

While the family lived on Kenilworth, Halla enjoyed the friendship of the lively Bellamy children next door. Stephen and his brothers would play games with her, such as Pick-Up-Sticks, which she could enjoy. Her mother, Dorothy Junior, was an afficiando of James Bond movies. To show her gratitude to the boys for time they spent with Halla, she would invite them to go to a movie. She actually needed their help to get Halla into the car and the theater.

An unusual kind of therapy for Halla resulted from a casual comment Dorothy made on the air. In thanking her viewers for the many Christmas cards she was receiving, she mentioned that her granddaughter Halla enjoyed them also. What she did not say on the air was that Halla was allowed to tear the cards into pieces as a way to strengthen her arm and hand muscles.

More cards than ever began to pour in to the Fuldheim residence. The Bellamy children and their mother recall seeing huge sacks of mail in the basement, where the children sorted the cards into piles according to size. Then Halla would engage in her therapy.

After William Ulmer's death Dorothy sold the Kenilworth Avenue home and moved to the Shaker Towers Apartments at 13900 Shaker Boulevard. She later purchased the spacious three-bedroom suite when the building was converted to condominiums.

Veiled references in Dorothy's books and snippets of correspondence in her papers hint at some love affairs or, at least, flirtations. Just as she had dispelled rumors about the Duke of Windsor, she also quelled those about Wendell Willkie, the 1940 Republican presidential candidate. She told of meeting Willkie in New York at the Pennsylvania Hotel, his campaign headquarters. "When I talked with him, [Willkie] he made it very clear that he was not impervious to my female charm, but that he was just too busy; and, in addition, as a candidate, he had to be circumspect." She quickly switched her comments to an evaluation of Willkie as a candidate. " . . . he would, I think, have made one of the great presidents of our country had he been elected."

Dorothy Fuldheim no doubt had long applauded Willkie's activities. When she herself was lecturing in the 1920s, Willkie, a native of Indiana who was practicing law with Mather and Nesbitt in Akron, was stumping for the need for international cooperation and responsible state government and also in opposition to the Ku Klux Klan. Known as an insatiable reader and for his enormous erudition, Willkie would certainly have found in Dorothy Fuldheim a woman who was a match for him intellectually. She does not indicate that they ever met when he was living in Akron from 1919 to 1929.

As a Republican presidential candidate, Wendell Willkie did not offer voters a clearcut choice. He agreed in principle with many of Roosevelt's New Deal programs as well as on foreign policy (which is why Dorothy, with her Democratic proclivities, endorsed his views). Willkie's loss at the polls kept FDR in the White House for an unprecedented third term. His book, *One World,* published in 1943, sold millions of copies. In it he took a global view and emphasized the need for international cooperation when the firestorms of the Axis war machines would finally be extinguished. Willkie would not live to see the war's end and the world embark upon the peace he envisioned. He died in New York of a heart attack in 1944.

Another man, whom Dorothy refers to only as "P," sent her wildly extravagant gifts. One Christmas Day she received a chinchilla wrap, and flowers arrived on New Year's Day. Each holiday thereafter she received lavish gifts—a jeweled evening bag, a velvet dress trimmed in white mink, a pearl necklace, baskets of exotic fruit. Always the card said, "To brighten your day," and was signed simply, "P." After two years Dorothy received a corsage of violets with the message, "This is to say goodbye." She never heard from him again. Dorothy asserted that she never learned "P's" identity, causing more than one skeptic to lift an eyebrow. A close friend says that she did, indeed, know him and that he once gave an elaborate party for her at a downtown Cleveland hotel.

A woman with a devil-may-care flair for the romantic and a genuine admiration for men could very well have fantasized some casual flirtations as well as deeply passionate affairs. Her good friend Sam Miller, who admired and respected Dorothy greatly, nevertheless admits with a fond smile that "Dorothy thought she was God's gift to men—a real *femme fatale.*" Another friend recalls an incident on a trip abroad when Dorothy insisted that one of the men in their party had made advances to her, had even chased her down the hallway of their hotel. Dorothy's friend scoffed at the probability of this story, saying, "He was about half her age."

Dorothy's neighbor at Shaker Towers, Taffy Epstein, recalls, "Dorothy loved men of all ages and played up to them—even my son, who was only seventeen at the time." When she would arrive at parties at Epstein's apartment, she would hold court, so to speak, lounging at one end of a tete-a-tete, her eyes roving, her manner compelling. Apparently, some men found her overbearing. "There was one man among my friends," Epstein says, "who would ask if Dorothy would be at a party before he would accept. If she was coming, he would decline."

In May 1980 Dorothy Fuldheim told *Cleveland Press* TV-radio editor Bill Barrett that there were two things in life she most wanted: for nothing to happen to her daughter and that she herself would die tranquilly with her wits about her. "When that great moment comes, I want to appreciate it." Although she attained wealth and recognition, life denied her these two wishes.

Dorothy Junior had achieved a solid professional career in her own right. Her teaching colleagues at Case Western respected her, and she moved among the educational and artistic circles in Cleveland. Students spoke highly of her and enjoyed her lively wit. She traveled frequently, and in 1977 she was in Moscow with a Case-sponsored group when their hotel caught fire. When this news aired, Dorothy Sr., whose television image was calm and unflappable, descended upon her across-the-hall neighbor and promptly went to pieces. "She was absolutely hysterical," Taffy Epstein remembers, though admitting she would have probably reacted the same way if her son or daughter had been involved.

The fire occurred on Saturday, making tracing Dorothy Jr.'s whereabouts on a weekend in Moscow very difficult. The day dragged painfully on. A friend arrived to take Taffy to dinner and to the Cleveland Play House, but leaving the distraught Dorothy was out of the question. "My friend went into Dorothy's apartment to use her phone, and I stayed on mine, trying to reach the group through the tour agency." At nearly midnight Taffy's friend at last reached someone in the American Embassy in Moscow who had seen Dorothy Jr. with the group from Case after the fire—at the circus.

"None of us had even thought of dinner," Taffy said. "I think I finally scrambled some eggs." Dorothy was probably so emotionally spent and so thankful for her daughter's safety that she didn't notice she was eating eggs, a food she detested.

In 1977 Dorothy Fuldheim Junior began wearing a pacemaker for a cardiac problem. She was fifty-seven at the time. Her mother's fears that something might happen to her daughter were valid. She could not help remembering that Milton, Junior's father, had died at age sixty-nine with heart trouble.

Before she began wearing the pacemaker, Junior suffered attacks when she would be unable to catch her breath. On one of these occasions, neighbor Taffy Epstein arrived home just in time to come to the aid of the Fuldheims. As she was unlocking her door, which faced theirs, Taffy could hear Dorothy's anguished voice and Junior's hoarse gasps.

Dorothy had already called Joan Davis [a doctor friend of Junior's] away from a Mt. Sinai [Hospital] bash at Oakwood Country Club. Junior was sitting with her back to the window, and Dorothy was alternately wringing her hands and pulling her hair out. Halla was already in bed, sleeping right through all the commotion.

When Joan arrived, she said, "Junior, I'm going to take you right down to the hospital."

Dorothy Sr. screamed, "Dorothy, don't you dare die. I'll kill myself. I'll kill myself. I'll jump out the window."

In the midst of hyperventilating, Junior gasped, "Mother, we live on the first floor. There's a two-foot jump. Now cool it."

Even in what could be a life-threatening crisis, Dorothy Jr.'s sprightly sense of humor surfaced.

Death took Dorothy Fuldheim's only daughter at age sixty, just before Thanksgiving in 1980. "My daughter's death blighted me. I'll never be whole again. No, there is no peace," said Dorothy Fuldheim.

While preparing dinner for her friend, attorney Ian Haberman, Halla, and herself, Dorothy Junior was watching her mother's evening commentary when her heart failed for the final time. Her mother arrived home as paramedics were lifting the cot into the ambulance. "It's Dorothy, isn't it?" she screamed. She had seen the flashing lights as her car approached Shaker Towers, and her driver had to wait to get into the parking lot until the ambulance moved.

Dorothy did not follow her daughter to St. Luke's Hospital that night; nor was she at her side the next morning when Junior died. She ordered her daughter's body cremated but refused to retrieve her ashes. After some time, at the request of the funeral director, friends collected Dorothy Junior's ashes and buried them. Case Western Reserve University held a memorial service for her at the Amasa Stone Chapel on the campus.

Dorothy could not accept her daughter's death; nevertheless, she eventually had to deal with questions from Halla, who was thirty-seven when her mother died. Dorothy described this conversation to her viewing audience in a tribute she gave to her daughter only a few days after Junior's death.

> I told her [Halla] . . . that we all have an appointment with God. My daughter received her summons last Monday. I told Halla that her mother was in heaven, and was free of all pain, and that someday she and I would join her. She said, "Will you be there?" I nodded. "And will God make you young again? . . . Will my mother be without pain . . . And when I go to meet her, will I walk without braces or crutches?"
>
> She reflected and then asked, "How did my mother get to heaven?"
>
> "God sent a messenger," I responded. "We all have our appointment in Samarra."

In this tribute that also appeared in the *Cleveland Press,* Dorothy stated, "Much of my happiness depended on my daughter Dorothy, who made my days and my years rich with affection and laughter." While she acknowledged to Halla the inevitability of death, she mourned her own "irretrievable loss" and said, " . . . the sun will never shine as brightly as it once did for me."

By making such a public statement of her grief, Dorothy perhaps was attempting to shore up her own acceptance of this grievous blow life had dealt her and somehow come to terms with it. Privately, though, she told her friend Richard Gildenmeister, "I am like a tree that will never have any more leaves." Though she would live nearly a decade longer than her daughter, she, in fact, was never whole again, at least in spirit.

12

"You Are Nine Feet Tall"

Immediately after her noon editorial on Monday, May 4, 1970, Dorothy Fuldheim breathed deeply of the heady perfume from the vase of lilacs on her desk and sat down to pen her commentary for the evening news. Her topic . . .

Voices in the corridor jabbed at her thoughts. A door slammed, causing the lilacs to tremble, and she caught the words "Kent State" uttered in terror. For a moment she froze. As the Vietnam War escalated daily, student unrest was mounting on a number of Ohio campuses that spring. Dorothy knew that students had torched the R.O.T.C. building at Kent State on Saturday in protest of U.S. troops in Cambodia. Her impulses flashed red alert. Within minutes she had commandeered a WEWS-TV vehicle and driver and was racing across the Ohio Turnpike to the normally serene northeastern Ohio campus.

By the time she arrived, thirteen bodies lay scattered about the grass. Four were dead; nine others were wounded. All were students at the University. All were attending classes regularly. They were victims of bullets fired by National Guardsmen whom Governor James Rhodes had ordered to the campus to maintain order and protect state property. Guardsmen had attempted to disperse throngs of milling, shouting students with tear gas. Students retaliated, hurling rocks and empty gas canisters. One shot rang out. Others followed.

According to a *Cleveland Plain Dealer* editorial, during the weekend Rhodes had called the situation at Kent State part of a national revolutionary conspiracy. He blamed outside agitators and threatened to outnumber demonstrators with troops ten to one. He called rioters "worse than fascists and vigilantes." The newspaper suggested that if the state's governor had had any evidence of such a conspiracy linking disturbances at colleges and university, he should make it public so that an impartial, national investigation could be made.

For her commentary that evening, Dorothy had no reason to write any words. She spoke from the grief and anguish borne of those hours spent in the sunshine of that May afternoon, searching for answers to the grim and unfathomable scenes she had witnessed. Unequivocal murder was Dorothy Fuldheim's assessment of the confrontation at Kent State. She began her commentary in her usual forthright and confident manner. But by the time she finished, she was weeping openly.

> There were no guns in the hands of the four who were killed and the nine who were wounded—they had no weapons, no iron rods in their hands, they were giving no speeches. Their sin was protesting against the war and the four that were killed were only bystanders. They were there to see what was going on; they were students who were curious about the excitement. There were crowds gathering on the campus to protest the war so they came along to see what was happening. No one told them that the governor of the state had called out the National Guard. The governor apparently decided it would show these long-haired troublemakers that protest meetings were not to be tolerated. There was some jostling, shouting and rock throwing but what prompted the National Guard to shoot? And who gave the National Guard the bullets? Who ordered the use of them? Since when do we shoot our own children? Ask the parents of these young people how they feel. When will their anguish be over? Tortured at the thought that their children were killed and without a reason, they exist with a pain in their hearts.
>
> So they died and I came back to Cleveland and went on the air and showed my emotion and anger about the killings. As I recounted their deaths I called it murder, for these four were no housebreakers, they were no killers, no drug addicts, no muggers, no rapists. . . .

Before she had dried her tears and returned to her office, the switchboard at WEWS-TV lit up like fairyland. Hundreds of viewers called that night, thousands more wrote the station in the days that followed. Ninety-five percent of the callers were vehemently critical of the position taken by the Queen of the News. *"Why are you sorry for those deaths? Too bad the National Guard didn't kill more. Those good-for-nothing bums, smart alecks—that's what they are. It's about time someone put them in their place. Good for the National Guard."* On and on and on.

A devastated Dorothy sought out Donald Perris, the station manager for whom she had worked for nearly twenty-five years.

She and Perris were close friends, yet she always expressed respect for his authority and high regard for his keen intelligence and perception. Knowing that her emotional outburst on such a sensitive issue had been unacceptable to the vast majority of those who called, Dorothy offered to resign.

Perris never hedged, never hesitated. "Nonsense, Dorothy," were his words. "You are nine feet tall."

In keeping with that early tradition of standing by its personnel and of giving Dorothy Fuldheim full rein over her commentaries, Perris says he gave no thought to reprimanding her, let alone accepting her resignation. "She came to me that night and said, 'I hope I haven't gone too far. I've been able to say what I thought without trimming my sails for over 20 years. I've never gone so far, so far that my judgment is impaired by my emotions.' It was the first time I've seen her really shaken.

"But then we heard from the others ... the others who saw it differently."

In a recent interview Perris said, "It actually all died down very quickly. When I told Miss Fuldheim I didn't want her resignation, I could make that decision on my own. I reported only to Jack Howard [of Scripps Howard]. He was the only person above me. I didn't have to consult with attorneys in those days."

If Perris had felt any compulsion to release the station's stellar talent, his finely chiseled intuition probably warned him he would arouse greater long-range ire among viewers. The reputation Dorothy had built in nearly a quarter-century of broadcasting at WEWS-TV could surely withstand this one passionate and overwhelming outpouring of disagreement.

Investigations into the Kent State killings by a Presidential Commission placed blame on both the National Guard and the rock-throwing, vandalizing students. It called for President Nixon to exert "reconciling moral leadership" on the campus. The report was largely ignored in Washington. A special grand jury of Portage County, Ohio citizens placed the blame squarely upon the administration of the University. It handed down twenty-five indictments of university personnel and totally exonerated the National Guard. The indictments were later dismissed.

In ensuing months, even years, hardcast opinions about the killings at Kent State by much of the general public would blur. Although Dorothy Fuldheim's comments on that May evening were charged with anger and disbelief, later exhaustive reports such as James Michener's *Kent State* and later William A. Gordon's *The Fourth of May* have upheld her initial reaction that the student protesters could have been controlled without the National Guard's firing upon them. " . . . the students could have been arrested," she said. "Any number of things could have been done. . . . Even an accused murderer or robber or kidnapper has a chance in the courts to disclaim any guilt and a jury of his peers will listen to this defense. But what chance did these dead students have? Did anyone accuse them of a crime? Were they told why they died? It was a senseless killing, as senseless as a tornado which tears down a tree just because it happens to be in the path of a storm."

Several years later she still grieved. She told the *Plain Dealer's* Mary Strassmeyer, "When I returned from Kent State I wept. . . . because part of the soul of America was sullied by such useless killing."

The morning after the Kent State shootings, Dorothy found a basket of spring flowers outside her office door. The card read, "We wept with you last night," signed, "Some students." A simple gesture, but one which cheered her through days when she would groan as bag after bag of mail, nearly all harsh and critical of her position, crowded her office.

Public wrath, like a Fourth-of-July sparkler, dies down quickly but leaves a searing burn if touched. And so Ohio and Dorothy Fuldheim began to put the Kent State killings behind and move to other things. The friends and families of the victims would try to assuage their grief; the university officials would shore up their campus against extremism; Governor Rhodes would be re-elected and have a government office building named for him in Columbus. Dorothy would write another book. Dorothy's fourth book was not about Kent State, although she perhaps could have written one. Instead, she tried her hand at fiction and produced *Three and a Half Husbands.*

Perhaps she felt the need to do something with a light touch to help lift her spirits. Those early 1970s were crisis-fraught years. The United States was conducting massive bombing raids against North Vietnam and bombing Vietcong supply routes in Cambodia. Vice-President Spiro T. Agnew resigned, pleading no contest to income tax evasion. When a cease-fire at last went into effect in Vietnam in 1973, the nation was becoming obsessed with the exposure of the Watergate burglaries that finally led to Nixon's being charged as an unindicted co-conspirator. Following three recommended articles of impeachment, Nixon resigned in August 1974. Economic gloom shrouded the country that year also. Arab oil-producing nations had cut off shipments to the United States, Europe, and Japan in retaliation for their support of Israel in the fighting in the Middle East, gravely affecting the United States' productivity. The American dollar was devalued for the second time in two years.

On all of these subjects, Dorothy Fuldheim's viewers heard analyses from her. She would also have delivered elegiac commentaries that year marking the passing of some world leaders she most esteemed—former President Harry Truman; David Ben-Gurion, Israel's founder and former premier; and Paul Henri Spaak, Belgian premier and founder of the Common Market. And she surely mourned the passing of that most captivating gentleman she ever interviewed, the Duke of Windsor.

On Sundays Dorothy began writing *Three and a Half Husbands.* Ever since she had brought her Aunt Molly back to life to supply one more needed chapter in *A Thousand Friends,* Dorothy had toyed with the thought of expanding her story into a full-length book. Although Aunt Molly and her near-incredible circumstances—three times a widow and nine stepsons—appear briefly in *I Laughed, I Cried, I Loved,* Dorothy claimed the expanded version was fiction and that it is not a veiled autobiography. "I may have had three and a half lovers, but I only had two husbands," she declared.

Dorothy said *Three and a Half Husbands* was her best book. The story rollicks along, spiced with Dorothy's keen wit. Its poignant ending brings tears and compassion for the "half-husband," the one her aunt never married. Although the book earned decent reviews, Dorothy regretted that it never became a play. Many readers suggested that it had dramatic possibilities. "The incredible Molly is clearly in the tradition of *Auntie Mame* and *Dolly*," wrote Jerome Lawrence for the book jacket. True enough, Molly's winsome charm and indomitable optimism suggested a role of those proportions. And a cast including nine children conjured up visions for Lawrence of another success to rival *The King and I*. The *Plain Dealer* reviewer, Alvin Beam, called *Three and a Half Husbands* a "delicious first novel" and suggested "an alert Hollywood should take a long look at the irrepressible Molly . . . "

Dorothy gave permission to Vincent Dowling, then producer/director of the Great Lakes Theater Festival in Cleveland (known at that time as the Great Lakes Shakespeare Festival), to adapt the story for the stage. By 1988 Dowling had left Great Lakes and become director of the Abbey Theater of Ireland, but he was still promising to produce *Three and a Half Husbands*. He wrote the book for the musical, and Thomas Tierney composed the score. Ted Durchman wrote the lyrics. Although a public reading took place in New York at the Dramatists Guild, sufficient financial backing never materialized. Perhaps even yet an enterprising producer will unearth *Three and a Half Husbands* and judge it worthy of a gamble. Then Dorothy and her Aunt Molly can smile down upon that producer's perspicacity and wisdom.

Biting disappointment stung Dorothy when she narrated a presentation of *Peter and the Wolf* with the Cleveland Orchestra. Loyal patron of the Orchestra that she was, Dorothy surely viewed this invitation as an opportunity to give back something of herself to the Orchestra.

But Dorothy's dramatic flair may have overpowered the production; Dorothy, Peter, and the wolf were not a good combination. Severance Hall received the performance with its traditional good manners, but the critics' comments were scathing. Dorothy chafed under what she felt was an unfair appraisal of her performance.

She was still feeling the sting a few years later when she told the *Cleveland Press's* Bill Barrett, "I squirm at criticism . . . But I certainly remember THAT one. That critic was nasty! There was no sense to what he wrote! How can you mess up 'Peter and the Wolf?' I thought he went out of his way to be nasty." Then to Barrett's follow-up question about criticism in general, the dauntless Fuldheim replied that No, she didn't think she could remember a criticism she ever truly deserved.

One might think Dorothy would literally have had a taste of humble pie a few months before that interview with Barrett. **Dorothy: "I Thought Everyone Loved Me"** screamed the front page of *The Cleveland Press*. Below the headline, a cartoonist depicted a terrified, aged Dorothy at a podium, receiving, not acclaim as was her custom, but a cream pie in the face.

Dorothy had nearly finished with her speech to the Citizens' League in Solon, a suburb east of Cleveland, when a tall man came onto the stage carrying a camera and shouting something about the Iran hostage situation, while a woman ran on stage from the opposite direction and hurled the gooey pie.

"I'm certainly not going to be down about a pie. It was good pie, too," Dorothy remarked to Fred Griffith the next morning when she appeared on *the* WEWS-TV *Morning Exchange*. "The audience in the Solon High School auditorium was in shock. No one rose from their seats for about twenty seconds. Then people came up and took their sweaters and wiped my face."

Miss Fuldheim testified against her assailants with her customary aplomb and theatrical flair. "It [the assault] was a sensation unlike any I have ever had," she said. She told Judge Joseph A. Zingales she still suffered nightmares.

The Revolutionary May Day Brigade, a self-styled group of revolutionaries took responsibility for the action the next day, according to the area newspapers. Marcella MacLean, spokesperson for the group called the assault "a political statement of what thousands of people in this city and country think of her [Dorothy Fuldheim]. She's not just some sweet old lady. She carries a heavy message." She claimed that Dorothy Fuldheim was frequently on the side of imperialism. Eventually two persons were arrested for their lead roles in the assault. Each of the perpetrators was eventually fined $500 and sentenced to sixty days in jail.

"The man carrying the camera was just a diversionary tactic," Dorothy explained to Fred Griffith. "It was all planned. Who goes out in the middle of a speech and buys a pie? I'd like somebody to strangle those people so I could watch. What did I ever do to them? I'm not political. I'm not running for office." She admitted she no longer felt safe and would probably take a private security officer with her to future public speaking engagements.

"What really griped me was that *The Plain Dealer* said I got the pie on my wig," she said to the *Morning Exchange* audience. "Well, I don't wear a wig—never have. Please put that in your paper. I dye my hair, but it's all mine."

To Griffith's thanks for her appearing on his nine-to-eleven morning show the morning after the pie-in-the-face incident, she remarked, "You'll have to admit, it is very valiant of me to get up this morning and do what I usually do. I even had to wash my own hair, something I never do."

To *The Cleveland Press*, but not in her interview on Griffith's show, she protested about her colleague at WEWS-TV, Ted Henry, and his comment on the eleven o'clock news the night before. In reporting the incident as a breaking news story, Henry said, in his sincere, empathetic manner, "That was a terrible thing to do to an eighty-six-year-old woman."

"How stupid," Dorothy retorted. "What difference does it make how old I am? The outrage is that this could happen to anyone."

"I should have gone to New York," she sometimes admitted. Evidence of one overall disappointment in Dorothy Fuldheim's professional life surfaces from time to time in her comments, especially in interviews that appeared frequently in area newspapers and magazines.

Although at age eighty-nine she received a new three-year contract from WEWS-TV, which included a substantial raise, Dorothy Fuldheim admitted she probably should have made the big move. "A bigger field. A bigger audience, bigger money. I should have done that, but it doesn't gnaw at me." Donald Perris concurs that the networks did make offers, one very tempting one, in particular.

By that time Dorothy's income had risen to a reported $100,000 a year, although neither she nor the television station ever issued an official statement of this. According to Perris, she received deferred income and a pension when she finally left WEWS-TV in 1985. Her guardian, Sam Miller, states that the pension was $500,000. He estimated her estate at one million dollars at the time of her death in 1989.

Money was always a prime motivating factor for Dorothy. She worked to support herself, she asserted, not from any driving force to achieve as a woman in a field dominated by males. Both Sam Miller and Donald Perris confirm that she was fearful that her orphaned granddaughter Halla would be left destitute. Dorothy had never forgotten the woefulness, the wretchedness of being poor. She often quizzed her guests about money.

Interviewing millionaire Nelson Rockefeller who became Vice President under Gerald Ford, Dorothy once asked, "How does it feel to be rich?" When Rockefeller, who at that time was governor of New York, replied that he didn't feel any different than she did, she retorted, "That's nonsense. How can someone with a vast amount of money understand a guy living on $240 a month?" She told him his ancestors must have been hijackers to make that amount of money. He laughed and said he had some poor friends.

If, in fact, money was such a decisive factor, what kept a television talent like Dorothy Fuldheim in the hinterlands of Ohio?

By 1971 the peppery little platform speaker who had arrived in Cleveland as a bride had lived and worked there for a half-century. She had seen the passing, in Cleveland, of her mother, a son-in-law, and two husbands. After William Ulmer's death, she moved her three-generational family—Dorothy Junior, Halla, and herself—from the English Tudor on Kenilworth Road to the close-knit community of Shaker Towers. There neighbors became family—Taffy Epstein across the hall, Taffy's mother next door. Upstairs was Maria Patrick (who later married Sam Miller). The friendships of both Taffy Epstein and Maria Miller sustained Dorothy through some of her darkest days, and the two women remained sincerely devoted to her until the day of her death.

As long as Dorothy Junior was living, enjoying the rewards of a satisfying career in her chosen field, her mother would not likely have considered asking her to go elsewhere. True, they were both grown, professional women, but they were two widows who were socially and emotionally supportive of each other and united in their concern for Halla's well-being.

After Dorothy Junior's heart problems developed, her mother lived in dread of the possibility of her daughter's death. She wished nothing to occur to disturb the pattern of their lives. Rather than accept a higher-paying offer from any of the networks, Dorothy drove herself to augment her income by continuing to accept nearly every speaking invitation offered to her. She would go anywhere to speak, dashing out at noontime or speeding away in her chauffeured Lincoln after the evening news. She addressed groups as diverse as the Auxiliary of the Cuyahoga County Bar Association and the Lorain County Farm Bureau, the Akron Dental Society and the Committee on Planning Services for the Aging of St. Eugene's Church in Cuyahoga Falls. Professional that she was, she could tailor her remarks to fit any group, time, or situation.

Dorothy herself claims that her loyalty to WEWS-TV kept her in Cleveland. In 1982 she told Larry King on his Cable News Network show that she refused offers from the networks out of loyalty to Don Perris. She mentions time and again the admiration she felt for General Manager Perris. He had been her staunch ally, standing alongside her at her most grave professional crisis, the Kent State debacle. Perris's words that night, "Dorothy, you are nine feet tall," had hammered themselves into her consciousness.

Perris feels the Kent State incident was a crossroad in Dorothy Fuldheim's relationship with WEWS-TV. "Many times she was tempted to leave. When the chips were down, she always stayed with us because . . . she was a person who believed in personal loyalty and gutting it out in a relationship. She was like that in everything she did."

These were questions Dorothy must have wrestled with: How could she leave such a manager? And how could she get along without the warm and wonderful camaraderie of the WEWS-TV staff? The *esprit de corps*, the chest-swelling feeling of being Cleveland's first television station, still existed. Dorothy gloried in the station's reputation and the fact that by the 1980s the city was inching its way back to respectability. For years, national attention had focused derision on Cleveland's polluted Cuyahoga River after a national magazine had pictured it in four-color flames. A newcomer to the city in 1975 asked where the tall buildings were. The Terminal Tower, built in 1930, was the only building that approximated skyscraper status. "Cleveland jokes" were nightly fodder for the talk shows. In the final days of 1978, the city had taken an ignoble slide into default that lasted nearly two years.

Now, in the early Eighties new office buildings, restaurants, and businesses began to inject life into the downtown. Lights burned brightly on Playhouse Square again in three restored, majestic theaters. Dorothy watched and waited. Like a homeowner surveying the painstaking tasks of renovation, she longed to see the completed project.

When Ted Turner's Cable News Network (CNN) had flashed onto the world scene in 1980, some of Dorothy's friends encouraged her to initiate a move to that organization. A serious all-news network and Dorothy Fuldheim would appear to be a consummate match. Fred Griffith feels Dorothy could have, indeed, fit in at CNN. "She could have worked as a pundit, an analyst at CNN. She used to do call-ins at WEWS-TV on the noon news," he said. Anyone who has watched Dorothy Fuldheim's interviews, even during the last decade of her career (1974–1984), has no difficulty picturing her in a Larry King-type format—interviewing a guest, then taking calls from around the world.

A call from CNN did not come, apparently, or Dorothy simply did choose to stay on in Cleveland. Some suggest that even if CNN had made advances toward her, bonds forged of well-disguised fears and insecurities would have held her back. Could she compete in a new setting against younger, more attractive women? At her age, would she identify with another station, another city? Others believe she savored her role as The Red-Haired Queen, ruler of "Dorothy's station" and trembled at the thought of never achieving a like status elsewhere if she were to move.

Her reflection on the matter, "It doesn't gnaw at me," defines her don't-look-back approach to her career. For all of her professional life, she had grasped opportunities as they came her way, making pragmatic decisions rather than ones based upon romantic notions. New York's lights may have burned brighter, but Cleveland's hearth was warmer.

13
One of a Kind—in Living Color

To Wilma Smith, who started at WEWS-TV in 1977 as a weekend anchor and reporter, Dorothy Fuldheim was a role model. "She was a fighter . . . a tiny woman who was a human dynamo," Smith says. "She saw how you could be strong and assertive and still maintain decorum."

Donald Perris says Dorothy believed deeply in equality for females. "She was militant but not in your face all the time. She knew she couldn't irritate others and still succeed." Yet, he saw her, as a woman, hassled by bosses, by people she interviewed, and by people in general. "Miss Fuldheim," as Perris consistently refers to her, "always found something in everyone that was wonderful. To her, there was nobility in all people—street cleaners to senators. Clients of the station, mostly conservative businessmen, loved her, even though their views and hers differed."

In her office Dorothy Fuldheim had an open-door policy. People drifted in to socialize, debate ideas, get advice. "She cared for a great many people," Greg Olsen says. He recalls being petrified at meeting her when he was hired in the 1960s. Although already regarded as "The Legend," she soon impressed Olsen as "up close and personal." He says, "I cared for Dorothy Fuldheim dearly. I respected her, related to her, and prayed to God she related to me."

Despite the pressures of preparing two commentaries a day and interviewing guests, Dorothy Fuldheim insisted upon answering her own telephone. Listeners called to praise her point of view in the

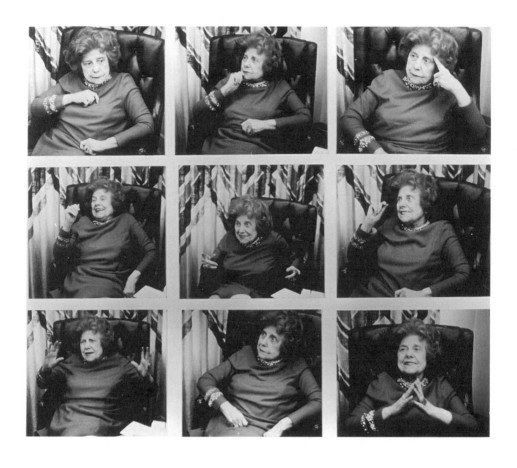

Photos by Donald Perris
Courtesy Greg Olsen
WEWS general manager Donald Perris captured Dorothy Fuldheim's vivacious expressions and gestures on film during an informal conversation with Greg Olsen.

When she visited Pearl Harbor, Dorothy laid a wreath on the grave of American war correspondent Ernie Pyle.

Hong Kong reporters interview Dorothy Fuldheim following her visit with just-released American prisoners of war in Taipei.

Photo courtesy John Carroll University Media
Archives/WEWS NewsChannel 5
1960s promotional photo.

A dog was always an important member of Dorothy's household. 1966 photo.

Sam Miller, Golda Meir, and Dorothy during Mrs. Meir's 1975 visit to Cleveland.

Miller, Dorothy, and Ohio Congressman Charlie Vanik during a tour of Israel.

Photo courtesy John Carroll University Media Archives
WEWS NewsChannel 5
Dorothy spent a quiet moment by the Suez Canal during a trip to the Middle East.

Wearing a white ermine coat and a black satin pant suit embroidered with dragons, Dorothy cut the ribbons to open Richard Gildenmeister's Bookshop on the Square in 1976. At left is Walter Kelly, then mayor of Shaker Heights. Behind Gildenmeister is his brother Douglas.

Dr. Benjamin Spock, authority on baby and child care, was an outspoken critic of the Viet Nam war.

Photo courtesy Cleveland Press Archives/
Cleveland State University Instructional Media Services
Dorothy Fuldheim, Junior, in March, 1980, eight months before her death.

*Dorothy wrote **Three and a Half Husbands** based upon the life of Molly Davidson, her favorite aunt. Richard Gildenmeister helps Dorothy prepare for a book signing.*

Photo courtesy John Carroll University Media Archives/
WEWS NewsChannel 5
Senator Hubert Humphrey and Dorothy Fuldheim made a lively pair.

With former governor of Ohio Frank Lausche.

Late in the evening, Dorothy made time to read for pleasure.

Photo courtesy John Carroll University Media Archives
WEWS NewsChannel 5
Cleveland native Bob Hope frequently appeared with Dorothy.

Photo by Will Richmond
Courtesy Baldwin-Wallace College

Dorothy often mounted a box to see over the lectern when she spoke.
Here she addresses graduates of Baldwin-Wallace College in June 1984.

Photo by Donald Perris
Courtesy Greg Olsen

Colleagues often gathered in the Fuldheim office for witty and mind-bending conversations with Dorothy.

Photo by Patricia Mote

*Fred Griffith, co-host of the popular **Morning Exchange**, now sits in the Fuldheim chair. Griffith joined WEWS-TV in 1966.*

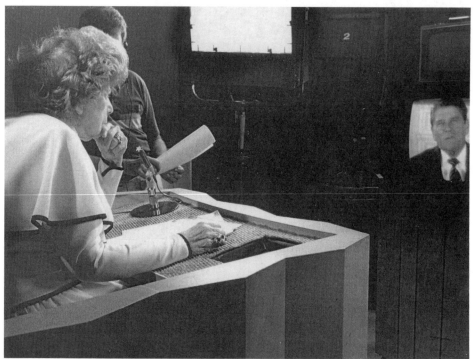

Photo courtesy John Carroll University Media Archives/
WEWS NewsChannel 5

In what would be her last interview, Dorothy spoke with President Ronald Reagan by satellite, July 27, 1985.

previous night's telecast or to take vehement issue with her. Sometimes a call from a listener would lead to his or her being invited to be a guest on her show.

When Fred Griffith joined WEWS-TV, nearly twenty years after Dorothy did, only three or four other women were on the staff—secretaries for each of the major departments. Now Griffith, who occupies one-half the former Fuldheim office, (now sub-divided with news anchor Ted Henry) has shouldered the role of what he calls "a second string Fuldheim." Griffith estimates he has interviewed more than 2,200 guests in his WEWS-TV career. For most of its twenty-five year history, he has co-hosted the station's popular *Morning Exchange*, a program acknowledged in the industry as a model for ABC's *Good Morning, America.*

"Dorothy was the preeminent air person in the building, nay, in the whole city," Griffith says. "Oh, there were some women in television, but no one with the stature she had, no one as up front." Griffith admits he doesn't quite know how she pulled that off, because lots of times if a woman was as assertive as Dorothy, she would be thought of as pushy and aggressive, difficult. He concludes that Dorothy Fuldheim was able to assume this persona because she had "a wonderful, elegant way about her, probably since she was born in 1893 and knew something about manners."

Understandably, since she entered the television industry in its infancy, most of Dorothy Fuldheim's colleagues were men. She was quite comfortable in this situation, however. Her intellect and her outspoken manner had attracted the attention of men for years. She relished finding her way around in male-dominated situations, dating back to those days she spent with her father, listening to lawyers in the Milwaukee County Court House. Then there were the rollicking tours of Europe in the 1930s, when she and the capricious Roseka dashed from one storybook-like encounter after another with wandering dukes or dashing noblemen. While gathering news and information for her lectures about what she recognized would be worldwide hostilities of disastrous proportions, Dorothy and Roseka easily attracted male attention and reveled in it. After all, how many pairs of vivacious American women were traveling unescorted about the continent in those times when Franco, Hitler, and Mussolini were rattling their sabers?

Although she insists that Dorothy Fuldheim was "fun" and "lovely to work with," Wilma Smith, now news anchor at WJW-TV, Cleveland's Fox network affiliate, admits "if you were female . . . you never knew what mood you were going to find her in." Smith agrees with occasional assertions that Dorothy got along better with men than women, but Smith feels this is nothing to be embarrassed about. "Dorothy did have relationships and friendships with women, but most of her close friends in the work force were men. She loved men, hilarity, cigars."

At about 4:30 on any afternoon, an unofficial meeting took place in Dorothy's corner office overlooking 30th and Euclid. Station manager Donald Perris would be winding down his duties for the day, as air time salesman Greg Olsen came in from a day of pavement pounding. For the next sixty to ninety minutes, near-equal portions of exuberance and serious conversation about any topic saturated the air in the Fuldheim office, no holds barred. She was a skillful interviewer, off camera as well as on, Donald Perris remembers. "She had a canny way of finding out stuff. She'd ask you half of something, then let it drop. Much later she'd come at you with the other half, then put it all together." Even late in the afternoon, with a commentary yet to do as part of the six o'clock news (the eleven o'clock commentary had already been taped and the six o'clock piece was presently being typed from her handwritten pages), Dorothy was always eager for these sessions of earnest debate. High-spirited conversation and rapid volleys of humor peppered the air. She thrived on these kinds of sessions with persons such as these two long-time associates, whose intelligence and judgment she respected. "She took us on," according to Olsen.

One day Perris positioned himself in her doorway with his own camera while she and Olsen were engrossed in one of these late-day, mind-bending discussions. The resulting photos captured treasured images of the ever-fascinating, never-predictable Fuldheim countenance with accompanying body language. None of the three noticed the clock's hands inching toward six. "Oh, my God," Dorothy screamed, "look at the time." Out the door she flew, clattering down the hall, heels clicking, bracelets jingling, before either Perris or Olsen could do much more than look helplessly at the clock.

Ted Ocepek, formerly a WEWS photographer, claims he was often her cameraman of choice. He credits this, in part, to the eye-to-eye rapport he established with her. She admired a person with a scalpel-sharp sense of humor who could match her repartee. Returning one night from Columbus where Dorothy had been tesifying as to the advisability of daylight saving time for Ohio, Ocepek, Jim Lowe, from the PR department, and Bert LeGrand, a youthful but efficient reporter who covered City Hall, stopped for a steak dinner at Marzetti's. Afterwards, bone-weary but unwound from the day's activities, they headed up I-71 toward Cleveland. Dorothy's tousled red head lolled against the back seat. She appeared to be dozing. Next to her, LeGrand, well-meaning but unaware quite where to draw the line with Dorothy, remarked, "I'm going to tell the world I slept with Dorothy Fuldheim."

"LeGrand, if you ate a baloney sandwich on the steps of the White House," Ocepek flung over his shoulder from the front seat, "you'd tell the world you dined with the President,"

In the half-light of the moving car, Dorothy's eyelids fluttered as amusement danced across her face. "How profound," she murmured.

During the Bobby Sands episode in 1981, Ocepek tells of traveling with Dorothy and producer Eric Braun to northern Ireland. Sands, who had been elected to the British Parliament, was an I.R.A. hunger striker and would die in prison after a sixty-six day fast. Dorothy alighted on Irish soil like royalty and played the imperial role to the utmost, according to Ocepek. She established herself near the airport baggage retrieval, graciously nodding and smiling at everyone who glanced her direction. She didn't offer to carry anything but her purse.

With 1500 pounds of equipment to move from place to place, plus personal luggage, photographer Ocepek soon bristled at Dorothy's "star" posture. "Hey, Dorothy, you got a free hand?" He motioned toward the pile of luggage and equipment.

A trace of annoyance whisked across her face, then disappeared . As she hoisted a small flight bag onto her eighty-eight-year-old shoulder, she drilled Ocepek with her blue eyes. "I like you, Ted," she said. "You treat me like one of the crew."

Ocepek had earned his stripes, however, working with Dorothy Fuldheim. Early in his career at WEWS-TV, she had given him a scathing dressing down in front of Senator Hubert Humphrey during an interview at the studio. Her complaint was trivial, easily corrected, and her actions before such a distinguished guest were unworthy and somewhat uncharacteristic of her. When the interview concluded, she swept out of the studio with her guest without a glance at the seething Ocepek. Days went by with no word of apology or even greeting from Dorothy. One day Ocepek was returning from an assignment, sprinting up the stairs two at a time, when he suddenly stopped short, eyeball-to-eyeball with Dorothy, who was taking her afternoon exercise by walking the stairs. Somewhat vague and flustered, she shifted her glance to a spot somewhere on the wall behind Ocepek and said, "Oh, Ted, about what I said the day of the Humphrey interview—I was harsher than I needed to be."

Looking up and down the stair tower, hoping to see some other human being who might have overheard this tardy bit of humility, Ocepek shrugged and sidestepped Madame Fuldheim. Instead, he turned and spoke to a cigarette machine standing on the stair landing. "Did you hear that? The lady does realize that even lowly cameramen have feelings."

Versatile Joel Rose, a WEWS-TV staff member—reporter, editor, writer, producer—for more than twenty years, remembers Dorothy sometimes bullied people who couldn't defend themselves, such as interns and the floor crew. "She could be a tyrant until someone stood up to her." Ocepek agrees. "If you made a doormat of yourself, she would use you." On one occasion she complained to then-news director Ed Cervenak that Rose had been rude to her. When Rose insisted that Cervenak go with him to confront her with this accusation, which Rose had denied, she told Cervenak she "never said such a thing about Joel." "After that," says Rose, "she treated me O.K."

In describing his work as a television producer, Richard Scott, now with Fox's WJW-TV, told *Plain Dealer* television reporter that his toughest television gig remains one of his first—serving as lighting director for the legendary Miss Fuldheim. When Scott started his career at WEWS-TV in 1983, she occupied the dowager queen position. Dorothy would call out to him, "What are you doing with those lights? Are you trying to blind me?"

Scott remembers she was always on him, but he tells this with a hearty laugh. "But, hey, I knew the lights were right so I'd just pretend to readjust them. I'd ask her 'How's that, Miss Fuldheim?' And she'd say, 'Better, better.'"

An incident described by Terence Sheridan for *Cleveland Magazine* divulges production supervisor Phil Parisi's encounter with the petulant ire of the great lady on one occasion. She dogmatically asserted that her on-screen image depicted her with a beard—a three-inch goatee! Even with her "allegedly weak eyes," she was confident she could see the beard, and why couldn't he and the lighting crew? Parisi admitted in an aside to Sheridan that the problem was in trying to keep a balance with the lighting—not too harsh, homage to the wrinkles—not too soft, aid for the TelePrompTer. After some cursory adjustments by the lighting crew and a second take of her one-minute, ten-second commentary on rising medical costs, a placated Dorothy Fuldheim, in her blue beaded gown and silver shoes, accepted the improvement as her due, thanked Parisi, and swept regally from the set.

Later, she gloried in her triumph in the beard incident. "A new light showed that I had a beard," she said to the reporter and others gathered in her office.

"A three-inch beard and nobody could see it, but I could. Dammit I know I am not young but that is no reason they should put a beard on me. In the end they all had to admit that there was a beard. This happened before, so I watched *Maude*, gave it my full attention, then I watched the show on TV after that, and I didn't see a beard in the carload. If they can be beardless, there's no reason I shouldn't."

"Of course," she added quickly, I have to admit it *was* getting funny."

Such brisk flashes of humor typify this veteran broadcast journalist's capability for sloughing off annoyances and minor difficulties that could easily have devastated a person of less maturity or professionalism. Donald Perris says, "Miss Fuldheim had everything that went with big talent—intelligence, appearance, and concern for details such as air time." And yes, she did have a temper. Every year arguments erupted about pay, but Perris denies several published reports that in 1976 she was paid $20,000 a year less than John Hambrick, popular male news anchor at WEWS-TV and brother to Judd Hambrick, currently appearing on WKYC-TV in Cleveland.

"She was well liked by people who knew her well," says Randy Culver. "Some who didn't know her well were in awe of her, or if they'd been chewed out by her, maybe they didn't like her. She would chew out lighting or cameramen if she didn't like lighting or angles."

Culver felt she was sometimes unjust simply because she actually didn't understand the technical aspects of what was going on. "She had many facets . . . could be kind and compassionate . . . [Yet] There were times I would get really angry with her when I'd see her treating others cruelly. She did think she was special."

Morning Exchange host Fred Griffith describes her as a "steel fist in a velvet glove." He admits that "she could slam down on you, and you knew you'd been hit, but you accepted it from her. You just knew she was good."

Dorothy Fuldheim was essentially insecure, Joel Rose feels. He observes that she was uncertain about her own abilities and feared being fired, probably because of her age. Thus, she looked at the newer people who came on at WEWS-TV as threats to her, fearing they would undermine her favored status with Donald Perris. This was particularly true when it came to blond, willowy Wilma Smith. "She was insanely jealous of Wilma," Rose remembers. This must have been a feeling that Dorothy revealed only to those who were closest to her. Smith herself remembers Dorothy as "the icon of icons for Cleveland television," one who would never be replaced. Smith sees no reason for Dorothy to have felt threatened. "Who could take it away from her?" she asked. "She was one of a kind. We will not see the likes of her again with television changing as it is."

Dorothy Fuldheim's director and producer for many years, Jim Breslin, adds that she did interview more men than women, yet he admits this is understandable since relatively few women were doing newsworthy things during much of her career.

In her book, *A Thousand Friends*, published in 1974, Dorothy commented upon interviews with such diverse and stellar female personalities as Helen Hayes, Madame Chiang, Helen Keller, Madame Pandit, Lady Astor, Gypsy Rose Lee, the Gabor sisters, Marian Anderson, Erma Bombeck, Margaret Mead, Beatrice Lillie. Others are notably absent. For instance, she is said to have interviewed every president from Franklin D. Roosevelt through Ronald Reagan, yet there are no accounts of visits with first ladies.

Absence of interviews with presidential wives may be indicative of their passive role until recent years. After Eleanor Roosevelt's activism (and surely Dorothy would have had some comment had she interviewed Mrs. Roosevelt), few others devoted their efforts to causes Dorothy would have found especially newsworthy. Perhaps she dismissed Lady Bird Johnson's highway beautification projects as inconsequential and Betty Ford's openness about her drug and alcohol addiction as too personal to deal with in an interview. If so, our interstate highways now blazing with wildfower varieties developed at the National Wildflower Research Center and the parade of noted personalities entering the Betty Ford Center for treatment of alcohol and drug abuse prove Dorothy erred in judgment.

Dorothy Fuldheim never interviewed people for their celebrity status alone. Instead, she focused on their activities, causes, or uniqueness. Of the singular magnificence of Helen Keller, Dorothy wrote, "I was humbled in her presence. She is a monument to the vigor of the human brain, a symbol of the dauntlessness of the human soul. After talking with Miss Keller, I knew that nothing is impossible, that whatever man dreams validates its possibility."

In the 1920s when Dorothy Fuldheim had burst on the Cleveland scene as a book reviewer, her first appearance was at the Women's City Club. Thus, when she wrote her book, *A Thousand Friends*, in 1974, WCC's popular *Meet the Author* series was the perfect place to launch it; at a special luncheon event members of the Women's City Club made her an honorary life member. Dorothy Fuldheim and the WCC "became friends forever," says longtime member of the group, June Kosich. She offers a perceptive rendering of the Fuldheim persona:

> Dorothy Fuldheim was a woman who through instinct, innate ability, and intelligence was able to see people and situations right down to the core and was never fooled by cover ups. Call it "Street Wise or People Wise," it was a gift she developed to the utmost.
>
> When I was in her presence I always felt she knew what I was thinking and going to say. She was vain and arrogant, commanded, sometimes demanded, attention, and yet she knew humility. Her comments were sometimes so harsh and biting that I often thought they came from a true caring and sensitive person who had lost patience with all the wrong around her.
>
> She was one of a kind, in living color, and had utmost admiration and respect from all who had the good fortune to know her and be touched by her life.

14
The Lady Speaks Her Mind

Her family's name was Schnell, which in German means "hurry" or "fast." She grew up in a city where labor unions flourished early, and where socialists held the mayor's seat for thirty-eight years. She knew the gnawing hunger that came from not having money for a school lunch and the chill that gripped a body that didn't own a warm coat. She endured the burning fevers and raging flus that frequently visited homes of poor children. Her family moved often, from one cold-water flat to another, groping for a little more space, a bit of comfort—a larger portion of the Promised Land.

Not surprisingly, as Dorothy Schnell Fuldheim became an adult, her thinking and attitudes tended to be progressive. This position intensified as she grew older. "I'm always for the underdog," she said on the anniversary of her thirty-fifth year in television. "I find myself always seeing the underdog's agony; I see the other side's reason, but I guess the agony distresses me more." She was an early champion of women's rights, birth control, Social Security, Medicare, civil rights. Yet, she understood history and recognized such changes were often, of necessity, evolutionary in nature. She was not a combative, for-ever-in-your-face type of liberal.

According to Donald Perris, "She realized the easy answers didn't work. She recognized that 'The Great Society' equaled 'The Law of Unintended Consequences.' Actually, her philosophy modified and [it] mirrored that of the country."

Greg Olsen, a co-worker who often matched wits with her, felt Dorothy was ahead of her time. "You either camped with her as a friend, or you broke camp with her as a person you didn't think knew what she was talking about. Yet, she was topical, whether you agreed with her or not. This is how she kept her sponsorships, her viewing audience."

"Like any great talent," Olsen adds, "she would have liked a perfect world. It made her a little *ongebroygest* (Yiddish for "a little crazy") because the world was not in order."

"I am intellectually honest, and I don't make any bones about it," Dorothy often said. Dorothy paraphrased the words of fiery nineteenth-century journalist William Lloyd Garrison, who wrote in *The Liberator*: "I am in earnest—I will not equivocate—I will not excuse. I will not retreat a single inch; and I will be heard." This was her credo. She said what she believed, and she flaunted the unequivocal support of her superiors and her sponsors. She worried little about ratings. With the exception of the public reaction to her position on the Kent State shootings, her fans far outnumbered her critics. Her comments on several still-polemic subjects illustrate her unbending stance:

On homosexuality: "They're entitled. But why so much publicity?" On *The Tonight Show* in 1977, Johnny Carson asked Dorothy Fuldheim what she thought about the case in California where the state ruled a gay teacher should lose his job. Dorothy replied, "Nature developed the sex impulse to procreate. Homosexuality is not normal. It is a deviation. However, it should not be considered immoral. The teacher should not lose his job."

On school prayer: "No, it's not appropriate. Prayer is sacred and should be engaged in with solemnity and real feeling. In the classroom it was as perfunctory as the Pledge of Allegiance."

On gun control: In 1972, when Governor George Wallace of Alabama was gravely wounded in an assassination attempt, Dorothy commented:

> In a decade we have four times tasted the horror of assassinations. The blood that poured from Governor Wallace's wound has once more stained the honor of America.
>
> Is it our fault? Well, haven't we exalted violence and killing in the movies and on television? "The Godfather" orders a murder with the same nonchalance we order

our groceries. We make heroes out of gangsters and let's get one thing straight . . . this crime could not have been committed without a gun . . . and anyone can buy a gun.

70% of crime would stop if guns were not available to everyone, and Governor Wallace's life would not be in jeopardy. And the Kennedys might still be alive.

The controversy swirling about ebonics or English that accepts some black idioms would surely have elicited Dorothy's opinion. She would have violently opposed the schools' acceptance of substandard usage. She might have made her point by asking, "Can you imagine Martin Luther King, Jr.'s speech having the impact in history that it did if he had said, 'I gots a dream' or "I done climbed to the mountaintop' (if such phrases could have passed Dorothy's lips)? Millions of immigrants, including Dorothy's own parents, came to America and learned English as a means to pursuing the promise this new country held for them. She would ask why we should coddle groups today, especially groups of American-born people, who may lack motivation and self-discipline to learn the English language properly.

On the most controversial issue of the late '60s and '70, the conflict in Viet Nam, Dorothy's advice to a young neighbor delineates her feelings. Stephen Bellamy was nine years old when the Fuldheim-Ulmer family and the Bellamys moved to adjacent homes on Kenilworth Road. He had grown up with enormous respect, tinged with awe, for the legendary lady who lived next door. Since his college deferment had expired, Stephen faced the draft with extremely ambivalent feelings. His mother had discussed this with Dorothy, who took it upon herself to phone Stephen and give him her advice. "I braced myself for some conventional adult advice," Stephen says, "but not for the first time, she surprised me."

> Steve . . . I know you're getting a lot of advice from your friends and relatives who aren't facing the draft. I won't add to that, I'll just offer some perspective.
>
> Historically, the United States has never granted amnesty . . . I know in spite of the conflicts that have arisen over the war, you're close to your family. If you flee the country you may not see them again. If you go to prison, its effects will mark you long after the war is forgotten. You're young and have to make a decision that will affect the rest of your life and you don't have the knowledge to make it.

> I just want you to know . . . that as your friend I'll support
> whatever decision you make, and if your decide to leave the
> country, my personal resources are at your disposal.

Although they might not always have agreed with her opinions, her viewers knew that she made them think. To Dorothy, this was the supreme compliment. In her view, being liked was not the quintessential role of a television news analyst. Dorothy Fuldheim embodied the antithesis of present-day thinking that "you don't want talking heads on TV." As Fred Griffith, thirty-year veteran at WEWS-TV, puts it, "Today's television news wants somebody on location who can walk and talk and chew gum simultaneously, not someone who can think up a topic and tell you what it is about." However, he points out that WEWS-TV has been an enormously successful television station doing exactly what today's television news opposes—having one person on camera, presenting commentary and analysis.

A well-respected reporter from the print media once told a *Cleveland Magazine* writer, "Dorothy is the best man they have in the joint. It tells you something about the decline of the newspaper business when the best known media person in the state is an eighty-year-old broad. . . .While those clowns at [WEWS-TV] Channel 5 smile and talk about Boy Scouts and marshmallows, we got to get the state of the world from an eighty-year-old woman." The reporter requested anonymity, and there is no record of how Dorothy reacted. Probably the references to her as the "best man" and an "eighty-year-old broad" would have irritated her, but the point the writer made would have given her a hearty chuckle.

Dorothy herself liked to tell of once being in the back of an elevator when two women got on. One said to the other, "I don't know why I'm going to hear that blankety-blank Fuldheim speak. The other said, "I can't stand her either, but I wouldn't miss her for anything." Dorothy most likely had to stifle a burst of undignified laughter in the rear corner of the elevator at that remark. To be thought of as a mind-prober pleased her far more than being at the top of a popularity list.

"I don't know what my political color is. I wouldn't tell you if I did."

"One year I vote Republican, another year Democrat. What is that? It's not bisexual, is it?"

Such banter put Dorothy Fuldheim on the favorite guest lists of the talk shows of her day—of Paar, Donahue, and especially Carson. To the host's delight, she would intersperse her serious comments with spicy morsels of her own brand of quick wit. She asked Carson, "How much do you pay for your shoes?" On Phil Donahue's show, discussing her interview with Nazi war criminal Albert Speer, she said, "I could have gone for him. For you, too."

As far as her politics were concerned, certainly her liberal views aligned her closely with the Democratic party. Yet, Dorothy Fuldheim tried to be fair in her assessment of political figures, regardless of party. She found President Jimmy Carter "dull," for example, and thoroughly criticized his handling of the Iran hostage situation in 1979. She suggested that he could have called for a session of the General Assembly of the United Nations and asked for action by the entire civilized world, or appealed to the Saudis and other Moslem nations to have talked sense to Khomeini. She ended a commentary in the *Lorain Journal* with, "Mr. Carter, act now. You're a humane man, but your dillydallying bewilders the nation."

She called Hubert Humphrey one of her favorites, but felt he lost his chance for the presidency "by being the Boy Scout and giving his allegiance to President Johnson during the Viet Nam War." When a telegram from President Reagan was read at a party honoring Dorothy's ninetieth birthday, she acknowledged his congratulations by quipping, "Oh, how I wish he were a Democrat." A year earlier, however, she had attacked the "so-called Reaganomics," saying that, despite the abuse of government aid by some, there are people who, by either from lack of fortune or ability, we will always have to take care of. She summed up her position on entitlements by saying, "I don't want my taxes reduced so some little old lady can't afford to take a bus."

Concerning Richard Nixon, whom she interviewed several times, she stated only three months before his resignation that nothing had been proved against him. Furthermore, she predicted, albeit incorrectly, that he will "postpone and postpone until he has stalled action against him and his term is finished." A story she loved to tell about President Nixon and Prime Minister Golda Meir of Israel perhaps best revealed her down-deep feeling about Nixon. The Prime Minister was said to have told Nixon: "I believe you, but I don't trust you." When he visited Israel, Nixon presented Mrs. Meir with a jewel box as a state gift. But somehow, someone neglected to put the jewel inside. The box was empty. Mrs. Meir reportedly said, "I told you I believe you, but I don't trust you."

At the height of the Watergate controversy involving President Nixon, Dorothy Fuldheim told an all-day seminar of career women in Akron that "the character of a president shall be a repository and example of the great ideals of this country." In studying the people around President Nixon, she added: "These people saw no difference in right or wrong. How can we have any business dealings with persons who don't know the difference?" She said a person couldn't even play tennis or cards with that type of person.

Dorothy and her daughter responded in their *Lorain Journal* column to President Carter's assertion in 1979 that Americans had lost faith in themselves. They answered,

> We have lost faith in our leaders . . . and the situation will not be reversed until old-fashioned character and integrity return to the leadership level of this country.
>
> Being powerful is not enough for greatness. Nazi German[y] was powerful. The Soviet Union is powerful. The moral vision of the writers of the Constitution is our glorious heritage. If we lose it, we will go down in the ashbin of history, like all the others.

What would Dorothy say about the charges against President and Mrs. Clinton that are currently being investigated? When asked this question, Dorothy's friend, Sam Miller, said bluntly, "She'd rip those people [the Clintons] to shreds." Obviously, she would apply the same standard: The President and those with whom he chooses to surround himself should exhibit exemplary character. In fact, she would extend this standard to include all government officials at every level, from the Speaker of the House to the township trustee who takes a bribe. But, like others who cry out for the need for higher standards of moral leadership, she offered no suggestions as to how to attract persons of high ethical standards to public service.

In a discussion with Barbara Walters, both television journalists agreed that contemporary leaders have lost some charisma, that today they possess a "streak of mediocrity." By contrast, both cited Anwar Sadat, the Egyptian statesman assassinated in 1981, as an example of greatness. Dorothy expressed an "enormous discouragement that courage and audacity are missing" in our modern leaders. Then-President [Reagan] was judged by Walters to be a good, caring man, but not superior. Dorothy did not disagree.

"Every so often we have an exciting mind," Dorothy Fuldheim remarked to David Bianculli, writer for *Beacon Magazine* in 1983. Asked if there was an exciting mind on the current political scene, Dorothy flashed a characteristic smirk.

"Are you kidding? Maybe the political leaders haven't had the courage to expect greatness from man. I cannot be reconciled to the fact that a figure in political life would continue to spend such an enormous amount of our wealth for armament . . . "

If Dorothy had been commenting upon the 1996 presidential election, she would have been highly critical of the age issue that was raised against the seventy-two-year-old Republican candidate, Senator Robert Dole. She would have emphasized his record of distinguished service to his country and the benefits to be gained from his experience. She would oppose the present momentum toward establishing term limits for members of Congress. Likewise, she saw no sense to forced retirement at age sixty-five for anyone, and spoke out emphatically on this subject:

> To force workers to retire at a certain age without regard to their physical and mental condition or their desire to work invalidates a person's constitutional right to work. . . .
>
> Pensions were established not to create jobs for younger people, but to take care of those who no longer desired to work or were not competent. Imagine the frustration, the agony for a person who has led a busy working life [?]. A job supplies a focal point to our lives. To suddenly be bereft of work and purpose in life is a damaging factor.

America's preoccupation with a youth-oriented society she referred to as "a disease we will eventually recover from." As always, the lady spoke her mind.

Although fair employment practices have now deterred mandatory retirement, the corporate downsizing in recent years has created an *ipso facto* forced retirement. For many, who have diversified skills and a broad education, this offers opportunities at age fifty-five or sixty to pursue another career or satisfying avocation; for others, the sudden loss of the stimulus of work may, indeed, wreak psychological, if not economic, havoc.

15
"Searching . . . Searching . . ."

Trying to unravel the mystery of the universe challenged all the powers of Dorothy Fuldheim's magnificent intellect. She wrote in *A Thousand Friends* Who am I? will be the question hurled at creation and what is my destiny? Perhaps then we shall have the answer to What is life and why do I die? If she were living today, she might have tackled *God and the Big Bang: Discovering Harmony Between Science and Spirituality* by theologian Daniel C. Matt. Repeatedly, she expresses her belief in a connectedness between spirituality and science.

"I always had a tremendous and accelerated interest in those things that were not human, especially science.

"Science is a field in which most people are not interested. I said to myself, 'One day, man will know where he came from, how he evolved . . .'

"I can remember there were stories written about going to the moon. Who'd have dreamed it? I was at a dinner party when the first men walked on the moon; no one [who was there] seemed to care."

Dorothy cared. Her idea of a bedtime story for two-year-old Tony, her neighbor's visiting grandson, was the story of men walking on the moon. Tony was wide-eyed, not as much about the men walking on the moon, perhaps, as sitting on the lap of the redhaired lady he often saw on television.

Dorothy knew a lot about science, especially astronomy. She also had strong views concerning the intellectual capacity of human beings.

"Man was encumbered by notions that weren't much higher than the animal's but maybe our great brain is expanding. I believe we're evolving; our brains and thoughts are growing.

"My dog doesn't understand things the way I do. The brain of man will someday be godlike. My one regret in dying, which we all have to do, is that I died too soon. The universe will be explained. It's inevitable. What else is there?"

That remarkable intellect intruded itself upon her consciousness and insisted upon absolute erudition as the ultimate end achievement for the human mind. Donald Perris perceptively sums up Dorothy's endless quest: "She couldn't rest until she could understand things. She couldn't accept anything she could not explain or understand."

Thus, unlikely among her books would be Asimov's *Guide to the Bible*, a weighty, verse-by-verse study of both the Old and New Testaments. A searcher can find in it facts of history, biography, and modern science to shed light upon cryptic passages.

Dorothy once described interviewing Bishop Fulton J. Sheen. She called him one of the most compelling personalities she had ever met. She listed his assets as great intellectual gifts, a rich vocabulary, personal charm, and his towering position.

> He also has what the Catholic calls the "gift of faith," she said. I once told the late Father Welfle, the head of John Carroll University, that Catholicism taxed my credulity, and his answer was "My dear, you will have to learn to do what all of us do. Use half of your brain for scientific growth and inquiry, the other half for faith." Since faith is a gift in itself, the equation Father Welfle spoke of is not obtainable by all.

Bishop Anthony M. Pilla of the Cleveland Diocese knew Dorothy Fuldheim well. "She had to understand everything," the Bishop says. "She had to reduce everything to an intellectual exercise. Faith, trust, and acceptance without full knowledge were impossible for her. She was such an independent, strong person. The whole question of dependency was tough for her to accept."

Her parents were Jewish immigrants, yet she apparently was not raised in the Jewish faith. She became an unflagging supporter of Israel and recorded her admiration for the small nation's courage in her book, *Where Were the Arabs?* But her allegiance to Israel's cause did not arise from any religious zeal; the crushing poverty of her youth had marked her forever with the missionary-like tendency to identify with the downtrodden, the weak, the unfortunate. Her knowledge of history impressed upon her the persecution of the Jewish people. When she asked Albert Speer in his garden at Heidelberg if he couldn't smell the dead flesh in the gas chamber, hear the cry of little children, realize that he was using slave labor in the factories pouring out instruments of destruction—she spoke from the depths of her soul, not from any urge to be eloquent.

A brief chapter in *A Thousand Friends* entitled simply Man's Destiny best encapsulates Dorothy Fuldheim's beliefs about the place of human beings in the scheme of things. Again rejecting any idea of immortality, she pays homage to "this wonderful, miraculous thing called the mind." From this she believes has emerged "a certain nobility, a certain capacity for feeling, an occasional glimpse of an individual endowed with goodness and an ability to understand and feel another person's pain and grief."

She cites Jesus Christ as the most passionate example of self-sacrifice the world has ever known, although she admits his story might be legend. Nevertheless, she sees in the avowed divinity of Christ an emergence of a concept that extols sacrifice of one's self for another and crowns human beings with nobility.

But where does the spark come from? Who gave to human beings this hunger for nobility, this need to assume part of another's burden? Where does humanity—with intellect and powers of reason— fit into the natural scheme of things? And with this superiority human beings cry out against the thought of a nothingness after death. "There is a maddening need to believe that whatever the pattern, there must be a logic, a purpose, a plan."

Dorothy's reverence and awe for the miracle that is the human mind is echoed in the words of Bill Gates, now-only-forty-something guru of the remarkable Microsoft Corporation. Gates told Walter Isaacson, writing for *Time*, "Religion has come around to the view that even things that can be explained scientifically can have an underlying purpose that goes beyond the science. Even though I am not religious, the amazement and wonder I have about the human mind is closer to religious awe than dispassionate analysis."

Like Gates, Dorothy acknowledged a purpose and a magnificent order about the universe, but the void in her life was a lack of a dimension of personal faith in what the *New Testament* calls "the evidence of things not seen."

This need set Dorothy on a quest that persisted throughout her later years, in particular, and intensified after her daughter's death in 1980. In the words of Sister Bernadette Vetter of the Orderof Humility of Mary, "Dorothy was searching . . . searching . . ." Early in 1984, a few months before Dorothy had her first stroke, Sister Bernadette was her guest. She recalls the interview well. "I expected it to focus education," she says. Sister Bernadette, a former high school principal, is co-founder of The Center for Learning, a publishing house for values-centered curriculum materials used in public and private schools throughout the nation and abroad.

But in her no-nonsense manner Dorothy disposed of education as a topic by observing that there is so much more for people to learn nowadays. Then she focused her laser-like questions on matters of the spirit. "Will we find out the whole mystery of the universe?"

Sister Bernadette's answer was swift and confident. "Certain key people help us to discover ourselves on our spiritual journey. Life is a mystery to be lived. We have to keep tuned into other people's hearts to find Him. Our relationship with God keeps growing." Dorothy's question was well directed. Thousands of students, as well as adults, have made their way through Sr. Bernadette's work-text, *My Journey, My Prayer*, in an ongoing process of self-discovery and growth. The nun, who was not wearing a habit but was dressed in a simple business suit, quietly emphasized her belief in the human need for reflection, for self-discovery; Dorothy Fuldheim focused upon the vast amount of new knowledge there is today, and the need to know and to unlock the secret of the universe.

Suddenly, the hostess demanded of her guest, "Are you as happy as you seem? How long have you been a nun?"

"Why, Dorothy," Sister Bernadette's face brightened. "I've been a nun for forty-five years."

Dorothy pressed on. "And would you live your life the same way again?"

"Yes, Dorothy." There was not a moment's hesitation. "Exactly the same."

"And are you happy because you established your relationship with God a long time ago?" Dorothy questioned.

"Yes," Sister Bernadette answered, hastening to add, "but it keeps growing."

"Interesting. Interesting." Dorothy's eyes scrutinized the nun's radiant face as if she hoped to find the key to a vast secret. "You are a happy person, one of the happiest I've ever talked to."

In any discussion Dorothy was likely to bring up the subject of some exotic mystery of the universe such as the Black Hole. But soon she would likely turn the subject to the spiritual rather than physical in nature. A reporter once asked her if it was possible that her interest in the faraway stars might be grounded in a distant memory of some prior life.

> "You mean do I believe in reincarnation," she asks with a sad smile. "No, I am sure there is some comfort to be found in that belief, but I never delude myself for the sake of comfort.
>
> "Nor do I believe in a life after death. I have observed that the stars die, the suns die. They become energy again. I don't think that immortality—life after death—would bring back my loved ones in a shape I'd recognize.
>
> "It is possible, though, that nothing is totally destroyed, that it merely takes on a different form.
>
> "But, no heaven, as hell. Just something within man that leads him to be noble and good rather than evil. And this is what helps him survive."

Inevitably, it seemed, Bishop Anthony M. Pilla found Dorothy Fuldheim seated with him at dinner parties, and just as inevitably she would bring up the subject of God and religion. He recalls,

> Mostly, she wanted to talk about did God exist? She considered herself an agnostic, but in my opinion she did have a faith. No one who claims not to believe in one [god] wants to discuss the subject as often as she did.
>
> Indeed, she was searching all the time. We'd get away from the subject and then come right back and talk about it. It wasn't that she was mocking or being insensitive. She was really searching. It was the kind of conversation I enjoy, not an adversarial conversation. It was very insistent probing. You couldn't give her fluff, you know.

He concurs that anything Dorothy could not reason through totally she struggled with. He would answer that you cannot understand God if you reduce him to yourself. That destroys the notion of God.

"I always spent time with her because I felt it was worthwhile. She genuinely was interested and appreciated the conversation."

After her daughter's death, Bishop Pilla again sat next to Dorothy at a dinner party. She questioned him as to what Catholics believe about afterlife. She concluded their conversation by saying, "You know, I desperately would like to believe what you believe. But I can't. For me, it's total finality and ending. I wish I could believe in something else."

"She did not deny the existence of a God or a power greater than herself," Greg Olsen says. "But she did not accept God's will, especially when Junior died."

"She always looked for science to come up with the means for eternal life," Randy Culver remembers. "She had faith in science but not much anywhere else." From doing continuity for Dorothy Fuldheim's telecasts for many years, Culver had observed her interviews with all sorts of people. In his mind is a clear-cut image of a conversation between Dorothy and Reverend Billy Graham that took place after Dorothy Junior's death.

Dorothy picked up on a comment by Graham. "Did I hear you say 'eternal life?'"

"Yes, I believe in eternal life. You can have eternal life, too." He told her, "If you believe in Jesus as your savior, you, too, can have eternal life."

Dorothy sat perfectly quiet for a moment. "Oh, if I could only believe that," she said sorrowfully.

Time and time again Dorothy's comments and writings reveal her unwillingness to accept anything on faith and her overwhelming need to place all things in a scientific framework. She reveals her belief that space exploration holds the key to the destiny of humanity.

> Somewhere in space must be our destiny. Somewhere in space we may meet creation itself. The beginnings of all things mature and grow only to crumble into dust; but for man there is a powerful revulsion at the thought of annihilation; that very revulsion validates the hope of some continuation after death . . .
>
> One of the most terrifying things about death for me is that I won't ever know when man has achieved that . . . when he has climbed to the very pillars of scientific achievement and can communicate with other worlds that I'll never know about.

> I am not preoccupied with my longevity. . . . I really don't
> have any fear of death, but I really don't think about it.
>
> I think it is almost impossible for a healthy person to
> think of himself as dead—a lot of people are living longer
> now.

Although she was Jewish, Dorothy practiced no formal religion. "I
am free of that burden," she said.

> I have a religion of my own, really a moral code. I don't
> have the kind of relationship where if I do so and so God
> will take me to heaven. Not at all.
>
> I think that mine [religion] is a superior one because I
> stand alone in the universe, and . . . I'm a human being; I
> do certain things. I share what I have.
>
> God is an entity far greater than any conception we have—
> this I believe. The very awesomeness of creation indicates
> something And I don't think it makes any difference to
> God whether you're a Catholic, Protestant, Jew, Moslem
> or whatever.

Abraham Lincoln exemplifies a person of deep compassion and
intellect who could openly acknowledge God's existence, although
he was not a member of any church. He stated unequivocally, "I will
join the church that carves these words over its door: "What doth the
Lord require of thee? To do justice, to love mercy, and to walk hum-
bly with thy God."

Lincoln, who early in life called himself an agnostic, did not attribute his knowledge of God to anything scientific but rather to his
serious study of the Bible as an adult. As the Civil War raged on and
in the months following the death of his young son Willie, Lincoln
spent long hours studying the Bible. The New Testament, which he
called "the true spirit of Christ," particularly engrossed him, and he
took it with all seriousness as the rule of life. While in the White
House, he wrote to his friend Josh Speed, "Take all of this book [the
Bible] upon reason that you can and the balance upon faith, and you
will live and die a better man."

Of all the books Dorothy read, there is no indication that she
ever read the Bible, or the Torah, or the Koran, for that matter. Had
someone whose wisdom she respected given her the advice Lincoln
gave to Speed, would she have searched the Scriptures or the Law for

some faith to grasp? Not likely. For an unaccountable reason, Dorothy regarded faith as a gift not possessed by all, and certainly not possessed by her. Although she acknowledged a creator of the universe, she regarded her entire life as a series of fortuitous events, opportunities that she seized and made the most of. Although she acknowledged a creator, she never saw any divine order at work in her life; every turn of events, in her eyes, occurred as a result of her own hard work and opportunism. Certainly, she had to make choices, but apparently, she never relied on any guidance other than intuition, based upon her own storehouse of knowledge.

Death was the one inexplicable human factor, and she linked it with the mystery of the universe. She wrote that she held her mother in her arms and tried to envelop her with love and keep her from death but that she could not. She told her, "You are not dead, for you will live in me forever, and I will hold your dreams in my heart."

Similarly, she once told Greg Olsen, "If you keep a person in your heart, that person will live forever." But this seemed little consolation for her when her daughter's life on earth ended at age sixty. Dorothy Fuldheim was then eighty-three, completing her thirty-third year as a news analyst at WEWS-TV. Life had been very lavish to her, but she felt it had taken its price, something that doesn't happen to everyone. Now her invalid granddaughter Halla was the only family she had.

Dorothy Junior died just before Thanksgiving in 1980. While friends flocked into the living room of the Fuldheim condominium to extend their sympathy, a large, self-assured woman sat at the kitchen table sipping tea. When neighbor Taffy Epstein, who was acting as one of several hostesses, came into the kitchen for another tray of pastries, she came face to face with Jean Melarvie. Epstein recognized her name as that of a former nun to whom Dorothy often affectionately referred as Sister Jean. She and Dorothy had been good friends for many years. Most likely, she is the unnamed friend Dorothy wrote about who taught at a parochial school in Cleveland years before and who regularly wheedled winter coats and boots for her poorer students from her good friend at WEWS-TV. Jean Bellamy recalls that Sister Jean and another nun often visited Dorothy when she lived next door to her in the 1950s and 1960s.

In all walks of life Jean Melarvie acquired friends. Donald Perris describes the former nun as very savvy about the stock market and business trends and probably very intellectual. "She had total accessibility to Dorothy Fuldheim." Perris says. She moved to a farm in West Virginia, but she had always promised Dorothy she would care for Halla if anything ever happened to her mother. Jean Melarvie was a strong, capable, educated woman who had known Halla since she was a child. Her promise to care for Halla offered a security Dorothy needed to placate one of her most gnawing fears.

After Dorothy Junior's death, Dorothy permitted Halla to move to West Virginia to live with Jean Melarvie. Halla required a great deal of care, and she had confidence Melarvie fit the role of an excellent caregiver. As Taffy Epstein says, "Caring for Halla required three people, and Jean *was* three people." Melarvie moved Halla to her three-story log home that she said she built on her farm at her own expense. Dorothy, of course, provided financially for Halla's complete care and comfort and installed such amenities as a Jacuzzi, a satellite dish, and a wheelchair lift. She talked often with her granddaughter by phone. Occasionally, Melarvie brought Halla to Cleveland for therapy and check-ups at the Cleveland Clinic.

Dorothy found living alone intolerable. Not only did she miss her daughter's companionship, but she was dependent upon others to do all of her routine personal errands such as banking and shopping. Since Taffy Epstein's mother had recently died, Dorothy invited her neighbor to move in with her. But Epstein was going through a difficult period of adjustment after her mother's death, and her doctor advised her against trying to live with anyone at that time.

Eventually, Dorothy left her condominium and moved to the spacious residence of her good friends, Sam and Maria Miller. To help her feel at home, the Millers arranged many of Dorothy's personal belongings in her new surroundings. They willingly assumed the day-to-day tasks that Dorothy herself was unable to handle. Sam, Maria, and Dorothy had been as close as family for many years. Now they actually were living as a family.

Although nearing ninety, Dorothy still kept her regular commentaries-and-interview schedule at WEWS-TV and continued to book a full calendar of outside speaking dates. Looking back, she felt life had taken its toll on her. "[Life] has chiseled me, like you do with a piece of marble," she said once. "It has disciplined me." She still kept searching, searching for the answers to the mysteries of the universe, but, more importantly now, she seemed to be searching inwardly for that wellspring of joy and peace she so craved.

16
Required: A Sense of Morality

"You are a moral man," Dorothy Fuldheim pronounced in a benedictory tone to her colleague, Peter Jennings, at the close of an interview with him in Cleveland early in 1984.

Jennings had just summed up a discussion about their mutual profession by stating emphatically, "The day we ignore morality and responsibility, we should be thrown out the door." The no-holds-barred conversation between the personable *ABC Nightly News* anchor and Cleveland's premier news personality had identified a broad plateau of agreement: Newspeople have access to a powerful medium, and their responsibility as they express their opinions is an enormous one; that responsibility begins with their own lives, whether analyst or reporter. Dorothy Fuldheim's response to Jennings was, "A newsperson must have a sense of his or her own morality or virtue before being perceived as moral by others."

When James Hanrahan hired Dorothy Fuldheim in 1947 and permitted her to fashion her one-of-a-kind version of a television news program, she had no model to emulate anywhere between New York and Chicago. Clevelanders had no other television station to watch at first, and Dorothy's way of presenting the news, as an analyst, became *the* way things would be done at WEWS-TV, at least, for the next four decades.

The vigorous, opinionated redhaired lady on the Channel 5 news took on the role of a wise but austere neighbor to thousands of households. Even young children recognized her. "Mom, 'Forfy Heim' is on now," one Cleveland mother's children would call out. The baby boomers grew up with a thrice-daily awareness of her commanding presence on their family's television screen. It was as punctual and reliable as mealtimes were in those days. "She came on right after Captain Penny," remembers Craig Peck, a Cleveland-area native. Although too young to understand why American troops were in Korea or to comprehend the fear of communism gripping the nation, many of that postwar generation remember Dorothy Fuldheim's don't-interrupt-me, forbidding manner as frightening. She was someone they put in the same memory pigeonhole as the Wicked Witch of the West.

Dorothy Fuldheim regarded herself as a news analyst, a title which set her apart from a host of others. She signed her letters with this title; she identified herself this way on the cover of her first book. Except for a few network personalities, such as H.V. Kaltenborn and Edward R. Murrow, few early newscasters, especially on local channels, were commentators or analysts; most just served up the daily happenings with few embellishments and a multitude of mispronunciations. In more recent decades both the network and local nightly news programs have concentrated on straight reporting of the news with an anchorperson or persons who shift from one news reporter to another. These roving reporters are strategically located as close as possible to the scene of crisis or conflict. They are always correctly attired for the climate or event taking place—Bob Simon in his fatigues on the dusty, potholed roads of Israel or Bosnia, a shivering Jill Dougherty bundled in scarf and earmuffs, on the snowy White House lawn. At times when a story does not surge with action, multi-faceted graphics leap across the screen to expand viewers' minds. As technology keeps spiraling, split-screen images and windows serving up weather advisories or lottery results encroach upon the viewer's turf.

Until the advent of CNN in 1980, news analysis or commentary was not an all-day, not even an everyday occurrence. Those citizens who sought the protracted opinions of pundits or commentators on national or international matters spun their dials to public television or public radio. After a major address by the President, the networks provided comments by a well-known, knowledgeable personality or their own news directors, and the management of local stations offered frequent editorials by the management, dealing with issues pertinent to their specific viewing areas.

As well as analyzing national and world situations, Dorothy Fuldheim's commentaries dealt with crucial local issues. A plethora of situations in Cleveland in the '60s and '70s provided her with ample material—a decaying downtown, race riots, forced busing of schoolchildren, a controversy over the sale of a municipal power plant, financial default, and an unsuccessful attempt to recall then-mayor Dennis Kucinich.

While airing her views to the public on vital matters, Dorothy saw in her television broadcasts a means of elevating language and promoting good taste. In her mind this was paramount. She forged ironclad standards that were embraced like the holy writ by WEWS-TV and likely influenced other stations in the city as well. In 1974 she wrote in *A Thousand Friends*:

> With the enormous impact TV has, it's up to those who appear to maintain a standard of good taste, good manners, good English, and integrity. I do not believe that the standards must be low, that one's vocabulary must be simple. To the contrary, people have much more sense, much more appreciation of the good and the fine and the important than they are credited with and it's up to TV performers, writers, and producers to recognize that fact.

Two unforgettable incidents transpired in Dorothy's career at the apex of the Me-generation. Both demonstrate the news analyst's strict adherence to her elevated standards. One was the highly-touted Jerry Rubin incident. Rubin was the unkempt, bearded and barefoot spokesperson for the Yippie movement, along with his sidekick, Abbie Hoffman. This was the militant Youth International Party, dedicated to questioning authority in whatever form. At their mock convention during the Democratic convention in 1968, the Yippies nominated a two-hundred pound pig named Pigasus for president, a direct slam at candidate-to-be Hubert Humphrey and at police. Chicago police subdued hundreds of demonstrators with clubs and hauled resisters away to jail.

> I threw Jerry Rubin off my program because his manners were bad and his arrogant attitude offensive. He wanted to show a picture of a nude with all the pubic hair showing.
> "Why?" I said.

> "Oh, ho," he cried triumphantly," you don't approve of
> nudes."
> "Why," I insisted, "do you want to show it? What is it
> germane to?"'
> No answer but another question hurled at me.
> "Do you take pot?"
> "No, of course not," he exclaimed before I had a chance
> to answer, "you drink and have a diseased liver."
> Me, a diseased liver! I have the best functioning liver in
> the whole country!
> Then he began the harangue on "the pigs," referring to
> the police. This was too much for me. I was suddenly filled
> with a violent rage.

The television screen blurred momentarily as the hostess slammed
down her copy of Rubin's book, *Do It!* "Out!" she cried. "This
interview is over." The camera caught a close-up of an astonished
Rubin, his face frozen in disbelief.

A myriad of lights flashed on the station's switchboard that afternoon from viewers who were incensed at the treatment the scruffy
Rubin received at the hands of Cleveland's Mother Superior of television. Some saw Rubin's hasty exit as a set-up, accusing Dorothy
of having planned all along to oust Rubin from the set. She was
vehement in her denial, but the incident still rankled when she recalled it in 1982. She told Diana Tittle of *Northern Ohio Live:*

> I didn't know that bird until he came in. And the reason
> that I threw him off was that he was vulgar. I have an el-
> egance of spirit. I don't want any vulgarity on my show.
> You know, that bird came back here and asked to be on my
> show again. Because I'm a reasonable person, I allowed him
> to come on, but I didn't believe him. I didn't believe that he
> stood for anything but to make a living. Well, I could un-
> derstand that. But when he said something—I've forgotten
> what it was—and I said, "Mr. Rubin, I threw you off once,
> and I can do it again."

Dorothy Fuldheim's reaction was not that of a prudish person
who was a throwback to the Victorian Era. In the 1960s, when there
were more students sitting on quadrangles and marching in protests
than there were in classrooms, Dorothy was more liberal in her attitude toward the young than many persons of her generation and of

their parents' generation. She criticized beards only if they were scraggly, hair only if it was dirty, blue jeans only because they were dull and ordinary. In fact, she demonstrated at the time of the Kent State episode that she could look past those kinds of habits which distinguished the youthful adherents to the protest movements of the times. Her concern for the dissident generation was that they seemed to be against so much, yet they seemed to be accomplishing very little as far as contributions to their culture and to society. She would smile smug approval today at Sonny Bono, occupying a seat in the United States Congress and at seeing Jane Fonda renowned as a fitness guru instead of scorned by many as "Hanoi Jane." She would delight in Paul McCartney's being a knight rather than the idol of screaming teens.

The lesser known but equally illustrative incident in which Dorothy Fuldheim held fast to her own rigid principles involved a non-appearance by *la* Fuldheim in her own commentary spot on the evening news. That afternoon a local radio station had done a show where everyone in the studio took off their clothes. The subject for discussion had been an article in a psychology journal on how clothing creates a cosmetic barrier to communication. A photographer from WEWS-TV, Clifford B. Feldman, happened to be on assignment in the same building where this was taking place. Someone with a radio clued him in to what was going on at station WERE. Rushing to the studio doors, he was told he could film the goings-on but only if he, too, agreed to remove his clothes. Feldman is said to have turned and left the studio door. Then he reconsidered, went back, and complied. He took the pictures of the two men and three women in the studio from the shoulders up, so it was said.

WEWS-TV did air the story on the evening news, but the anchorman read a statement as to why Dorothy Fuldheim would not present her commentary. She had told manager Donald Perris she was not physically ill but that she was " . . . mentally nauseated. I'm sick of having my life style [traditional values] besmirched and I propose expressing my disdain and disapproval." At Perris' suggestion, she wrote a statement of her position and delivered it to the anchorman.

Mind you, Dorothy was no prude. She had nothing against nudity for the sake of appreciation of the human form. In fact, she delighted in it. Countless sketches and paintings of standing and reclining nudes enhanced the pristine blue and white walls of her Empire-furnished Shaker Towers apartment, and a sculpture in classic Greek style adorned the glass-topped coffee table. She opposed nudity, however, for the sake of titillation in the same way she objected to writers and screenwriters whose characters rip their clothes off each other and in her words, "roll in the hay," when they first meet. She felt the act of lovemaking should employ protracted and subtle techniques such as wooing and coquetry that would result in a high degree of excitement in sex. Just as she felt Jerry Rubin's entire persona was an attention-getting device to make money, she believed that exploiting nakedness and physical love was reprehensible.

These two incidents clearly demonstrate that she was not just giving lip service to the idea of values and high standards. She was willing to buck public opinion and walk the walk herself, not just talk the talk, as the saying goes. Dorothy Fuldheim clung to her criteria for excellence at a time when Sunday school classes debated "situational ethics" and time-honored standards were crashing down all around.

If his studio had boasted a television set instead of a gramophone, Professor Henry Higgins of *My Fair Lady* could have transformed every flower girl in London's Covent Garden into a grand duchess. Just as his training and her diligent practice removed every trace of Cockney from Eliza Doolittle's speech, television can have a powerful and positive impact upon fostering proper, even elegant, speech. This is nowhere more apparent than when comparing newscasters as a group with members of the Congress, whose daily endeavors are observable on C-span. Who can find but of a modest trace of a Texas drawl in Dan Rather's speech compared with that of Senator Phil Gramm? Even Peter Jennings' clipped, brittle Canadian accent goes virtually unnoticed until he says "aboot" for "about." By contrast, the eloquent Senator Robert Byrd, second in longevity in the Senate, still retains his thick-as-honey West Virginia tonality, as distinctive as his sartorial splendor and his courtly demeanor. Quite understandably, members of Congress very likely strive to preserve their native speech patterns as a means of making their states more identifiable. In fact, regional dialects and accents are a distinctive element in our rich cultural fabric, and we would not wish to have a homogenized American speech. But the point is, if a person wishes or needs to do so, speech patterns can be changed. If motivated, people can train themselves to speak well, and the best way to do so is by listening and imitating others who do. There are television newspersons in top positions today who have even conquered speech impediments as well as distracting dialects, accents, and incorrect usage. The public has little regard for opinions of television personalities whose speech makes them appear ignorant. The days when Dizzy Dean, a backwoods base-ball-great-turned radio announcer, could get by with declaring that a runner "slud" into first base have faded into the distant past.

In her thirty-seven years of broadcasting daily into homes in north-east Ohio, Dorothy Fuldheim's polished speech and mind-bending vocabulary must have had a positive effect upon her viewers. Just as some readers today keep a dictionary close at hand when they read William F. Buckley or George Will, many of Dorothy Fuldheim's fans surely enriched their own word power, perhaps even unconsciously, as they watched her broadcasts through the years. Dorothy did not flaunt her vocabulary, however. In fact, because her commentaries were so short, she wrote in a rather compressed style, and she de-pended upon creating images her listeners would relate to. In her commentary on America's bicentennial, for example, she spoke of the early settlers of this nation calling them " . . . the malcontent, the dreamer who dreamed of a land freed from the tyranny of kings where he coud worship God as he saw fit and where his sons could walk erect freed from the scourge of poverty."

The catch-phrase "Ken-and-Barbie" television journalism has emerged to refer to the growing numbers of male-female news anchor teams. While in 1972 only eleven percent of anchorpersons were female, by 1985 nine out of ten network affiliated stations had a female anchorperson. Today, most stations in even small cities seem to have a female anchorperson; some stations even have a duo-female team. When female newspersons first blossomed on television screens, their hairstyles, clothing, and jewelry all seemed to be mass produced by Mattel. No one emerged with the panache and individuality—and accompanying wisdom—of a Dorothy Fuldheim. Whether airing thought-provoking commentaries or interviewing visiting celebrities, she opened an informed window on the world, one that she always enhanced with charm and wit.

Barbara Walters, who celebrated twenty years with ABC in 1996, came up through the ranks. For twelve years she worked as a writer for NBC's *Today* show before being made its co-host in the 1960s. Her move to ABC in 1976 to co-anchor the evening news with vet-eran newscaster Harry Reasoner at an unprecedented salary carved a new niche in television history—the first female anchorperson *for a major network.* Walters has observed many changes in the delivery of television news. She recently stated to *TV Guide* that good looks on camera are not as important for television newspeople as being good at their jobs. Also, she feels that because there are more middle-aged viewers today, being young is not the prerequisite it once was.

In the year Dorothy Fuldheim turned ninety, a thirty-eight-year-old anchorwoman named Christine Craft won a half-million dollar damage verdict against the owners of the Kansas City station that dropped her in 1981. Dorothy Fuldheim is said to have been supportive of Miss Craft who had revealed the station manager told her she was "too old, unattractive, and not deferential to men." In a *Time* magazine account, Dorothy was hailed as a "notable survivor," in a field in which Roone Arledge, ABC News President, stated, "It is a fact of life—when your face is out there as your byline, cosmetic factors are involved." Others cited as having survived were Barbara Walters, of ABC, then fifty-one; Pauline Frederick, who retired in 1974 at age sixty-five from NBC, and reporter Taris Savell, fifty-two, of Pensacola's WEAR.

If Dorothy Fuldheim were at the peak of her career today, picturing her at CNN or any of the all-news cable channels is not difficult. She would probably have toned down her appearance, however. The female newspeople at CNN bear out Walters' opinions: They are obviously selected for their ability and their intelligence, not necessarily for their appearance. Their clothing is muted, even drab at times; their hairstyles often appear as if they do their own—and sometimes in a hurry. But one only needs to observe interviews by CNN personalities such as Judy Woodruff and Mary Tillotson to realize that these are knowledgeable, astute women who are skilled interviewers, not talking heads or dolls with movable parts. If Dorothy Fuldheim were watching television today, she would give her blessing to the CNN ladies and regard them as serious newspeople.

Television as an industry has changed in its mission in the second and third generations, and this affects the state of broadcast journalism today, says Walter Cronkite. In a recent *Frontline* interview, Cronkite expressed a concern that there is a lack of clear-cut responsibility in broadcasting today—a responsibility that was pounded into the pioneers in the industry. Today it is a business, not a gut feeling about the future of broadcasting and what broadcasting will do for the country by bringing the nation together, linking cities. "Today the concern is maximizing profit," Cronkite says. "You do that by entertainment, primarily."

Commenting when appearing on *Larry King Live*, Barbara Walters called this the age of "tabloidmania," meaning that anything can be asked or printed. "We just have to live with it," she said. Walters, whose stellar career as an interviewer eclipsed her stint as a news anchor on CBS, and King, currently appearing six nights a week for an hour on CNN, both draw an array of high-powered personalities and probe relentlessly into their lives. Stating that television journalists must be aware of changes in viewers' tastes, Walters added that "people don't want to see politicians today at 10:00. They want to see the notorious and famous—O.J. Simpson, Colin Powell, Mike Tyson, Christopher Reeve . . . "

Cronkite, the dean of newscasters of the mid-twentieth century, was definitely not an entertainer. Priding himself on taking a totally objective position on all news reports, Cronkite presided over some of America's proudest and most tragic moments—the moon landing, the asassinations, the race riots of the Sixties, the resignation of President Nixon, the nation's Bicentennial. He regarded himself as a news presenter, however, rather than an analyst. In discussing today's news broadcasting, Cronkite emphatically states that news presenters should not pretend to be journalists.

Upon retirement in 1993, NBC's John Chancellor echoed his CBS colleague's feelings about the need to be profitable. He sees this as affecting the way the news is presented in that it has become more entertainment-oriented. It lacks the honesty it had in the 1950s, he says.

John Chancellor emerged as a commentator after twelve years of being a reporter. He and a colleague, career newsman Walter Mears, vice president of the Associated Press, have produced a handbook for newswriters, *The New News Business*. In a chapter on Analysis, Chancellor and Mears define the essense of analytical or commentary writing. Chancellor sees it as a sort of logical brief: facts put together in such a way that they lead to an inescapable conclusion. News commentary is not "someone sitting there on your television set giving out his opinions on why he doesn't like Senator So-and-so because of the color of his eyes." Mears agrees. Commentaries should be logical essays that make a point. They must supply background, perspective, explanation, motives. He suggests that he did not write that changing campaign managers wasn't going to rescue George Bush's losing campaign in 1992. "Instead," he said, "I did that one this way: 'In big-league baseball, they fire losing managers in the hope that a new one can get more out of the old team. But the same players still take the field. That goes for big-league politics too.' "

Dorothy Fuldheim's commentaries were well-researched and founded upon her cerebral grasp of world and domestic affairs. Yet, from her throne in northeast Ohio, she sometimes bared her iron fist of the velvet glove. Her techniques were often more direct, sometimes more scathing, less subtle than these two journalists describe. For example, on the oil crisis in 1974, she said, "The gods must be playing with Americans' emotions. We have seen ourselves blackmailed and hijacked as no other country."

Although she expressed her views forcefully and with unwavering conviction, they were not flagrant or unfounded opinions tossed across the airwaves. She knew and used to full advantage a variety of persuasive techniques to win over her viewers. According to the study made by rhetorician Judith Reisman, the main lines of argument which flow naturally from Dorothy Fuldheim's premises use inductive and deductive reasoning, arguing from example, analogy, authority and causal relations (in particular, specific instance and cause to effect), to persuade her audience to her idea of the good and the noble. She was daily able to reinforce her image as a person of virtue and of gigantic character in whom trust can confidently be placed.

The format of the nightly news appears to be undergoing continual change, In his 1980 book, *The Third Wave,* futurist Alvin Toffler predicted the computer age would usher in what he called the "de-massifying" of all the media. He cited changes that were occurring even then: fewer daily newspapers, yet more area and neighborhood papers; fewer general interest magazines but many more in number and variety, catering to every interest imaginable, and more specialized radio offerings such as stations offering only pop, rock, gospel, or oldies and more ethnic and racial stations.

In television, Toffler foresaw a proliferation of news broadcasts aimed at individual interests instead of three network news organizations delivering the news to the nation. As he predicted, today we have nightly programs dispensing specialized, bite-sized helpings of business news, investment news, sports, tabloid news, entertainment news, international news, and politics. Cable television and the internet offer us indescribable numbers of choices. The result is a loss of a common ground, a lessening of community. People can get the news spun to their particular frame of reference. Critics maintain that television newspeople talk *about* the news but often do not discuss the issues from all sides. For example, the business news report jubilantly reports how a corporate merger will increase earnings and drive stock prices up, but on a local channel in the city where the company is headquartered, the news report may emphasize the several thousand jobs to be eliminated as a result of the merger.

Evening network news shows have lost more than ten percent of their audiences in just three years and "they haven't the faintest idea what to do about it," says Robert Lichter, head of the nonprofit Center for Media and Public Affairs in Washington. What they seem to be doing about it is featuring fewer headline stories on the nightly news. Viewers have probably heard these already via local news, radio, or the internet. Instead, more in-depth features are appearing such as CBS' *Eye on America* and NBC's *In Depth*. ABC's *Person of the Week* often profiles an ordinary citizen whose accomplishments the network deems noteworthy. Because the public's taste in literature and film has swung heavily in favor of nonfiction and true stories, weekly television news magazines now are thriving on every channel. Perhaps the stalwart ratings of CBS' *Sixty Minutes* have proven the investigative and human interest formats to have enduring appeal.

If Dorothy Fuldheim were on the television news scene today, she could find a niche in the myriad of forms in which television news is now being delivered. Nowhere, though, would there likely be the kind of journalistic freedom she experienced in the early days of television. The specters of excessive litigation and political correctness hover in the wings of the studio during every broadcast.

17
Just Before Sunset

Icon, monument, legend—what metaphor is bold enough, vivid enough, encompassing enough to describe Dorothy Fuldheim?

In June 1983 her friends formed a living metaphor at Blossom Music Center to honor their acclaimed First Lady of Television on her ninetieth birthday. As seven hundred friends and associates finished a sumptuous buffet meal, served in The Restaurant at Blossom and adjacent tents, two thousand more well-wishers began settling their blankets and lawn chairs on the gentle slopes of the peaceful, verdant setting, the world-class Cleveland Orchestra's summer home.

The last rays of splendid midsummer sun dimmed, and the deepening twilight cast long violet shadows across the amphitheater. Like a lone sapphire, the evening star hung low on the horizon. Honeysuckle's heavy fragrance saturated the air, and an aura of joy surrounded Dorothy and her friends as they made their way toward the pavilion. Guest conductor Mitch Miller and Dorothy bantered talk-show style before he took up his baton to lead the pop concert. Wearing a stunning off-white sheath, a high-spirited Dorothy danced about the flower-filled stage to the delight of the cheering crowd.

A year later, just before Dorothy turned ninety-one, ABC's Ted Koppel interviewed her for *Nightline* from her office at WEWS-TV. She announced to Koppel she knew she was a better news analyst than she had been thirty years previously. Further emphasizing her attitude toward age, she suggested criteria for electing a president that would include an intelligence test, far more indicative of ability, she told Koppel, than age. The year was 1984. In November Americans would re-elect President Ronald Reagan, at age seventy-three, the oldest man ever elected to that office.

At the conclusion of the *Nightline* interview, Dorothy removed the earpiece and looked annoyed. The lines in her face seemed deeper that day, and she remarked to the cameraman in a peevish tone: "I hope it's OK. That's an awful lot of time and energy to spend for a such a short segment." As she waited to find out if the taping was satisfactory, she asked the cameraman, "Who was I talking to?" Upon hearing his name, she nodded in vague recognition and affirmed that he [Koppel] was a "knowledgeable man." Her face showed obvious relief when she learned that the taping did not have to be done again.

Only one month and a day after her comparatively subdued ninety-first birthday, Dorothy interviewed President Ronald Reagan by satellite. Some of the discussion surrounded the President's newly nominated Democratic opponents for the approaching November election and, in particular, that party's history-making choice of a woman, New York Congresswoman Geraldine Ferraro, as the vice-presidential nominee. The interview was taped for future airing.

When she finished on that Friday afternoon, Dorothy chatted with audio engineer Bill Kozel about the president's warm and colloquial manner. While Kozel gathered his equipment, Dorothy reached for her yellow pad to review her evening commentaries before sending them to the typist. She reached for her phone and told her assistant she was now available to take calls.

"The interview went well. It was about six minutes long," Kozel remembers. "She didn't complain about not feeling well when we were talking afterwards." But such a confession would have been nearly as out of character for Dorothy as if she had said she neglected to have her gingersnaps with her French coffee that morning.

That night some viewers thought it unusual that Dorothy Fuldheim's taped commentary at eleven o'clock had also been used for the six o'clock broadcast. But by that time, Dorothy had been rushed to Cleveland's Mt. Sinai Hospital where surgeons removed a fist-sized blood clot from her brain. Even as she was admitted to the hospital, Dorothy's sense of humor buoyed her along, according to

Dr. Michael Devereaux, the hospital's chief of neurology. "When we asked her if she had any allergies, she said, 'Yes. To men.'" Seemingly, an out-of-character statement for Dorothy, but Devereaux knew her well enough to read it as a facetious comment. Saturday's *Plain Dealer* carried only a brief article on an inside page, quoting a Mt. Sinai Hospital spokesperson as saying Dorothy Fuldheim "was there for tests and was feeling fine."

Sunday morning's banner headline declared, **Fuldheim in Coma after Brain Surgery.** At after-church coffees, Sunday brunches, and golf outings, the comments were the same: "We just watched her on the late news last night. She seemed fine." (Many viewers never realized the 11 p.m. commentary was taped earlier.) The entire WEWS-TV viewing area waited and prayed for its Queen of Television. President Reagan phoned to voice his concern. *The Plain Dealer* and WEWS-TV issued bulletins and asked the public not to call the hospital. But there was nothing to report. Dorothy Fuldheim remained in a coma. On Monday doctors refused to speculate on a prognosis. Their only comment was that she was in no pain but was still in danger.

Day after day after day Dorothy's cogent commentaries, her refined and gracious manner toward her guests, her feathers and beads and oversized rings no longer sparkled on television screens in Cleveland area homes.

"I will never retire," she had often said. "Life will have to retire me." It did.

Around 9:30 every morning Greg Olsen would think he heard the purr of Dorothy's Lincoln nearing the back door at WEWS-TV. Then the ad salesman would remind himself that his favorite TV lady would not be coming through that door today. Other staff members huddled in doorways and asked one another if there was any change in her condition. They told their favorite Dorothy stories, maybe because in the telling they felt closer to her; maybe they thought she could somehow know that she was giving them a laugh to start their day.

"One day, when I was still new and timorous at WEWS-TV," Wilma Smith was saying to a group outside her office, "I still thought of myself as little Wilma Pokorny from Garfield Heights. I had trouble thinking of myself as a member of the same television staff as Dorothy Fuldheim. After all, I had grown up with her as a daily presence in my parents' living room." Smith continued, as more listeners joined the group. "This particular day was very cold, so I just planned to dash across the street and back very quickly to do an errand. But Dorothy's commanding voice stopped me in my tracks as I was passing her office. 'Where do you think you're headed with no coat on?'

"After I explained, she made some comment about young people's hardiness and foolishness. Then she called out sternly, 'Well, come in here. You can wear my coat.'

"And that's how I happened to be walking across Euclid Avenue in a mink coat one cold winter morning. The scent of Dorothy's French cologne lingered on the fur, and I felt totally pampered and elegant. Never mind that the sleeves came only to my elbows!" Wilma Smith's delightful laugh rang through the hallway.

Someone else recalled one of Joel Rose's favorite stories. Joel had left the station a few years before, but he had often told of passing Dorothy's office one day and hearing her laughing heartily as she hung up her phone. "Come in here, Joel," she called, "and I'll tell you a crazy story." Rose told how he stepped inside her office and prepared to be entertained. Dorothy was still chuckling. "You know, bankers are the most stupid people on the face of the earth," she announced. "I'm eighty-seven years old, and my bank just gave me a twenty-five-year loan to buy my condominium."

Outside the studio, cab drivers who often took "Red" to noon speaking engagements slowed at 30th and Euclid, as if they expected to see someone hailing a cab for her. Or perhaps this was the cab drivers' way of keeping her in their thoughts or feeling they were doing something for her. Viewers continued to deluge the WEWS-TV switchboard with calls, although reports of Dorothy's condition were given daily. Hundreds of get-well cards arrived for her every day. Still, her condition did not change significantly.

After two weeks Dorothy regained consciousness and was able to speak. News releases contained vague phrases such as "gradual response to her environment" and "some limited verbal response." Doctors described her vital signs as "strong," however, and she no longer required a respirator. She remained at Mt. Sinai until September 26 when she was moved to the Margaret Wagner House, part of the Benjamin Rose Institute. By coincidence, the highly regarded nursing home stands on Euclid Heights Boulevard in Cleveland Heights, only a few blocks from the gabled bungalow Dorothy and Milton Fuldheim had purchased some forty years before.

Because Dorothy Fuldheim had been in public view for so long, many people felt entitled to know every detail of her illness, to chart her daily progress. Although she was ninety-one years old and had suffered a serious stroke, some viewers refused to accept that she should remain in a nursing home. A local group evolved purporting to be "Citizens to Save Dorothy Fuldheim." They distributed buttons and T-shirts (for a fee, of course). Some members of the National Organization for Women (NOW) picketed the Margaret Wagner House and said that if such a prominent person could be kept in a nursing home against her wishes, "how often does it happen to thousands of others?"

The efforts of these groups were encouraged in January by a story that appeared in a newspaper in an adjacent county. In an interview with Dorothy Fuldheim, a reporter quoted her as saying she wanted to leave the Margaret Wagner House and go back to her own Shaker Heights condominium, but that Sam Miller, who was by this time her legal guardian, would not allow this. When Miller had applied for guardianship in October, Dorothy had signed the application. Now she stated she had no recollection of doing so. In November Cuyahoga County Probate Judge John J. Donnelly had declared Dorothy Fuldheim "incompetent by reason of physical disability." Samuel H. Miller was appointed her legal guardian. He also applied for and was granted resident guardianship of the estate of Halla Urman, Dorothy's granddaughter.

Papers in surrounding cities picked this story up from the wire service. Dr. Michael Devereaux was quoted as saying Dorothy would need round-the-clock nurses seven days a week if she were to go home. "She remains intellectually impaired. She can fool a lot of people. We feel she would be better protected in Margaret Wagner. Part of keeping her there is to protect her memory in the community—her own image." Devereaux had urged the appointment of Sam Miller as Dorothy's guardian. He claimed that due to Dorothy's recent illness, as well as her advanced age she was not presently able to care for herself or her property. He added that her desires to go home should not be considered to be without merit. Most friends who were urging her release and were quoted in the story were not named.

The *Akron Beacon-Journal* printed several stories concerning the loss of freedom a person experiences when entering a nursing home. These stories kept attention focused upon what some perceived as

Dorothy's unfortunate plight. Sam Miller is quoted in one of the articles, saying, "If I had known at the time when I took on this guardianship of all the travail and so forth that my family and I have been put through, I would still take it because it's the right thing to do.

"If there's someone you loved all your lifetime and they've come to an impasse," he said, "it behooves someone to step into the picture and make sure everything goes properly and correctly. But because this was a lady who had been in public life for so long, I was set up as a target by well-meaning friends."

The same Lake County reporter that interviewed Dorothy traveled to West Virginia to interview Halla and Jean Melarvie. The resulting stories described Halla as being totally happy in her surroundings with no wish to return to Cleveland. She told the reporter she is where her grandmother wanted her to be. Halla is now in her early fifties and remains in West Virginia with Melarvie who is what is known in West Virginia as the "Committee for Halla Urman." She receives a salary from Dorothy's estate. Since her care for life is provided by Dorothy's estate, as administered by Sam Miller, who is still guardian of the estate, Halla will never be left penniless, as her grandmother so feared.

With the insatiable curiosity the public displays for the intimate lives of its celebrities, political leaders, and the notorious, a news reporter walks a fine line between what is good journalism and what is a violation of the subject's privacy. At a press conference after Dorothy Fuldheim's stroke, an unnamed Cleveland journalist summed up this position: "Sometimes being a good human being supersedes being a good reporter." The Cleveland news media seemed to take this stance where Dorothy was concerned. **Public is Protective of Dorothy Fuldheim** declared the headline on *Plain Dealer* television editor Maria Riccardi's column two days after the interview that was picked up by the wire service. Although Riccardi acknowledged Dorothy had been saying that she wanted to go home, her column focused on Dorothy's right to privacy and that "the truth of Fuldheim's impaired state was difficult for many folks at home to accept."

To allay the concerns aroused and inflamed by the stories in newspapers of surrounding cities, Sam Miller invited several highly respected Clevelanders to visit Dorothy Fuldheim at the Margaret Wagner House a few days later. Present were Bishop Anthony M. Pilla of the Cleveland Catholic Diocese; his assistant, the Rev. Michael

Dimengo; the Cleveland Metropolitan General Hospital neurosurgeon, Dr. Robert J. White, and Mary Strassmeyer, staff writer for *The Plain Dealer*. As they clustered about Dorothy's easy chair, she sat, erect and unnatural, somewhat confused by the number of visitors. She wore a blue, knee-length brunch coat, white socks and white sports shoes. A black afghan lay over her knees. A walker and a wheelchair stood nearby. Her neatly combed hair was the familiar orange-red, and she had a fresh manicure. Neither a book nor a newspaper was in the room, but paintings on the walls and masses of flowers declared that Dorothy Fuldheim lived here.

Dorothy talked readily, though some of her speech was what her neurologist, Dr. Michael Devereaux, explained as confabulation, (filling in gaps in the memory with detailed, but more or less unconscious, accounts of fictitious events). She talked a great deal about going home and taking care of herself. In response to Strassmeyer's questions about cooking for herself, she snapped, "I never cooked in my life and I don't intend to start now." Then came a typical Fuldheim-like quip: "If you don't stop interrogating me, you may be dismissed."

Several times she mentioned that people were seeking her out "for her mind," including President Reagan. She could not remember having spoken with a reporter the previous week, but she seemed agitated by stories about her appearing in the newspapers. She answered everyone's questions, but her attention span proved short. Her blue eyes lacked their customary glint of intelligence, and the hand and arm actions she used so well on television were missing. Furthermore, she confused Bishop Pilla with her doctor.

Another resident of the Margaret Wagner House, Milt Widder, a former *Cleveland Press* columnist, told a *Plain Dealer* reporter, "She [Dorothy] wants to get the hell out," he said. "But she's not ready to go. She doesn't have the mental capacity. Sometimes she's very good. Other times she doesn't remember."

Widder and Dorothy Fuldheim had known each other for more than forty years. By sad coincidence, they were drawn together by more than their journalistic professions. Milt Widder's wife, also named Dorothy, had died at age seventy-one in that same dreary Thanksgiving week in 1980 as Dorothy Fuldheim, Jr. Now Widder and Dorothy sat together at meals like two worn, propped-up dolls exchanging weak, wistful smiles.

Those who agitated for Dorothy's return to her own condominium never implied she did not receive good care at the well-respected Margaret Wagner House. But the wishes of a person who could afford proper twenty-four-hour care should be granted, they claimed. A person of means should not be restricted to a nursing home.

Anyone who is confined to an institution, no matter how comfortable or even luxurious it is, longs constantly to return home; it becomes an overwhelming obsession. Home is the ultimate, the shining perfection where all things are idyllic. Dorothy gave no thought to the logistics of managing her home—hiring help, handling finances, doing necessary shopping. She envisioned a return to the world she knew before her stroke. This world would materialize, she thought, if only she could just move back to her condominium. She seemed to have forgotten that she had been unhappy there and had, in fact, not lived there for several years before her stroke. Actually, if she returned, her life would be much the same as it was the Margaret Wagner House, except there would be many days she would very likely see only one other person, her caregiver. Friends would continue to call on occasions, but Dorothy's condition would not permit her to resume her active social life. A friend might invite her out for a drive or for a quiet dinner. That would be as much as she could hope for. Her stroke and her advanced age had physically incapacitated her, and her mental state was inconsistent.

At the Margaret Wagner House the staff and residents respected Dorothy, but she received no special treatment. Glimpses of the legendary television news queen still shone through her impairments, however. Rae Richie, a social worker assigned to Dorothy, said, "She commanded attention, held her head high. You could tell she knew she was still an important person. She kept her red hair even though it wasn't always easy to get her out to a salon." Richie frequently read to Dorothy. One day she was reading some of Harry Truman's letters to his wife Bess. "He was just like that," Dorothy said, perking up for a moment. She had always admired President Truman for his dignity and his forthright manner.

Sheila Niles, then assistant director of nursing at Margaret Wagner, said, "She [Dorothy] had a vibrant mind trapped in an uncooperative body. She was frustrated. You could see it in her demeanor."

Ten months after her stroke Dorothy was said to have contacted the Legal Aid Society to help her return home. Two lawyers visited the Margaret Wagner House to interview her. Her doctors still maintained she should be in a nursing home. "Her condition has not changed in any significant way," said her physician, Dr. Devereaux. "She's incapable of contacting Legal Aid, so someone probably did it for her. . . . . Any lawyer that has enough brains to be able to blow his nose will see that she's unable to go home."

Devereaux said Fuldheim often did not know where she was. "She's a puppet in the hands of some people," he said. "And that's tragic."

In early June 1985 all talk of Dorothy's returning home subsided. She suffered a second stroke. "Dorothy's circuits are down and some will never be connected again," said Sam Miller.

Mary Strassmeyer visited Dorothy once more and found her immaculately groomed and well dressed. But she responded listlessly to questions by answering only yes or no. She indicated that she felt very well and that she no longer wished to go home. When Strassmeyer left, Dorothy said to her, "I appreciated your coming. It's nice to see somebody alive once in awhile."

Friends celebrated Dorothy's ninety-second birthday with her on the shady grounds of the Margaret Wagner House a few weeks later. She wore a dark dress, most of which was covered by a pastel-colored plaid shawl. Sam Miller pushed her wheelchair out under the trees where a bouquet of ninety-two roses towered over the refreshment table. A cake resembling a basket held more roses made of frosting. "That cake must weigh ten pounds," one of the guests remarked. Enough of the Fuldheim spark ignited for her to pan her friends' musical rendition of "Happy Birthday." Don Webster of WEWS-TV read a telegram of congratulations from Nancy and Ronald Reagan, while tuxedo-clad waiters passed glasses of champagne. A second, smaller cake was served to honor Sam Miller's birthday. The effects of Dorothy's second stroke were apparent. Her mouth was drawn to one side. She spoke very little and with difficulty. Her hand trembled as she attempted to gesture in her familiar fashion. Whenever this happened, Maria Miller, who was never far from Dorothy's side, kindly took her hand in her own.

In the months that followed, honors and awards continued to rain upon Dorothy Fuldheim, although she no longer could accept them personally. Her alma mater, Milwaukee Normal College, had become the Milwaukee campus of the University of Wisconsin. Her friend and colleague, Fred Griffith, traveled to Milwaukee to accept a Distinguished Alumnus Award on Dorothy Fuldheim's behalf.

The Scripps Howard Corporation, owner of WEWS-TV, named her news analyst emeritus and established a $10,000 yearly Dorothy Fuldheim scholarship at John Carroll University for a student entering broadcast communications. At Kent State University the Scripps Howard Foundation created a fund to award a $5,000 Dorothy Fuldheim Scholarship each year to a student residing in the seventeen-county area in northern Ohio served by WEWS-TV.

Her ninety-second birthday was the last party for Dorothy, but it was not the last birthday. She would spend four and one-half more years at the Margaret Wagner House before she entered Mt. Sinai for the final time in mid-October 1989. "Complications from a stroke" took Dorothy to her final rest on November 3 of that year. Services were private for this woman who had lived such a public life.

When her daughter died, nearly a decade before, a distraught Dorothy had cried out, "Why didn't God take me?"

Trying to comfort her, Yvonne Breslin, wife of Dorothy's long-time director, told her, "Dorothy, God isn't ready for you, yet."

"No one is ready for me," Dorothy said.

How many times during more than five years did Dorothy Fuldheim wonder again and again, "Why doesn't God take me?" She had said she wanted to die with all of her faculties. People who knew her well grieved for her. "She should have gone out in a rocket ship," says her neighbor from the 1950s and 1960s, Jean Bellamy. She and her husband Peter and their five children were close to Dorothy in the days when her television career was on the rise and she was totally in control. Jean Bellamy went to visit her once at Margaret Wagner, but, sadly, Dorothy did not recognize her former neighbor.

Throughout her life Dorothy had passionate longings—for knowledge, money, luxuries, ecstatic experiences. All of these things consumed her mind for decades. Yet, she kept searching, longing for answers to questions she could sometimes not even phrase. Dorothy had always known death was beyond her control.

In a 1982 interview with Barbara Walters that evolved into an intimate conversation, Dorothy said, "I have a curiously Olympic feeling toward the tumult and turmoil of the world, yet the enigma of life haunts me. I know stars die, butterflies die, human beings die. It torments me. I would like to know . . . " The concept of immortality remained incomprehensible to her.

Those who knew her spiritual longing perhaps hoped that in those final, silent years Dorothy Fuldheim could have had a renascence such as the poet Edna St. Vincent Millay described when she wrote, "The soul can split the sky in two/And let the face of God shine through."

Dorothy's metaphorical comments about life, spoken on a televised documentary, "Great Moments in the Life of Dorothy Fuldheim," provide her own fitting epitaph:

> Life is like a great cathedral. At the beginning of a service there are a few candles lighted, then more, until the whole cathedral is illuminated. When the service is over, sooner or later they go out, no matter how sonorous the music or how great the light was they gave off. But for one hour there was the splendor of light.

Epilogue

Yes, Dorothy, the light went out—in the red glints in your hair, in your ice-blue, piercing eyes, in your sparkling jewelry and glittering clothes. But the radiant aura you left with the world—your mesmerizing intellect, your elegance of spirit, your staccato wit—will remain.

You often said that when you were a little girl you used to climb to a hidden spot on a rooftop, high above the smoke and steam of the city of Milwaukee. You would crouch down among the gritty chimneys and watch the wondrous splendor of the sunset. As the rivulets of color silently collided and transmuted themselves from one glowing tint to another, you promised yourself that someday you'd have dresses made of all those colors. But when the light vanished and dusk shrouded the rooftops in pearly sameness, you'd flee your dream world to face the fact that tomorrow you'd go to school once more in a patched and faded dress.

But life treated you lavishly in many ways. Not only did you own the dresses, but you also earned attention, distinction, and scores of accolades for decades of tireless dedication to noble causes. Spent in the glaring light of high noon, your life was both exemplary and precious. You left a legacy of inestimable worth to others in your profession and to all human beings who knew and revered you.

Reach out for the sunset, Dorothy. You will surely add to it one more vibrant, timeless hue.

Commentaries

Included here are some of Dorothy Fuldheim's well known personal commentaries as well as some that reflect upon historic moments in our nation's history. These commentaries are found in the Dorothy Fuldheim papers in the Kent State University Special Collections. They are reproduced here in chronological order and as they appear in the Special Collections.

DOROTHY FULDHEIM

IN MEMORIUM OF SENATOR ROBERT KENNEDY
(not dated but presumed to be June 6, 1968)

The sun rose on Tuesday and the hours passed—morning to sunset and then the hours of darkness until midnight when in Los Angeles word came that Robert Kennedy had achieved a victory.

He stood there boyish and gay, jubilant and weary, thanked his supporters and, to avoid the crowd, walked through the kitchen to get to the rear elevators.

Who knew, who could have dreamed that Death walked a few steps ahead of him to claim him?

For the shot, it rang out and destroyed the brain of Robert Kennedy, destroyed something precious in the world.

Ask not for whom the bell tolls, for if one man dies all men die a little.

In all of us some sense of security, some sense of happiness has been taken away.

Robert Kennedy in the full flower of his manhood was struck down wastefully and wantonly and the sun will never shine as brightly again.

Fate has encircled the Kennedy family with so tragic a pattern that only a Shakespeare will able to put it into words.

As the bells toll their mournful song that a man has died, grey envelops the world.

What shall man pray for? For some assuagement of anguish for the mother of Robert Kennedy and the father whose hearts are already scarred with other anguishes?

Some peace for their tortured hearts?

For the soul of our nation that we shall walk in the future in more righteous paths?

For Robert Kennedy and John Kennedy there is forever carved in our hearts that once there was a Camelot, and its golden glory shall not be forgotten.

Commentary
Thursday, August 8, 1974, 11 p.m.

NIXON RESIGNS

I return from my vacation because this evening is historic. Our children's children will read of this somber event in their history books and not for a thousand years can a similar episode occur.

His farewell talk tonight had great grace free of any bitterness, a sad regret and a review of what his administration had accomplished, and only one reference to Watergate. But the truth is the President has folded his tent and disappeared into the night and the nation is numb that it could have happened to our proud and valiant land. Though there is relief, there is also a sense of unbelief for the price is great—a President and Vice President sent into oblivion by their lack of honesty and integrity. There is no vindictiveness in our hearts, just a sense of horror that it could have happened. One wonders at the stupidity of recording the conversations and keeping the tapes instead of burning them.

But at long last it is finished, the horror is over. The vigor and the fundamental sense of right and wrong of the American people has won out. No wrongdoer ever had more opportunity to plead his case before the tribunal of the Americans than Mr. Nixon did. Not one redeeming fact was registered to break the blackness of the offense; and, yet, there is pity, too, for Mr. Nixon. He might well have cried out with Cardinal Wolsey, " . . . had I but served my conscience with half the fervor I served my ambition, I would not now be the bereft of my honor."

But now there is a new day, day of hope and light for the Constitution and our democracy has been affirmed. Legality and integrity rules this land. In another time, in another country it might have led to dictatorship. This moment affirms our form of government and the justice of our code of honor.

Tomorrow sees a new president who comes to this exalted position, the highest honor 200,000,000 Americans can bestow on any man. Because of the double tragedy of Spiro Agnew and Richard Nixon, may we forever remember that the character of the president determines our people.

DOROTHY FULDHEIM

Commentary
Monday, July 5, 1976 6 p.m.

THE DECLARATION OF INDEPENDENCE
AND THE CONSTITUTION

Bells rang, ships silhouetted the skyline, songs were sung, there was dancing in the streets, the skies were lighted with fireworks—people around the nation drank toasts to the birthday of our nation. The highways buzzed with the sound of Americans on their way—forever moving, forever on the go. But mostly throughout the nation parts of the Declaration of Independence and the Constitution were read aloud for the Declaration of Independence and the Constitution are our guarantees for freedom.

Written by a group of men—Jefferson, Franklin, Adams, Washington, who in a few noble and endearing words enunciated an emancipation for the common man that dethroned kings and placed upon the common man the right and responsibility for his destiny.

Perhaps only once before in history did fate give such a group to any peoples and that was in Athens under Pericles when with a great leap of magnificent intellectual flowering they crowned Greece with a heritage of art and philosophy.

One of the most moving scenes was the swearing in of new citizens in Chicago and Miami. For them it was a solemn moment, the opportunity to swear allegiance to our country. They, too, constitute the common man who with his brain, his inventiveness, his courage, his dreams turned this forbidding continent into the greatest engine of production and distribution that man had ever conceived of.

The dukes didn't emigrate. It was the malcontent, the dreamer who dreamed of a land freed from the tyranny of kings where he could worship God as he saw fit and where his sons could walk erect freed from the scourge of poverty. For this they labored to see their dreams come true. For this they planted and seeded. For this they built roads, log cabins, and schools. And they soon grew rich. They cherished their freedom. They built cities, and their buildings towered to the skies. They invented the harvester, the automobile, the planes, they rode the skies, they walked on the moon. They give generously to the rest of the world.

Billions and billions of dollars all were animated and sustained by the noble words and philosophy of the Declaration and the Constitution. This was man's gift to man and yesterday we reaffirmed our faith in our dream.

COMMENTARIES

America Has Lost Faith—In Leadership (excerpt)
The Personal Commentary Of Dorothy Fuldheim Sr. And Jr.
From *The Lorain Journal*, September 2, 1979.

Rarely does a day pass that the newspapers don't carry a story about a political figure who is being investigated for dipping into the public till or for fraud. How greed has grown since the Vicuna coat of Harry Truman's day. The spectacle of Nixon and the Watergate gang profiting by writing books and talking on TV shows in enough to turn the entire nation cynical.

The courts agonize over the right of a criminal with nary a thought of the rights of the victim. How soon will Sirhan Sirhan and Charles Manson be paroled? How many criminals are turned loose over legal technicalities? Law and justice are not always the same especially if the accused has money.

LABOR LEADERS OFTEN draw such immense salaries that they can no longer understand the problems of their membership. And often they have questionable associates or are even accused of shooting one another.

Then there is the continuing story of the military drill instructors brutally causing the deaths of green recruits.

In Cleveland there is the remarkable mystery of where has all the money gone and who is responsible, and why can't the citizens, who after all paid in that money, get any straight answers from City Hall. The taxes got higher and the chuckholes deeper.

If all this was not enough to sour the entire land, there is the spectacle of disappearing gas lines and disappearing shortages as the price passes the dollar mark.

YES, MR. PRESIDENT, we have lost faith. But in our leaders, and the situation will not be reversed until old-fashioned character and integrity return to the leadership level of this country.

Being powerful is not enough for greatness. Nazi German[y] was powerful. The Soviet Union is powerful. The moral vision of the writers of the Constitution is our glorious heritage. If we lose it, we will go down in the ash bin of history like all the others.

DOROTHY FULDHEIM

The "Richness and Security" of Marriage
The Personal Commentary of Dorothy Fuldheim Sr. and Jr.
May 27, 1979

Some weeks ago, I interviewed Lauren Bacall. She was promoting her book, "Be Myself." It is not a great book, but it is a good book.

What is more extraordinary, it is an honest book, and so rare is an honest book that it has received enormous attention. In just one bookstore, in one day, in Cleveland, 900 copies were sold.

THERE ARE A few moving chapters in Miss Bacall's book, as when she described hearing her husband, Humphrey Bogart, welcoming their first child. When she first told him that they would have a child he was upset, fearful that it would come between them; that it would take some of her time with him away for the baby. But after the baby was brought home, Miss Bacall says she heard Bogart in the baby's room looking down on the infant in the crib.

It was Bogart's first child. He was 47 years old and had been married twice before. "You are only a little fellow, aren't you?" he whispered. "Welcome home, I'm father." Words that make one choke up with emotion.

In the interview I asked Miss Bacall if she was thinking of marrying again. Sadly and ironically she answered, "Who gets married these days? Everyone just does their thing."

She had had a bizarre experience with Sinatra, who had helped her through the first years after Humphrey's death, who planned to marry her and then left her, as it were, at the church door. She described Sinatra's conduct by the use of one noun—a four-letter word which ordinarily offends me, but in this case it took a vigorous obscenity to describe Sinatra's conduct.

Marriage has been tested for many centuries, and it has stood firm like the Rock of Gibralter until this generation. It is being chipped away, assaulted, ridiculed, ignored, cheapened, but it still stands as the one great moral shelter in our lives.

IT IS TRUE that bearing a child outside of marriage is no longer the disgrace it used to be. No longer would a famous actress be publicly insulted as was Sara Bernhardt who was announced by the butler at a reception as Mademoiselle and son.

Today the Ms. does away with the Miss or Mrs. No longer is a family disgraced by a daughter who though not married is having a baby. In the past it may have been annoying to have a son father a child outside of marriage, but never the disgrace as when such a thing happened to a daughter. And it's about time. Just as it is unreasonable to arrest a prostitute who is selling her wares, but not the male who is the buyer. Injustices are being wiped out.

But doing one's thing instead of getting married is no substitute for the richness and security of marriage. Life is a lonely business at best. We are each imprisoned by our own natures. In marriage, there is a touching of heart and of soul. In marriage the husband knows that his happiness, his strength, is guarded by the woman who is his wife, while she knows that he is her security, her strength, that their fates are entwined and that she is first in his concern and he is in hers.

It is an intertwining of destinies. If there are children, it is the fruit of some sweet and sublime hour. A child is (or should be) the blossom of a moment of exquisite tenderness. There is a holiness to such fruition, and in marriage there is also the protective quality.

ONE MAY BE cynical and skeptical of marriage. So many are dismal relationships. What once was beautiful, may become a burden and end in divorce, for not all human relationships are perfect.

But for those who experience a happy marriage, for those who know the joy of looking into the eyes of a trusting child, who draw the blanket over the young body to keep it warm during the night, for those who turn to the shelter of the arms of one's lover, know the comfort of "doing one's thing" in the security of marriage and permanence.

This copy from the archives is from the *Lorain Journal* dated August 12, 1979 from the Fuldheim column, "The Personal Commentary of Dorothy Fuldheim Sr. And Jr." The commentary was originally aired on WEWS-TV on Dorothy Fuldheim's eighty-sixth birthday. The station received more than fifteen thousand requests for reprints.

THIS OLD HOUSE HAS BEEN GOOD TO ME

The house I lived in is 86 years old.

It has lost some of its original color, much of the red and pink is gone, and the white is not as white as it used to be. It doesn't stand quite as straight—it seems to have sunk a little and sometimes it tilts slightly. But its heating apparatus, its disposal plant, its illuminating system all are functioning remarkably well.

It has talked with many people all over the world—from Chinese cooks to the priests of Bangkok. The house I live in traveled extensively and still does, though more infrequently. It has been fanned by the perfumed winds of Hawaii, and made thirsty by the deserts. It has tasted of the good of all people—from the Scandinavian to the Hindu food.

ITS WINDOWS HAVE looked upon God's earth—from the villages in Spain to the glories of French art; it has looked out on the Swiss mountains and the Russian steppes. Through these windows my house gazed into the heavens and once watched the first human step out into space and walk on the moon.

That house, which I inhabit, has heard music singing the sonorous sound of the great masters—from Bach to Ravel. That house has talked to the great and the insignificant, to the world-famous individuals and to humble people.

My house has rumbled with delight and been shaken with laughter at the Bob Hopes and the Jack Bennys of the world, and the gaiety of my friends over the years.

That house has look upon Albert Einstein, and felt the warmth of his handshake. My house, that I inhabit, has known the sweetness of tender love and been torn with stormy, glorious and ecstatic passion.

My house has been with friends and known quiet smiles and serenity, and torn with sobs for friends who left this strange and absorbing planet, even as you and I must someday, but whose memory is stored in the computer which runs my house.

THIS HOUSE HAS known agony, and has been repaired by specialists so that it is whole again, able to withstand any storms. Sometimes the house creaks as though old, but always it has stood sturdy and staunch, withstanding pain, storm, snow and rain.

It has stored away secrets revealed to it, and treasured. The attic is full of memories, someday in a leisure hour to be taken out and remembered.

Its brain is its most important room, for here are to be found new ideas, concepts, contents of books, philosophies, poems, the treasures of the world in print, and been awed by knowledge of the expanding universe. It is like an expanding library—each new idea creates more room for other ideas. It is the one room in my house that attests to my relationship with divinity.

In another chamber, known as the heart room, are all the loves, the compassion, the hurts, the triumphs, the exquisite passions for those I love. This is a sacred room, for its has known happiness and sorrow. Its colors are radiant yellows and golds, somber greys and blues.

I look at the house and I see an aging house, needing a coat of paint, but covered with the bushes and trees of experience, willing to stand sturdy for more years.

EIGHTY-SIX YEARS ago my parents gave me a deed to this house with the understanding that I use it and enrich it. I have done so, and I think that on this day it deserves my thanks for giving my spirit a resting place where I could see and hear and feel and love and learn.

It is a house now crammed with many memories, but still stands staunch and valiant waiting the years until it must finally be closed with a sign saying, "SOLD TO GOD."

DOROTHY FULDHEIM

From *The Cleveland Press*, Wednesday, December 3, 1980

DOROTHY FULDHEIM'S TRIBUTE TO HER DAUGHTER
The following tribute to her late daughter was delivered by Dorothy Fuldheim on Channel 5 on Monday. Like her audience, The Press was deeply touched by it and is printing it for those who missed it—or would want to hear it again.

I would like to thank my many friends and viewers who expressed their sorrow at my loss. It is irretrievable. Much of my happiness was dependent on my daughter, Dorothy, who made my days and my years rich with affection and laughter.

She was full of grace, and she lived her life with both grace and felicity. She was tender and quick with understanding and sympathy. She was proud, too proud, to ever engage in anything but integrity and beauty. She drank in life with greed. Every sound of music, every challenging idea, every drama, all new ideas in the scientific world won her interest. She looked upon life as a rich garden, and the perfume of life intoxicated her with great excitement.

She lived fully as an aristocrat—one of the noble ones of life. Life to her was a gift, and she wore it proudly and appreciatively. Her death has not only saddened me, but I will never be whole again.

I told her daughter, Halla, my granddaughter, that we all have an appointment with God. My daughter received her summons last Monday. I told Halla that her mother was in heaven and was free of all pain and that someday she and I would join her.

She said, "Will you be there?" I nodded. "And will God make you young again? Will my mother be without pain? And when I go to meet her, will I walk without braces and crutches?"

She reflected and then asked, "How did my mother get to heaven?" "God sent a messenger," I responded. "We all have our appointment in Samarra."

Hers was too soon, and I am left with an enormous loneliness. But while she lived she graced life. Those who knew her shared her warmth, understanding, and her enormous loyalty. She was gallant and heroic and took her anguishes quietly, with no reproaches against fate—a true aristocrat in spirit.

She was blessed with an incomparable intellect. She was a gift given to me, and for those of you who have walked in the valley of anguish, and for those of you who must someday walk through that valley, as all of us must, our tears will join and the sun will never shine as brightly as it once did for me. The sound of her voice, the music of her laughter are now denied to me.

Notes

1
"Everyone Ought to Have Been Born Poor"

15   A GREAT WALL SEPARATED Dorothy Fuldheim, *I Laughed, I Cried, I Loved,* Cleveland: The World Publishing Co., 1966), 1.
NO ONE WHO HAS Ibid.
EVERYONE OUGHT TO Mary Strassmeyer, "A Monument Named Dorothy," *The Cleveland Plain Dealer Magazine,* May 9, 1976.

16   THE MORNING SUN Dorothy Fuldheim, *Three and a Half Husbands,* (New York: Simon and Schuster, 1976), 9-10.
TEA IS GOOD Ibid., 23.
SO WHAT SHOULD I Ibid., 16.

17   DON'T WALK STRAIGHT Ibid., 37.

18   BEGAN HER PROMENADE Dorothy Fuldheim, *A Thousand Friends,* (New York: Doubleday & Co., 1974), 8.

19   SHE WAS A QUEEN BUT Greg Olsen, interview with author, Rocky River, Ohio, May 15, 1996.

20   AT AN OPENING DAY William Hickey, "The Redhead Sets a Record," *The Cleveland Plain Dealer Magazine,* October 1, 1972, 6.
WITH MUCH WISDOM Samuel H. Miller, interview with author, Cleveland, Ohio, March 23, 1996.

2
Growing Up in Milwaukee

21   DOROTHY REMEMBERED Fuldheim, *I Laughed, I Cried, I Loved,* 7-8.

22   I LEARNED FROM THIS EARLY Ibid., 10
TO FILL AN HOUR Ibid., 152
FOR MY FATHER, GOOD Fuldheim, *Three and a Half Husbands,* 92.

23   I LEARNED THE POWER "Tribute: Great Moments in the Life of Dorothy Fuldheim" WEWS-TV, tape #4053.
THE POWER OF WORDS Fuldheim, *Three and a Half Husbands,* 92.
SOMEDAY YOU WILL HAVE Fuldheim, *I Laughed, I Cried, I Loved,* 3.
DOROTHY LATER WROTE Ibid.

24   ALICE ROOSEVELT WAS "TR: The Story of Theodore Roosevelt." Public Broadcasting System, WVIZ-TV, October 7, 1996.

25   THEN TO THIS EARTHEN Edward Fitzgerald, trans. *Rubáiyát of Omar Khayyám, First Edition,* (New York: Crowell, 1964), XXXIV, LX, LII.

26   DOROTHY WROTE THAT Fuldheim, *I Laughed, I Cried, I Loved,* 12.
      SHE ATE AND DRANK Emily Dickinson, *Poems,* (Cleveland: Fine Editions Press, 1947), 47.
      HER AUNT MOLLY, DOROTHY Fuldheim, *Three and a Half Husbands,* 9.

27   ALTHOUGH THE POPULATION Anthony M. Orum, *City-Building in America,* (Boulder: Westview Press 1995), statistics quoted from U.S. Bureau of Census, 79.
      RECORDS SHOW THAT Golda Meir, *My Life,* (New York: G.P. Putnam's Sons 1975), 53.
      DOROTHY'S CLOSE FRIEND Miller, interview.
      HAD THEY BEEN CLOSER Meir, *My Life,* 87.

28   OF GREAT INFLUENCE Fuldheim, *I Laughed, I Cried, I Loved,* 10.

3

From the Schoolroom to the Stage

29   I HAVE NEVER FOUND. *The Echo,* Yearbook of the Milwaukee Normal School, 1912, 58
      A RESIDENT OF *Bulletin of the State Normal School,* (Milwaukee: J.S. Bletcher & Co., 1912.

30   PREPARATION FOR TEACHING Ibid.
      BECAUSE OF THE LARGE "Dorothy Fuldheim: How She Got into Television," WEWS-TV. August 12, 1987.
      IN 1910 THREE-FOURTHS Robert W. Wells, *This is Milwaukee,* (Garden City: Doubleday, 1970), 182.

31   THE FIRST MONEY I EARNED Fuldheim, *I Laughed, I Cried, I Loved,* 15.
      THE SCHOOL BOARD, HEADED Ibid.

32   HIS GOAL WAS TO MAKE Wells, Ibid.
      I WANDERED LONELY AS William Wordsworth, "I Wandered Lonely As a Cloud," from Dudley Miles and Robert C. Pooley, *Literature and Life in England,* (Chicago: Scott Foresman and Company 1943), 397.
      GIRLS SHOULD HAVE Diana Tittle, "Fuldheim on Fuldheim," *Northern Ohio Live,* January 1982, 33.

33   THE SCHNELLS NOW HAD Fuldheim, I Laughed, I Cried, I Loved, 16.
      DOROTHY HAD SO MANY Ibid.
      I NEVER HAD A DATE Bill Barrett, "'The Theater—'That's Where I Really Belong,'" *The Cleveland Press,* May 29, 1980.
      HIS NAME WAS HERBERT David Bianculli, "Dorothy," *Beacon Magazine,* June 19, 1983, 6.
      LIFE WAS MAGNIFICENT Fuldheim, *I Laughed, I Cried, I Loved,* 16.
      BASED UPON HIS AGE Milwaukee Archives, data extracted from the 1910 Census.
      LESS IS KNOWN ABOUT Milwaukee Historical Society, information extracted from *Milwaukee City Directories, 1910–1918.*
      IN HER PINK BALLET Fuldheim, *I Laughed, I Cried, I Loved,* 9.

34   IN 1958 WHEN HER Bertha Schnell, Death notice, *The Cleveland Plain Dealer,* September 18, 1958 (from Necrology File, Cuyahoga County, Ohio Library).
      MILTON'S OCCUPATION Milwaukee Historical Society, information extracted from *Milwaukee City Directories, 1918–1920.*
      SHE WAS OUR SANCTUARY Fuldheim, *I Laughed, I Cried, I Loved,* 9
      BERTHA SCHNELL SEEMED Fuldheim, *I Laughed, I Cried, I Loved,* 4.
      WASN'T THAT WHY ONE Ibid., 5.
      FOUR DIFFERENT ADDRESSES from *Milwaukee City Directories, 1918–1923.*
      IN 1929 MRS BERTHA from *Milwaukee City Directory, 1929.*
      MY FATHER WAS A MAN OF Fuldheim, *I Laughed, I Cried, I Loved,* 4.

35   HE DID NOT DIE IN from *Milwaukee City Directories, 1922-1929.*
SHE WAS STILL LISTED AS Judith Simonsen, letter to author, April 25, 1995.
I HAD ALL THIS EMOTION William Hickey, "The Redhead Sets a Record," *The The Cleveland Plain Dealer Magazine,* October 1, 1972, 6.
ALTHOUGH SHE WROTE LATER Fuldheim, *I Laughed, I Cried, I Loved,* 16.

36   'TIS BUT THY NAME THAT IS William Shakespeare, *Romeo and Juliet,* Act II, Sc. III, (New York: Dell 1965), 57.
DECADES LATER DOROTHY Dorothy Fuldheim, *A Thousand Friends,* (Garden City: Doubleday & Co.,1974), 196.
I'M SURE I WOULD HAVE "The Redhead Sets a Record, 6."

37   FEW ACTRESS ARE INTERESTED "The Theater—'That's Where I Really Belong.'"
ALTHOUGH NOT MARXIST IN Wells, *This is Milwaukee,* 176.
THE SOCIALIST TRADITION Ibid., 178.

38   I PERCEIVE THAT YOU FAIL Ibid., 181.
IRONICALLY THE OWNERS "Floating Palaces," Arts & Entertainment Network, January 12, 1997.

4
On the Lecture Circuit

40   THE STATE WON'T LET Sada Cowan, "The State Forbids" from *Pomp and Other Plays.* (New York: Brentano's, 1926), 209-210.

41   I WAS AWED Fuldheim, *I Laughed, I Cried, I Loved,* 16.
SO I WENT TO PHILADELPHIA Terence Sheridan, "Dorothy Fuldheim and Mother News," *Cleveland Magazine,* April 1973, 48.
DOROTHY WROTE LATER Fuldheim, *I Laughed, I Cried, I Loved,* 18.
I TOLD THE AUDIENCE Ibid

42   HICKEY, WHO BY THIS TIME "The Redhead Sets a Record," 6.
THE YOUNG FULDHEIM FAMILY *City Directory of Cleveland,* 1927.
AS FINANCES ALLOWED *City Directory of Cleveland, 1951.*

43   ONE DAY I WAS WALKING "Dorothy Fuldheim and Mother News," 58.
I HAD A SENSE OF DRAMA Ibid.
ON HER WAY Taffy Epstein, interview with author, Shaker Heights, Ohio, August 8, 1996.

44   SHE CLAIMED TO READ Nancy Gallagher, "Here's Dorothy Fuldheim!" *Cleveland Press,* August 8, 1959, 33.
IT DOESN'T MATTER IF Ibid.

45   BY 1910 CLONES OF Theodore Morrison, *Chautauqua: A Center for Education, Religion, and the Arts in America.* (Chicago: University of Chicago Press, 1974), 178.

46   BRYAN'S UNEQUIVOCAL REPLY Ibid., 187.
IT WOULD TAKE A FULL "The Redhead Sets a Record." 6.

47   MANY PEOPLE UNDERRATE "Dorothy Fuldheim and Mother News," 48.
WHEN HE WAS CAMPAIGNING Fuldheim, *I Laughed, I Cried, I Loved,* 153-154.
I'M NEVER UNAWARE OF MY Mike Clary, "Durable Dorothy," *Beacon Magazine,* March 1975, 11.
AT A HIGH SCHOOL GRADUATION Mary Sidoti, conversation with author, Canton, Ohio, October 5, 1996.
AT A WHITE TIE DINNER IN Fuldheim, *I Laughed, I Cried, I Loved,* 159-160.

48   SHE PRIDED HERSELF "Durable Dorothy," 11.

5
While Storm Clouds Gathered

49   I COULD NOT FOLLOW Fuldheim, *I Laughed, I Cried, I Loved,* 58.

50   ADOLF HITLER WALKED Ibid.

51   THE JEWISH INTERNATIONAL Ibid., 59.
HE CARRIED A RIDING Ibid.
LUCKILY, HE DIDN'T EVEN "The Redhead Sets a Record," 6.

51 A 1937 NEW YORK TOWN Fuldheim, *I Laughed, I Cried, I Loved,* 156.
52 HER MOTHER NEVER Ibid., 5.
BERTHA SOMETIMES Ibid., 6.
WITH TYPICAL WRY Ibid., 46
53 AT AN AUDIENCE WITH Ibid., 49.
HIS FACE WAS STONY Ibid., 50.
WHEN HE WAS PRESENTED Ibid.
IT SHOWS HOW MANY OF Ibid.
54 SHE KNEW THAT SHE WAS Ibid., 53-54.
AFTER FINALLY HEEDING Ibid.
SEASONED WHITE HOUSE "FDR," A & E Television Network, November 1996.
55 COFFEE THAT WOULD Fuldheim, *I Laughed, I Cried, I Loved,* 160.
SHE REMEMBERS THE PRESENT Dorothy Fuldheim, "My Fondest Christmas Memory," *Elyria Chronicle-Telegram,* December 24, 1978.
56 WHEN DOROTHY STEPPED Fuldheim, *I Laughed, I Cried, I Loved,* 158-159.

6
Radio: A Brief Interlude

58 IN THE 1930'S DOROTHY Fuldheim, *A Thousand Friends,* 13.
THE SOVIETS . . . WILL Ibid., 14-15.
59 FOR THESE VIEWS SHE Ibid.
EDUCATORS HOPED SHE Ibid., 13-14.
HER FEE FOR THE YEAR Nancy Gray. "Before Barbara Walters There Was Dorothy Fuldheim," *Ms.* , December, 1976, quoted by David H.Hosley and Gayle K. Yamada in *Hard News: Women in Broadcast Journalism,* (New York: Greenwood Press, 1987), 68.
ONE DAY DOROTHY FOUND Fuldheim, *I Laughed, I Cried, I Loved,* 165.
60 WHY WON'T BLUE CROSS PAY Fuldheim, *A Thousand Friends,* 174-175.
SHE MENTIONS A SERIES Fuldheim, *I Laughed, I Cried, I Loved,* 162.
DOROTHY JUNIOR AFTER "Dorothy Fuldheim-Urman, 60," *The Cleveland Plain Dealer,* November 27, 1980.
HAL WAS THE SON OF SAMUEL *City Directory of Cleveland,* 1941.
61 THE DEATH IN THIS CASE S. R. Gerber, Coroner's Verdict #56531, Cuyahoga County, Ohio, July 25, 1944.
SHE IS THE SHADOW OVER "Here's Dorothy Fuldheim!" 33.

7
Television and Dorothy Debut in Cleveland

63 THE HUNGER AND FASCINATION Roger Brown, "Electrifying History," *Cleveland Plain Dealer,* January 7, 1996.
64 GOD, I WAS OLD. FIFTY-FOUR "Dorothy Fuldheim: How She Got into Television," WEWS-TV, August 12, 1987.
65 HER EARLY DAYS Harry F. Waters with Jon Lowell, "The First Lady of TV News," *Newsweek,* June 11, 1979, 91.
I OWED HIM [HANRAHAN] SO MUCH "The Redhead Sets a Record," 6.
THIS EPISODE SET THE TONE Russell Cook, "Dorothy Fuldheim's Activist Journalism and the Kent State Shootings," E. W. Scripps School of Journalism: Athens, Ohio, 1941, 14.
SHE SAID WHAT SHE WANTED TO James Breslin, telephone interview with author, October 3, 1996.
TO BE ABLE TO HUMANIZE Fuldheim, *A Thousand Friends,* 175.
66 DOROTHY FEELS IF THE NEWS "Here's Dorothy Fuldheim!" 33.
ONE OF THESE WAS COMEDIAN Randall Culver, interview with author, Berea, Ohio, September 26, 1996.
UNDOUBTEDLY THE MOST ROMANTIC Fuldheim, *A Thousand Friends,* 10.
67 SO FANTASTICALLY ERRONEOUS "Dorothy Fuldheim and Mother News," 60.
BUT APPARENTLY SHE Ibid.

69   NEVER I BELIEVE HAS Fuldheim, *I Laughed, I Cried, I Loved*, 188.

THE PRESS BALLOONED David Halberstam, *The Fifties*, (New York: Villard, 1993), 56.

NUMEROUS SENATORIAL CAMPAIGNS Ibid., 55.

HE CAME AND I INTERVIEWED Fuldheim, *I Laughed, I Cried, I Loved*, 198.

70   HE ATTACKED THE SENATOR'S A. M. Sperber, Murrow: His Life and Times, (New York: Freundlich Books, 1986), 438.

BECAUSE ONE MAN OF SUCH Ibid., 439.

LONELINESS THAT ACCOMPANIES Fuldheim, *I Laughed, I Cried, I Loved*, 189.

71   SOMEBODY IS GETTING AWAY Louis Seltzer, *The Years Were Good*, (Cleveland : The World Publishing Co., 1956), opposite 256.

DOROTHY ASKED ARIANE *A Thousand Friends*, 63.

72   I HAVE A SIMPLE PHILOSOPHY Fuldheim, *The Years Were Good*, 267.

THE PAPER WAS INDEPENDENT Ibid., 264-265.

73   IF I HAVE TO APOLOGIZE "Here's Dorothy Fuldheim!" 33

WEWS DID NOT SIGN ON William Hickey, "30 Years of Memories WEWS-TV," *The Cleveland Plain Dealer Magazine*, December 11, 1977, 62.

ONE EVENING AS I BEGAN Culver, interview.

74   HIS INDIVIDUALISM IS SO Fuldheim, *I Laughed, I Cried, I Loved*, 184-185.

MAY BE ALL THE AWFUL Ibid., 191.

TO HAVE A SOMEWHAT BRUSQUE Ibid., 194.

BRILLIANT BUT Fuldheim, *A Thousand Friends*, 31.

TO BE SOFT-SPOKEN, SERIOUS *I Laughed, I Cried, I Loved*, 194.

WHAT A SUPERB PICTURE Ibid., 180

IT MAKES NO DIFFERENCE Ibid., 181.

75   THE GREAT INEXTINGUISHABLE Fuldheim, *I Laughed, I Cried, I Loved*, 176.

WHAT DOES ONE SAY Ibid.

THE MOST NERVOUS AUTHOR Ibid., 196.

THERE WAS A UNITY Olsen, interview.

YOU SAID WHAT YOU Donald Perris, interview with author, Gates Mills, Ohio, April 15, 1996.

DON PERRIS WAS THE Wilma Smith, interview with author, Cleveland, Ohio, August 20, 1996.

8

The Incomparable One O'Clock Club

78   SHE NEEDED BILL Bill Gordon, telephone interview with author, November 15, 1996.

WASN'T THAT AUDIENCE Ibid.

DOROTHY WAS THE EPITOME Bill Gordon, "Dorothy," *Cleveland Magazine*, February 1990, 22.

RANDY, HOLD MY HAND Culver, interview.

SO TELL ME, MR GR-R-R-ROZA "Dorothy," *Cleveland Magazine*, 22-23.

79   HOW MANY HOME RUNS Culver, interview.

DOROTHY FULDHEIM WAS "Dorothy," *Cleveland Magazine*, 22.

80   MRS. KELLUM LIVED BY Mary Cayet, conversation with author, Middleburg Heights, Ohio, May 12, 1996.

81   THEY ALWAYS SEEMED TO LOSE Perris, interview.

JIM HANRAHAN TOLD "Here's Dorothy Fuldheim!" 33.

SHE HAD THE ABILITY Perris, interview.

A SORT OF POPULIST NOTION Gordon, interview.

DURING BILL GORDON'S Ibid.

82   THE STATION MANAGEMENT Ibid.

9

All in a Day's Work

99   SHE LIKED TO *DOONK* Culver, interview.
HER PALATE SENSED "Dorothy Fuldheim and Mother News," 50.
SHE STAYED HEALTHY *Larry King Live*, Cable News Network, in "Dorothy Fuldheim: A Great Lady, A Great Loss," WEWS-TV, November 4, 1989.
I'D PICK IT UP THERE Taffy Epstein, interview with author, August 8, 1996.

100   LOATHES EGGS AND THE HENS "Dorothy Fuldheim and Mother News," 50.
TRIED TO CONSUME A LOT Mary Strassmeyer, "A Monument Named Dorothy," *The Cleveland Plain Dealer Magazine*, May 9, 1976, 10.
WE KEEP MOTHER Jenny Crim, Interview with Dorothy Fuldheim Jr., WEWS-TV, October 29, 1979.
DOROTHY WAS QUITE CONTENT Bill Barrett, "I Don't Have Fear of Death, I Don't Think about It," *Cleveland Press*, May 28, 1980.
THESE WERE REPORTED TO BE "Here's Dorothy Fuldheim!" 33.
I RUN MY HOUSE "The Theater,— 'That's Where I Really Belong.'"
DOROTHY SHOWED SOME PIQUE Epstein, interview.
A DRIVER LOOKED IN HIS "A Monument Named Dorothy," 10.

101   GOOD MORNING, LADY Olsen, interview.
THE REDHEAD WHO ONCE "A Monument Named Dorothy," 7.
FLASHY DRESSING WAS PART Smith, interview by author.

102   SOMETHING HAPPENED WHEN Stephen Bellamy, telephone interview with author, February 24, 1997.
DOROTHY DETESTED SLACKS "The Theater, 'That's Where I Really Belong.'"
I LIKE ONLY LARGE ROMANTIC Fuldheim, *I Laughed, I Cried, I Loved*, 154.
SHE WAS NEVER WITHOUT Smith, interview.
WHAT A FLAIR HE HAD Fuldheim, *I Laughed, I Cried, I Loved*, 19.
I OFTEN WONDERED WHY "Dorothy Fuldheim and Mother News," 58.
I WAS PAGED TO COME TO Smith, interview with author.

103   I DO 10 A WEEK AND EACH "A Monument Named Dorothy, 7.
HOW DO I DO IT David Bianculli, "Dorothy," *Beacon*, June 19, 1983, n.p.
SHE ALWAYS KNEW MORE Perris, interview.
FURTHER EVIDENCE THAT Fred Griffith, interview with author, Cleveland, Ohio, August 20, 1996.

104   THE GLUE PERSON WHO HOLDS Perris, interview.
I ALWAYS THOUGHT THE BEST Ted Ocepek, telephone interview with author, October 28, 1997.
WHEN I PUT SOMETHING "I Don't Have Fear of Death."
THERE ARE DAYS WHEN Ibid.

105   IT'S QUITE A TRICK "Durable Dorothy," 8.
DOROTHY KNEW HOW TO Joel Rose, telephone interview with author, November 21, 1996.
SOME CRITICIZED HER "Durable Dorothy," 10.

106   I'M SUPPOSED TO BE Fuldheim, *I Laughed, I Cried, I Loved*, 181.
BY THE WAY, WHAT DO YOU J. Breslin, Culver, interviews.
I ALWAYS ENJOYED WATCHING Congressman Louis Stokes, letter to author, July 29, 1996.

107   THE INTERVIEW WITH YOU John H. Chafee, letter to Dorothy Fuldheim, February 2, 1972, The Dorothy Fuldheim Papers, Kent State University Special Collections, Kent, Ohio.
I ENJOYED THE INTERVIEW Senator Hubert H. Humphrey, letter to Dorothy Fuldheim, January 29, 1969, The Dorothy Fuldheim Papers.
RARELY HAVE I BEEN Nelson A. Rockefeller, Governor of New York, letter to Dorothy Fuldheim, October 4, 1973, The Dorothy Fuldheim Papers.

107   I REALLY ADMIRED HER Bishop Anthony M.Pilla, telephone interview with author, August 13, 1996.

108   AND THIS IS WHY I'm no phoney, you know," "Durable Dorothy," 11.
FIRST OF ALL, I CHARM Ibid.
SHE TREATED EVERYONE THE J. Breslin, interview.
I FEEL LIKE A CORNED BEEF Olsen, interview.
ONE DAY DOROTHY WAS ON THE J. Breslin, interview.

109   LINDA OF SOLON General references to miscellaneous correspondence, Kent State Special Collections.
URGING HER TO DO ANOTHER Diane Cleaver to Dorothy Fuldheim.
January 19, 1973, The Dorothy Fuldheim Papers.
ASKING HER TO DO A Cuyahoga County commissioner Seth Taft to Dorothy Fuldheim September 14, 1973, The Dorothy Fuldheim Papers.
LETTERS ON FILE FROM Rex Humbard to Dorothy Fuldheim, August 31,1973 and November, 1973, n.d.,The Dorothy Fuldheim Papers.

110   THANKING HER FOR HER Tony Poderis to Dorothy Fuldheim,
February 11, 1974, The Dorothy Fuldheim Papers.
NOW WHY IN THE Tony Poderis, conversation with author, January 8,1997.
IF SHE WERE Richard Gildenmeister, interview with author, March 28, 1997.
SHE WOULD GO ANYWHERE Miller, interview.
TINY DOROTHY FULDHEIM ARRIVE Chris Bade, conversation with author, April 16, 1996.

111   WITH THE HEAT AND Ibid.
COMPLAINED VIGOROUSLY "Dorothy Fuldheim and Mother News," 54.
SHE DIDN'T WANT TO DRESS Diana Tittle, "Fuldheim on Fuldheim," *Northern Ohio Live,* January 1982, 32.
HER CLASSES IN RUSSIAN "Dorothy Fuldheim-Urman, 60," *The Cleveland Plain Dealer,* November 27, 1980.
IT'S SATISFACTORY. IF I Jenny Crim, interview with Dorothy Fuldheim, Jr.

112   SOMETIMES HER MOTHER WOULD J. Breslin, interview
SHE AND HER MOTHER ALTERNATED Dick McLaughlin, "The Other Dorothy Fuldheim," *The Cleveland Press,* April 30, 1980.
THE THINKING MAN'S REDHEAD *Lorain Journal,* May 12, 1979.
IF THERE IS ONE THING THAT I Laughed, I Cried, I Loved, 153.
TO BE ENTERTAINING AS WELL George Steinbrenner to Dorothy Fuldheim June 26, 1973.

113   BUT NOT WELL ENOUGH TO "Durable Dorothy," 20.

10

The Fuldheim Phenomenon

114   AN ELDERLY WOMAN SHE Johnny Carson, "The Tonight Show," interview with Dorothy Fuldheim, NBC-TV, October 10, 1977.
SHE DIDN'T WORK BECAUSE "Fuldheim on Fuldheim," 32.

115   WHEN DOROTHY ENTERTAINED Miller, interview; Rose, interview.
SHE REFUSED A SUGGESTION *The Cleveland Plain Dealer Rotogravure Magazine,* July 6, 1958, n.p.
BERTHA SCHNELL DIED THE Death notice, Bertha Schnell, *Cleveland Plain Dealer,* September 18, 1958.
DOROTHY FULDHEIM WAS THE "Dorothy Fuldheim, TV News Legend, Dies."

116   SUM UP HER TOWERING *Hard News: Women in Broadcast Journalism,* 70.
IN THOSE EARLY YEARS SHE Gioia Diliberto, "Profiles of Three Newswomen," Master's thesis, University of Maryland, 1975, quoted in *Hard News,* 64.
PAULINE HAS BEEN DOING *Current Biography, 1954,* 293, quoted from *New York World-Telegram & Sun,* March 12, 1954.
A TALL, LISSOME BRUNETTE Ibid., 292
EVENTUALLY PAULINE *Hard News,* 65.

117   IF PAULINE FREDERICK Ibid.

117   GOD IS NOT BLESSING *Dorothy Fuldheim*, interview with Danny Thomas, WEWS-TV, February 8, 1978.

118   WHEN JUNKETING AUTHORS Griffith, interview.

119   LIKE MONET AND DOROTHY Ibid.

       TELL ME, I ASKED HIM Fuldheim, *A Thousand Friends*, 60-61.

120   I ASKED HERR Phil Donahue, interview with Dorothy Fuldheim, *Donahue*, ABC Television Network, May 15, 1984.

       THE FORMER NAZI OFFICIAL Ibid.

       WITHIN THE INFANT William Shakespeare, *Romeo and Juliet*, Act II, Sc. III, (New York: Dell, 1965), 57.

121   ABSOLUTELY NOT SHE Dorothy Fuldheim, *Where Were the Arabs?* (Cleveland: The World Publishing Company, 1967), 16-17.

122   I WAS TORN WITH Ibid., 45-46

123   MILLER WHOSE PARENTS HAD "Israel Honors Miller, Son of a Junk Peddler," *Cleveland Plain Dealer*, December 30, 1975.

124   MILLER HAS BEEN TWICE Ibid.

       SUFFERING HAS NO POLITICAL "A Letter to a Friend," *Cleveland Plain Dealer*, June 26, 1996.

       THE SAME FIRE IN THE BELLY Miller, interview.

       I DON'T KNOW MUCH ABOUT Ibid.

       DOROTHY AND I BECAME Miller, interview.

125   HE [MILLER] HAS THAT "A Letter to a Friend."

       SHE WAS MUCH MORE Perris, interview.

       SHE GREW UP IN Ibid.

126   THE PREMISES FROM WHICH Judith Reisman, "A Rhetorical Analysis of Dorothy Fuldheim's Television Commentaries." Case Western Reserve University, Ph.D. dissertation 1979, 61.

       SHE SUPPORTED THE POSITION Fuldheim, *I Laughed, I Cried, I Loved*, 193.

11

Another Side of Dorothy

127   SHE HAD NO PERIOD Miller, interview.

128   MY MOTHER LIVED Fuldheim, *I Laughed, I Cried, I Loved*, 7.

       SHE WAS AN INVALID Jean Bellamy, telephone interview with author, February 19, 1997.

       HER MOTHER'S VISITING Fuldheim, *I Laughed, I Cried, I Loved*, 6.

       BERTHA WAS THEIR Ibid., 9.

129   AT ONE TIME "Milton H. Fuldheim Dies," *Cleveland Press*, August 8, 1952.

       MY FATHER WAS A Dick McLaughlin, "The Other Dorothy Fuldheim." *Cleveland Plain Dealer*, April 3, 1980.

       BECAUSE OF HER AVERSION J. Bellamy, telephone interview.

       HE WAS AN AGREEABLE "W. L. Ulmer, Husband of Dorothy Fuldheim," Cleveland Press, January 19, 1971.

       STEPHEN AND HIS Stephen Bellamy, telephone interview with author, February 24, 1997.

       THE BELLAMY CHILDREN J. Bellamy, S. Bellamy, telephone interviews.

130   SHE TOLD OF MEETING "Dorothy Fuldheim and Mother News," 60.

       HE WOULD I THINK Fuldheim, *I Laughed, I Cried, I Loved*, 189.

131   ANOTHER MAN, WHOM Fuldheim, *A Thousand Friends*, 2.

       A CLOSE FRIEND SAYS Epstein, interview.

       DOROTHY THOUGHT SHE Miller, interview

       WHEN SHE WOULD ARRIVE Epstein, interview.

       THERE WERE TWO THINGS "The Theater—'That's Where I Really Belong.'"

132   WHEN THIS NEWS AIRED Epstein, interview.

0# NOTES

MY FRIEND WENT INTO Ibid.

133   DOROTHY HAD ALREADY Ibid.

MY DAUGHTER'S DEATH "Dorothy," Beacon, 33.

ITS DOROTHY ISNT Gildenmeister, interview.

AFTER SOME TIME Miller, interview.

134   I TOLD HER [HALLA] "Dorothy Fuldheim's Tribute to Her Daughter," The Cleveland Press, December 3, 1980. Samarra reference to works by W. Somerset Maugham and John O'Hara.

MUCH OF MY HAPPINESS Ibid.

I AM LIKE A TREE Gildenmeister, interview.

12
"You Are Nine Feet Tall"

135   THE GUARDSMEN ATTEMPTED "4 Killed, 10 Hurt at KSU as Students, Guards Clash, The Cleveland Plain Dealer, May 5, 1970.

DURING THE WEEKEND RHODES "Nightmare at Kent State," The Cleveland Plain Dealer, May 5, 1970.

136   THERE WERE NO GUNS Fuldheim, A Thousand Friends, 75-76.

137   NINETY-FIVE PERCENT Ibid., 76.

PERRIS NEVER HEDGED Ibid., 77.

SHE CAME TO ME THAT "Dorothy Fuldheim and Mother News," 52.

IT ACTUALLY ALL DIED Perris, interview.

138   INVESTIGATIONS INTO THE James A. Michener, Kent State: What Happened and Why, (New York: Random House, 1971), 520-533.

THE STUDENT PROTESTERS "Fuldheim on Fuldheim," 32.

EVEN AN ACCUSED Fuldheim, A Thousand Friends, 75.

WHEN I RETURNED FROM "A Monument Named Dorothy."

139   I MAY HAVE HAD THREE Attributed to Dorothy Fuldheim.

140   THE INCREDIBLE MOLLY Jerome Robbins, book jacket of Three and a Half Husbands.

A DELICIOUS FIRST Alvin Beam, "Molly the Merry, and the Marryer," The Cleveland Plain Dealer, November 28, 1975.

HE WROTE THE "Mary, Mary," The Cleveland Plain Dealer, March 3, 1988.

I SQUIRM AT CRITICISM "Dorothy Fuldheim: 'I Don't Have Fear of Death.'"

141   A POLITICAL STATEMENT OF Elyria Chronicle-Telegram, March 22, 1980.

EACH OF THE PERPETRATORS The Cleveland Plain Dealer, June 21, 1980.

142   WHAT REALLY GRIPED ME Morning Exchange, Fred Griffith, interview with Dorothy Fuldheim, WEWS-TV, March 22, 1980.

THAT WAS A TERRIBLE Jim Marino, "Dorothy: 'I Thought Everyone Loved Me,'" The Cleveland Plain Dealer, March 21, 1980.

HOW STUPID, DOROTHY Ibid.

A BIGGER FIELD "The Theater—'That's Where I Really Belong.'"

ALTHOUGH AT AGE EIGHTY-NINE William Hickey, "Dorothy Fuldheim Gets 3-Year Contract, Raise," The Cleveland Plain Dealer, March 30, 1983.

NETWORKS DID MAKE Perris, interview.

THE PENSION WAS Miller, interview.

SHE WAS FEARFUL THAT Miller, Perris, interviews.

143   HOW DOES IT FEEL "Durable Dorothy," 10.

144   SHE REFUSED OFFERS "Larry King Live," Quoted in Cook, 9

MANY TIMES SHE Perris, interview, November 30, 1990, quoted in Cook, 14.

IN THE FINAL DAYS OF David D. Van Tassel and John J. Grabowski., eds. The Encyclopedia of Cleveland History, 2nd Edition. (Bloomington: Indiana University Press, 1996), 352.

145   DOROTHY COULD HAVE Griffith, interview.

13
One of a Kind—In Living Color

146 SHE WAS A FIGHTER Smith, interview.
146 MISS FULDHEIM ALWAYS Perris, interview.
SHE CARED FOR Olsen, interview.
163 HAS DONE SOME 2,200 Griffith, interview.
ACKNOWLEDGED IN THE *Encyclopedia of Cleveland History*, 1058.
A WONDERFUL, ELEGANT Griffith, interview.
164 FUN AND LOVELY TO Smith, interview.
AT ABOUT 4:30 Perris, Olsen, interviews.
SHE HAD A CANNY WAY Perris, interview.
SHE TOOK US ON Olsen, interview.
ONE DAY PERRIS Ibid.
CLAIMS HE WAS Ocepek, interview.
165 OCEPEK TELLS OF Ibid.
SHE HAD GIVEN Ibid.
166 SHE COULD BE A Rose, interview.
IF YOU MADE A DOORMAT Ocepek, interview.
WHAT ARE YOU DOING WITH Roger Brown, "The Man Behind the Camera,"
The Cleveland Plain Dealer, April 14, 1996.
167 EVEN WITH HER "Dorothy Fuldheim and Mother News,"49.
A NEW LIGHT SHOWED Ibid.
MISS FULDHEIM HAD Perris, interview.
SHE WAS WELL LIKED Culver, interview.
168 A STEEL FIST IN A Griffith, interview.
SHE WAS INSANELY Rose, telephone interview.
THE ICON OF ICONS Smith, interview.
SHE DID INTERVIEW J. Breslin, telephone interview.
169 I WAS HUMBLED IN Fuldheim, *I Laughed, I Cried, I Loved*, 194.
BECAME FRIENDS FOREVER June Kosich, letter to the author, August 3, 1996.
DOROTHY FULDHEIM WAS Ibid.

14
The Lady Speaks Her Mind

170 I'M ALWAYS FOR THE "Fuldheim on Fuldheim," 32.
SHE REALIZED THE EASY Perris, Ibid.
171 YOU EITHER CAMPED WITH Olsen, Ibid.
I AM INTELLECTUALLY "Dorothy Fuldheim: A Great Lady..."
WEWS-TV, November 4, 1989.
THEY'RE ENTITLED "The Theater—'That's Where I Belong.'"
JOHNNY CARSON ASKED *The Tonight Show*, interview with Dorothy
Fuldheim, NBC Television Network, October 7, 1977.
ON SCHOOL PRAYER "The Theater—'That's Where I Belong.'"
IN A DECADE WE Dorothy Fuldheim, Commentary, "Responsibility of Free
Accessibility of Guns," WEWS-TV, May 16, 1972.
172 STEVE I KNOW Stephen Bellamy, telephone interview. Many young Americans did
leave the country rather than fight in Viet Nam. They were later granted amnesty by
President Gerald Ford. Bellamy, as a conscientious objector, chose to serve his country
in a noncombat military role. His account of Dorothy Fuldheim's advice to him first
appeared in *Cleveland Free Times*, October 28, 1992.
173 TODAY'S TELEVISION NEWS Griffith, interview.
DOROTHY IS THE BEST MAN "Dorothy Fuldheim and Mother News," 60.
ONCE BEING IN THE BACK OF "The Redhead Sets a Record," 6.
I DON'T KNOW WHAT MY "Dorothy Fuldheim: A Great Lady..."
ONE YEAR I VOTE Ibid.

174 I WANT TO BE RICH *The Tonight Show,* interview with Dorothy Fuldheim, NBC Television Network, October 7, 1977.
I COULD HAVE *Donahue,* interview with Dorothy Fuldheim, ABC Television Network, May 15, 1984.
SHE FOUND PRESIDENT *Akron Beacon Journal,* February 28, 1974.

174 MR CARTER, ACT NOW Dorothy Fuldheim, Sr. and Jr., "Carter's Dillydallying Confuses Us," *Lorain Journal,* November 18, 1979.
ONE OF HER FAVORITES "Dorothy Fuldheim: A Great Lady..."
OH, HOW I WISH HE "Dorothy Fuldheim: Ninetieth Birthday," WEWS-TV, June 23, 1983.
SHE HAD ATTACKED "Fuldheim on Fuldheim." 32.
NOTHING HAD BEEN PROVED Joe Blundo, *Kent Stater,* "Fuldheim—Witty, Astute," May 17, 1974.
I BELIEVE YOU BUT Joan Rice, "Answer to a Shrinking Violet Pulls No Punches," *Akron Beacon-Journal,* February 28, 1974.

175 THE CHARACTER OF A Ibid.
WE HAVE LOST FAITH Dorothy Fuldheim, Sr. and Jr., *The Lorain Journal,* September 2, 1979.
SHE'D RIP THOSE Miller, interview.
CONTEMPORARY LEADERS HAVE "Dorothy Fuldheim: A Great Lady..."

176 TO FORCE WORKERS TO Dorothy Fuldheim, "Commentary: Mandatory Retirement" WEWS-TV, October 13, 1975.
AMERICA'S PREOCCUPATION "Donahue," interview with Dorothy Fuldheim, May 15, 1984.
EVERY SO OFTEN "Dorothy," *Beacon Magazine,* 6.

15

"Searching . . . Searching"

177 WHO AM I *A Thousand Friends,* 82.
SCIENCE IS A FIELD "Dorothy," *Beacon Magazine,* 7.
HER IDEA OF A BEDTIME Epstein, interview.

178 MAN WAS ENCUMBERED "Dorothy," *Beacon Magazine,* 7.
MY DOG DOESN'T Ibid.
SHE COULDN'T REST Perris, interview.
SHE LISTED HIS ASSETS Fuldheim, *I Laughed, I Cried, I Loved,* 197.
SHE HAD TO UNDERSTAND Bishop Pilla, telephone interview.

179 BUT HERR SPEER Fuldheim, *A Thousand Friends,* 61.
THIS WONDERFUL Ibid., 81
CITES JESUS CHRIST Ibid., 80.
THERE IS A MADDENING Ibid., 81.

180 RELIGION HAS COME Walter Isaacson, "In Search of the Real Bill Gates," *Time,* January 13, 1997, 57.
EVIDENCE OF THINGS *The Holy Bible,* Hebrews 11: 1.
WILL WE FIND OUT THE "Dorothy Fuldheim," interview with Sister Bernadette Vetter, WEWS-TV, May 1, 1985.

181 YOU MEAN DO I BELIEVE "The Theater—'That's Where I Really Belong.'"
MOSTLY SHE WANTED TO TALK Bishop Pilla, telephone interview.

182 YOU KNOW I DEPERATELY Ibid.
SHE DID NOT DENY THE Olsen, interview.
SHE ALWAYS LOOKED FOR Culver, interview.
YES I BELIEVE IN Culver, interview.
SOMEWHERE IN SPACE Fuldheim, *A Thousand Friends,* 82
ONE OF THE MOST TERRIFYING "Durable Dorothy," 20.

183 I AM NOT PREOCCUPIED "Dorothy Fuldheim: 'I Don't Have Fear of Death, I Don't Think About It.'"

I AM FREE OF THAT "Durable Dorothy, 20.

GOD IS AN ENTITY Ibid.

AND I DON'T THINK "The Theater—'That's Where I Really Belong.'"

WHAT DOTH THE LORD *The Holy Bible:* Micah 6:8.

183   THE NEW TESTAMENT WHICH Lord Godfrey Rathbone Benson Charnwood, quoted by Paul Angle, *The Lincoln Reader.* (New York: Holt, 1947), 493-495.

184   SHE HELD HER MOTHER IN Fuldheim, *I Laughed, I Cried, I Loved,* 7.

IF YOU KEEP A PERSON Olsen, interview.

WHEN NEIGHBORS Epstein, interview.

THE UNNAMED FRIEND Fuldheim, *A Thousand Friends,* 4-5.

185   TOTAL ACCESSIBILITY TO Perris, interview.

SISTER JEAN AND ANOTHER J. Bellamy, telephone interview.

CARING FOR HALLA REQUIRED Epstein, interview.

SHE PROVIDED FINANCIALLY, Marcia Myers, " Fuldheim, 'I'm Locked Up Against My Will,'" *The Lorain Journal,* January 17, 1985.

EVENTUALLY DOROTHY LEFT Miller, interview.

[LIFE] HAS CHISELED ME "Dorothy Fuldheim and Mother News," 50.

16
Required: A Sense of Morality

186   THE DAY WE IGNORE Dorothy Fuldheim, Interview with Peter Jennings, December 10, 1983.

A NEWSPERSON MUST HAVE Ibid.

MOM FORFY HEIM Comment, unidentified patron at Cuyahoga County, Ohio, Library, Fairview Park Branch, December, 1996.

187   THE BABY BOOMERS Comments, Nick Bogojevich, Craig Peck, Brian Tomek, et al.

188   WITH THE ENORMOUS IMPACT Fuldheim, *A Thousand Friends,* 71-72.

THE YIPPIES NOMINATED *This Fabulous Century 1960-1970,* (Alexandria, Virginia: Time-Life Books, 1970), 173.

I THREW JERRY Fuldheim, *A Thousand Friends,* 69-70.

189   THE TELEVISION SCREEN "Tribute: Great Moments in the Life of Dorothy Fuldheim," WEWS-TV.

I DIDN'T KNOW THAT "Here's Dorothy Fuldheim!" 33.

190   A NON-APPEARANCE BY "Dorothy Fuldheim and Mother News," 54.

MENTALLY NAUSEATED I'M Fuldheim, *A Thousand Friends,* 71.

COUNTLESS SKETCHES AND "Dorothy Fuldheim and Mother News," 54.

191   SHE OPPOSED NUDITY Ibid.

IT WAS THE MALCONTENT Dorothy Fuldheim, "Commentary: The Declaration of Independence and The Constitution," WEWS-TV, July 5, 1976.

192   ONLY ELEVEN PERCENT Marlene Sanders, *Waiting for Prime Time* (Champaign/Urbana: University of Illinois Press, 1988), 168.

BY 1987 THIRTY-EIGHT PERCENT Daniel Paisner, *The Inside Stories of Television Newswomen.* (New York: William Morrow & Co., 1989), 23.

193   GOOD LOOKS ON CAMERA *TV Guide,* "Barbara Walters: Two Decades at the Top." April 27, 1996, 26.

IT IS A FACT OF LIFE "Requiem for TV's Gender Gap?" *Time,* August 22, 1983.

TELEVISION AS AN INDUSTRY "Smoke in the Eye." Frontline, WGBH Educational Foundation, www.wgbh.org

194   WE JUST HAVE TO LIVE "Larry King Live," Cable News Network, interview with Barbara Walters, June 20, 1996.

NEWS PRESENTERS SHOULD

JOHN CHANCELLOR ECHOED Neil Hickey, "Chancellor: Retiring but Not Silenced." *TV Guide,* July 17, 1993, 33.

THIS AS AFFECTING Neil Hickey, "Chancellor: Retiring, but Not Silenced, *TV Guide,* July 17, 1993.

CHANCELLOR SEES IT John Chancellor and Walter R. Mears, *The New News Business,* (New York: HarperCollins, 1995), 84.

HE DID NOT WRITE Ibid.

195   THE GODS MUST BE PLAYING Joan Rice, "She's the Answer to a Shrinking Violet Pulls No Punches," *Akron Beacon Journal*, February 28, 1974.

PENSIONS WERE ESTABLISHED Dorothy Fuldheim, "Commentary:Mandatory Retirement," WEWS-TV, October 13, 1975.

196   THE MAIN LINES OF ARGUMENT Reisman, "A Critical Analysis of the Dorothy Fuldheim's Television Commentaries," 60.

PREDICTED THE COMPUTER Alvin Toffler, *The Third Wave,* (New York: Bantam Books), 161-162.

EVENING NETWORK NEWS Robert Lichter, quoted by David Bauder, "NBC Showing Gains Against ABC News," *Cleveland Plain Dealer*, January 10, 1997.

17

Before the Sunset

197   FRIENDS FORMED A *Dorothy Fuldheim*. Ninetieth Birthday. June 27, 1983, tape #4018.

198   I HOPE IT'S OK Ted Koppel, interview with Dorothy Fuldheim, *Nightline*, ABC-TV. Segment taped at WEWS-TV, June 20, 1984.

THE INTERVIEW WENT Bill Kozel, telephone interview, March 12, 1997.

WHEN WE ASKED "Fuldheim's Condition Is Critical," *The Cleveland Plain Dealer,* July 30, 1984.

199   WAS THERE FOR TESTS "Dorothy Fuldheim, 91, Hospitalized, July 28, 1984.

FULDHEIM IN COMA "Fuldheim in Coma after Brain Surgery," *The Cleveland Plain Dealer,* July 29, 1984.

SHE WAS IN NO PAIN "Fuldheim's Condition is Critical."

I WILL NEVER RETIRE "The First Lady of Television News," 91.

ONE DAY WHEN I WAS Smith, interview.

200   COME IN HERE JOEL Rose, telephone interview.

CONTAINED VAGUE PHRASES "Fuldheim Is Out of Coma," *The Cleveland Plain Dealer,* August 10, 1984.

201   SOME MEMBERS OF Maria Riccardi, "Fuldheim Asks Legal Aid to Help Her Return Home," *The Cleveland Plain Dealer,* May 4, 1985.

SHE WANTED TO LEAVE Maria Riccardi, "Public Is Protective of Dorothy Fuldheim," *Cleveland Plain Dealer,* January 19, 1985.

WHEN MILLER HAD Marcia Myers, "I'm Locked Up Against My Will," *Lorain Journal*, January 17, 1985.

DOROTHY WOULD NEED Ibid.

DUE TO DOROTHY'S RECENT Ibid.

RESIDENT GUARDIANSHIP Joseph Gibbons, telephone conversation with author, April 3, 1997.

202   IF I HAD KNOWN AT William Canterbury, "Fuldheim Case Spotlights Loss of Freedom," *Akron Beacon Journal*, December 29, 1985.

SHE IS WHERE HER "Fuldheim Guardian Seeks Charge of Granddaughter," *The (Lake County) News Herald,* n.d.,from the Dorothy Fuldheim Papers.

SHE WILL NEVER BE Miller, interview.

SOMETIMES BEING "Public Is Protective of Dorothy Fuldheim."

THE TRUTH OF Ibid.

203   SHE SAT ERECT AND Mary Strassmeyer, "Dorothy Fuldheim Receives Some Guests," *The Cleveland Plain Dealer,* January 21, 1985.

IN RESPONSE TO Ibid.

PEOPLE WERE SEEKING Ibid.

SHE WANTS TO GET Ibid.

MILT WIDDER'S WIFE "Dorothy Widder," Obituary, *Cleveland Plain Dealer*, November 27, 1980.

204   SHE COMMANDED ATTENTION "Dorothy Fuldheim: A Great Lady..."

HE WAS JUST LIKE THAT Ibid.

204   SHE HAD A VIBRANT Ibid.

205   HER CONDITION HAS Maria Riccardi, "Fuldheim Asks Legal Aid to Help Her Return Home," May 4, 1985.

DOROTHY'S CIRCUITS "Dorothy Fuldheim Suffers Second Stroke," *The Cleveland Plain Dealer,* June 9, 1985.

FRIENDS CELEBRATED "Dorothy Fuldheim: Ninety-second Birthday," WEWS-TV, June 27, 1985.

206   WHEN HER DAUGHTER Yvonne Breslin, telephone interview with author, October 3, 1996.

SHE SHOULD HAVE GONE J. Bellamy, interview.

I HAVE A CURIOUSLY Dorothy Fuldheim, interview with Barbara Walters, WEWS-TV, February 9, 1982.

207   THE SOUL CAN SPLIT Edna St. Vincent Millay, "Renascence." *Collected Lyrics of Edna St. Vincent Millay,* (New York: Harper & Row, 1939), 3.

LIFE IS LIKE A "Tribute: Great Moments in the Life of Dorothy Fuldheim."

Epilogue

209   YOU USED TO CLIMB Fuldheim, *A Thousand Friends,* 8.

Selected Bibliography

BOOKS

Angle, Paul, ed., *The Lincoln Reader.* New York: Holt, 1947.

Barnard, Ellsworth. *Wendell Willkie: Fighter for Freedom.*
Marquette, Michigan: Northern Michigan University Press, 1966.

Bartlett's Familiar Quotations. Fourteenth Edition. John Bartlett, ed.
Little, Brown and Co.: Boston, 1968.

Bent, Rudyard K. and Henry H. Kronenberg. *Principles of Secondary
Education.* New York: McGraw-Hill Book Co., Inc., 1949.

Bulletin of the State Normal School, July 1911. Milwaukee, Wisconsin:
J.S. Bletcher & Co.

Candee, Marjorie Dent, Ed. *Current Biography.* Bronx, New York:
H.W. Wilson Co., 1954.

Chancellor, John and Walter R. Mears. *The New News Business. A Guide
to Writing and Reporting.* New York: HarperCollins, 1995.

City Directories of Cleveland. Cleveland Directory Company, Publishers,
1927–1941; 1947–1951.

Cooper, Cynthia L. and Sam Reese Sheppard. *Mockery of Justice: The True
Story of the Sheppard Murder Case.* Boston: Northeastern University
Press, 1995.

Cowan, Sada. *Pomp and Other Plays.* New York: Brentano's, 1926.

Current Biography. Bronx, New York: H.W. Wilson Co., 1954.

Dickinson, Emily. *Poems.* Cleveland: Fine Editions Press, 1948.

Ellis, Edward Robb. *A Diary of the Century: Tales from America's Greatest
Diarist.* New York: Kodansha International, 1995.

Fallows, James. *Breaking the News: How the Media Undermine American
Democracy.* New York: Pantheon Books, 1996.

Feehan, John M. *Bobby Sands and the Tragedy of Northern Ireland.* Sag Harbor, New York: Permanent Press, 1983.

Fuldheim, Dorothy. *A Thousand Friends.* Garden City: Doubleday & Co., 1974.

———. *I Laughed, I Cried, I Loved.* Cleveland: The World Publishing Co., 1966.

———. *Three and a Half Husbands.* New York: Simon & Schuster, 1976.

———. *Where Were the Arabs?* Cleveland: The World Publishing Co., 1967.

Gabler, Neal. *Winchell: Gossip, Power and the Culture of Celebrity.* New York: Alfred A. Knopf, 1994.

Gordon, William A. *The Fourth of May: Killings and Coverups at Kent State.* Buffalo: Prometheus Books, 1990.

Halberstam, David. *The Fifties.* New York: Villard, 1993.

Hosley, David H. and Gayle K. Yamada. *Hard News: Women in Broadcast Journalism.* New York: Greenwood Press, 1987.

Khayyam, Omar. *The Rubáiyát.* FitzGerald, Edward, trans. New York: Random House, 1947.

Meir, Golda. *My Life.* New York: G.P. Putnam's Sons, 1975.

Millay, Edna St. Vincent. *Collected Lyrics of Edna St. Vincent Millay.* New York: Harper & Row, 1939.

Morrison, Theodore. *Chautauqua: A Center for Education, Religion, and the Arts in America.* Chicago: University of Chicago Press, 1974.

Matt, Daniel C. *God and the Big Bang: Discovering Harmony Between Science and Spirituality.* Woodstock, Vermont: Jewish Lights Publications, 1996

Michener, James A. *Kent State: What Happened and Why.* New York: Random House, 1971.

Orum, Anthony M. *City-Building in America.* Boulder: Westview Press, 1995.

Paisner, Daniel. *The Inside Stories of Television Newswomen.* New York: William Morrow & Co., 1989.

Sanders, Marlene. *Waiting for Prime Time.* Champaign/Urbana: University of Illinois Press, 1988.

Shakespeare, William. *Romeo and Juliet.* New York: Dell Publishing Company, 1965.

Sperber, A.M. *Murrow: His Life and Times.* New York: Freundlich Books, 1986.

Seltzer, Louis. *The Years Were Good.* Cleveland: The World Publishing Co., 1956.

The Echo. Yearbook of the Milwaukee Normal School, 1912. Milwaukee Urban Archives.

This Fabulous Century 1900-1910. Alexandria, Virginia: Time-Life Books, 1969.

This Fabulous Century 1960-1970. Alexandria, Virginia: Time-Life Books, 1970.

Toffler, Alvin. *The Third Wave.* New York: Bantam Books, 1980.

VanTassel, David D. and John J. Grabowski, eds. *The Encyclopedia of Cleveland History*, 2nd Edition. Bloomington: Indiana University Press, 1996.

Wells, Robert W. *This Is Milwaukee.* Garden City: Doubleday, 1970.

PERIODICALS

Akron Beacon Journal

Canterbury, William. "Fuldheim Case Spotlights Loss of Freedom." December 19, 1985.

McGowan, Marianne. "Sands Drama Touches Veteran Newswoman." May 11, 1981.

Rice, Joan. "Answer to a Shrinking Violet Pulls No Punches." February 28, 1974.

Beacon Magazine

Bianculli, David. "Dorothy." June 19, 1983, 4, 6.

Clary, Mike. "Durable Dorothy." March 9, 1975, 8-10.

Cleveland Magazine

Griffith, Fred. "The Last Word." October 1991, 128.

Gordon, Bill. "Dorothy." February 1990, 22.

Sheridan, Terence. "Dorothy Fuldheim and Mother News." April 1973, 48ff.

Cleveland Plain Dealer

"A Letter to a Friend." June 26, 1996.

"Bash to Honor Fuldheim." June 21, 1983.

Bauder, David. "NBC Showing Gains against ABC News." January 10, 1997.

Beam, Alvin. "Molly the Merry, and the Marryer." November 28, 1976.

Bernstein, Leonard M. "2 Held in Fuldheim Pie Attack." March 22, 1980.

Brown, Roger. "The Man behind the Camera." April 14, 1996.

————."Electrifying History." January 7, 1996.

"Costly Use of Ohio Guard Pays Off with Restored Peace." May 4, 1970

Fuldheim, Dorothy, "Dorothy Fuldheim's Tribute to Her Daughter," December 3, 1980

"Dorothy Fuldheim Hit in Face with Pie at Solon Talk." March 21, 1980.

"Dorothy Fuldheim, 91, Hospitalized." July 28, 1984.

"Dorothy Fuldheim, TV News Legend, Dies." November 4, 1989.

"Dorothy Fuldheim-Urman, 60." November 28, 1980.

"Fuldheim's Condition is Critical." July 30, 1984.

"Fuldheim Better, Is out of Hospital." September 27, 1984.

"Fuldheim in Coma after Brain Surgery." July 29, 1984.

"Fuldheim Is out of Coma." August 10, 1984.

"Fuldheim Is Released from Intensive Care." August 27, 1984.
"Fuldheim Taken off Critical List, Is Able to Talk with Gestures."
    August 21, 1984.
Hickey, William. "Thirty Years of Memories: WEWS-TV."
    December 11, 1977.
————. "Dorothy Fuldheim Gets 3-Year Contract, Raise."
    March 30, 1983.
Kovac, Carl. "Kent ROTC Office Ablaze." May 3, 1970.
Marino, Jim. "Dorothy: 'I Thought Everyone Loved Me.'" *The Cleveland
    Plain Dealer*, March 21, 1980.
Miller, William F. "Israel Honors Miller, Son of a Junk Peddler." Decem-
    ber 30, 1975.
"Mrs. Meir Closely Guarded Here." December 30, 1975.
"Nightmare at Kent State." Editorial. May 5, 1970.
"Reagan and Fans Worldwide Sending Fuldheim Their Best."
    July 31, 1984.
Riccardi, Maria. "Public is Protective of Dorothy Fuldheim."
    January 19, 1985.
————. "Fuldheim Asks Legal Aid to Help Her Return Home."
    May 4, 1985.
————. "Fuldheim Stricken Third Time." October 9, 1985.
"Schnell, Bertha, Death notice." September 18, 1958. Obtained from
    Cuyahoga County Library necrology file.
Strassmeyer, Mary. "Dorothy Fuldheim Receives Some Guests."
    January 21, 1985.
————."Dorothy Fuldheim Suffers Second Stroke, Is Weakened."
    June 9, 1985.
Cleveland Plain Dealer Magazine
Strassmeyer, Mary. "A Monument Named Dorothy." May 9, 1976, 6-10.
Hickey, William. "The Redhead Sets a Record." October 1, 1972, 6.
"Who Is This?" July 6, 1958, n.p.
Cleveland Press
Barrett, Bill. "Dorothy Fuldheim: 'I Don't Have Fear of Death, I Don't
    Think about It.'" May 28, 1980.
————."The Theater—'That's Where I Really Belong.'" May 29, 1980.
Bernstein, Leonard M. "2 Held in Fuldheim Pie Attack." March 22, 1980.
"Dorothy Fuldheim Hit in Face with Pie at Solon Talk." March 21, 1980.
"Dorothy Fuldheim Interviews Barbara Walters." February 9, 1982.
"Dorothy Fuldheim's Tribute to Her Daughter." December 3, 1980.
"Dorothy Widder, Obituary." November 27, 1980.
Gallagher, Nancy. "Here's Dorothy Fuldheim!" August 8, 1959.
McLaughlin, Dick. "The Other Dorothy Fuldheim." April 3, 1980.
"Memorial Service Planned for Dorothy Fuldheim, Jr." November 27, 1980.

"Poll on '70s Has Dorothy, Dennis on Top." December 26, 1979.
"W.L. Ulmer, Husband of Dorothy Fuldheim." January 19, 1971.
Lorain Journal
Fuldheim, Dorothy Sr. and Dorothy Jr. "The 'Richness and Security' of Marriage." May 27, 1979.
———. "This Old House Has Been Good to Me." August 12, 1979.
———. "America Has Lost Faith in Leadership. September 2, 1979.
———. "Carter's Dillydallying Confuses Us." November 18, 1979.

"Barbara Walters: Two Decades at the Top." *TV Guide*. April 27, 1996, 24-26.
Blundo, Joe. "Fuldheim—Witty, Astute." *Kent Stater*. May 17, 1974.
The Bulletin of the Normal Schools of Wisconsin. 1911-1912. Madison, Wisconsin, 1912.
"Fondest Christmas Memory." *Elyria Chronicle Telegram*. December 24, 1978.
"Fuldheim Guardian Seeks Charge of Granddaughter." Horvitz Newspapers, n.d.
Henry, William A. III. "Requiem for TV's Gender Gap." *Time*. August 22, 1983, 57.
Hickey, Neil. "Chancellor: Retiring but Not Silenced." *TV Guide*. July 17, 1993, 33.
Isaacson, Walter. "In Search of the Real Bill Gates." *Time*. January 13, 1997, 44-57.
Ruth, Daniel. "Tribute to a Small Giant: Bright TV Light Goes Out," *Chicago Sun-Times,* November 16, 1989.
Tittle, Diana. "Fulheim on Fuldheim." *Northern Ohio Live*. January 1982, 31-33
Waters, Harry F. with Jon Lowell. "The First Lady of TV News." *Newsweek*. June 11, 1979, 91.
Weigel, Tom. "Channel 5 Counts to 30 with Lots of Memories." *TV Guide*. December 9, 1977, 49-50.
Women's City Club Bulletin. September 1974.
Women's City Club Bulletin. September 1976.
Women's City Club Bulletin. May 1981
Zoglin, Richard. "The News Wars." *Time*. October 21, 1996, 58-63.

UNPUBLISHED SOURCES

Chafee, John H. Letter to Dorothy Fuldheim, February 2, 1972.
Cleaver, Diane. Letter to Dorothy Fuldheim, January 19, 1973.
Cohen, Rabbi Armond. Letter to author, January 8, 1997.
Cook, Russell. *Dorothy Fuldheim's Activist Journalism and the Kent State Shootings.* Paper completed in partial fulfillment of Ph.D. degree, E.W. Scripps School of Journalism, Ohio University, March, 1991.

Fuldheim, Dorothy. "The Declaration of Independence and the Constitution." Commentary, WEWS-TV, July 5, 1976, 6 p.m.

———. "Mandatory Retirement." Commentary. WEWS-TV, October 13, 1975, 6 p.m.

———. "In Memorium." Commentary. WEWS-TV, n.d.

———. "Responsibility of Free Accessability of Guns." Commentary. WEWS-TV, May 16, 1972, 11 p.m.

Gerber, S.R., Coroner's Verdict #56531, Cuyahoga County, Ohio, July 25, 1944.

Humbard, Rex, Letters to Dorothy Fuldheim, August 31, 1973; November n.d., 1973.

Humphrey, Hubert H. Letter to Dorothy Fuldheim, January 29, 1969.

Kosich, June. Letter to author, August 3, 1996.

Milwaukee County Historical Society, information extracted from the 1910 U.S. Census and *Milwaukee City Directories, 1918-1929*.

Mottl, Ronald M. Sr., Letter to author, August 13, 1996.

Poderis, Tony, Letter to Dorothy Fuldheim, February 11, 1974.

Reisman Judith. *A Rhetorical Analysis of Dorothy Fuldheim's Television Commentaries.* Case Western Reserve University: Ph.D. Dissertation, 1979.

Rockefeller, Nelson A. Letter to Dorothy Fuldheim, October 4, 1973.

Simonsen, Judith. Curator, Milwaukee County Historical Society, Milwaukee, Wisconsin, letter to author, April 25, 1995.

Steinbrenner, George. Letter to Dorothy Fuldheim, June 26, 1973.

Stokes, Congressman Louis. Letter to author, July 29, 1996.

Taft, Seth. Letter to Dorothy Fuldheim, September 14, 1973.

FILM

"FDR." *Biography*. A & E Television Network. November 1996.

"Floating Palaces." A & E Television Network. January 12, 1997.

Larry King Live, CNN. June 20, 1996.

Nightline. Dorothy Fuldheim interviewed by Ted Koppel. ABC-TV, taped at WEWS-TV. June 20, 1984.

"TR: The Story of Theodore Roosevelt." *The American Experience.* Public Broadcasting System. October 7, 1996

Selected WEWS-TV videotapes from The Media Archives, John Carroll University:

    "Dorothy Fuldheim: A Great Lady, A Great Loss." WEWS-TV, November 4, 1989.

    Donahue. ABC Television Network. May 15, 1984

    Dorothy Fuldheim. Book review. October 8, 1968, n.d.

    "*Dorothy Fuldheim:* How She Got Started in Television," August 12, 1987.

    Dorothy Fuldheim. Ninetieth birthday. June 27, 1983, tape #4018.

Dorothy Fuldheim. Ninety-second birthday. June 23, 1985.

Dorothy Fuldheim. TV and Lifestyle Changes. December 28, 1977.

Dorothy Fuldheim. With Barbara Walters. February 9, 1982

Dorothy Fuldheim. With Danny Thomas. February 8, 1978.

Dorothy Fuldheim. With Peter Jennings. December 10, 1983.

Dorothy Fuldheim. With Sister Bernadette Vetter. May 1, 1984.

Jenny Crim: Interview with Dorothy Fuldheim, Jr. October 29, 1979.

Larry King. With Dorothy Fuldheim. June 1983

One O'Clock Club. With Dr. Tom Dooley, n.d.

One O'Clock Club. Book review, n.d.

The Morning Exchange. WEWS-TV, March 22, 1980.

The Tonight Show. NBC Television Network. October 7, 1977.

"Tribute: Great Moments in the Life of Dorothy Fuldheim" WEWS-TV, tape #4053.

Index